SQUEEZING SILVER

A true story

Minpeco S.A. v. Hunt
(New York, February–August 1988)

Squeezing Silver

Peru's Trial Against Nelson Bunker Hunt

by
Mark A. Cymrot

Twelve Tables Press
XII

www.twelvetablespress.com

P.O. Box 568
Northport, New York 11768

Library of Congress Cataloging-in-Publication Data

Name: Mark A. Cymrot
Title: Squeezing Silver
Description: Northport, New York: Twelve Tables Press, 2018
ISBN: 978-1-946074-19-5
Subjects: Law—United States/Law,
LC record available at https:lccn.loc.gov/

Twelve Tables Press, LLC
P.O. Box 568
Northport, New York 11768
Telephone (631) 241-1148
Fax: (631) 754-1913
www.twelvetablespress.com

Printed in the United States of America

Cover Art: Rebekah Feldman

Table of Contents

Prologue

Nelson Bunker Hunt comes striding down the center aisle of the packed courtroom, shoulders back, head up, eyes focused forward. Short, rotund with a pudgy face and sandy hair, he is wearing a gray business suit, presumably tailormade, although Bunker might be proud to tell you he bought it off the rack. On his doughy frame, the difference might not matter. With a blue shirt, simple blue tie and white pocket square, he looks poised. This is the moment the jurors—four women and two men—have been waiting for; they are sitting erect, three of them on the edges of their seats. Bunker's wife Caroline, brothers Herbert and Lamar, and friends are sitting among reporters and the curious. TV news artists are drawing on sketchpads resting across their laps. The courtroom is silent. Bunker steps up to the witness box, raises his right hand, and intones the oath in a strong voice.

As Bunker settles into the hard, wooden witness chair, he turns toward his lawyer who was standing across the well of the courtroom waiting to ask him questions. I am watching Bunker's every move. I know he is nervous; so am I. In different ways, we are confronting turning points in our lives.

Our young trial team is accusing the infamous Texas oil tycoon of executing a scheme to manipulate silver prices. When prices spiked from $9 to $51, Bunker and his cohorts pocketed billions while thousands were cheated, our client Minpeco S.A. among them. Ultimately, the scheme was calamitous when silver prices collapsed, driving Bunker and his family into default and the US economy to the verge of a major financial crisis. The jury can save Bunker and cleanse him of the embarrassment and shame of his very public failure or label him a manipulator and wretched crook.

Bunker will tell his story before I have my chance to cross-examine him, a confrontation that might determine the outcome of the case. I can soar or crash and, with me, our team that has been tireless for five years. Can I stand with the renowned lawyers who have lined up for the defense, or will I fade and be forgotten, one more pretender unfulfilled?

Before Bunker arrived, the jurors patiently listened for three months to our witnesses lay out the complex events of the fall of 1979. We hope to prove that two groups secretly working together bought virtually the entire inventory of silver bullion in US commodity exchange warehouses, which caused the extraordinary price rise. Bunker Hunt and his family made up one group, and a second group that included the brother-in-law of the Saudi Crown Prince, dubbed the "Conti Group," was trading through a flamboyant broker,

Norton Waltuch at ContiCommodity Services, Inc., a sub-
sidiary of the commodity conglomerate Continental Grain.
We are accusing the two groups of a scheme to commit racketeering, monopoly, and fraud designed to make spectacular
profits at the expense of other traders. "A small group of
men, acting for themselves, ignoring others, uncaring
about innocent people, innocent traders, manipulating the
silver markets," is the way I described their scheme to the
jury.

A single silver futures contract bought for $4,500 before
the price spike could be sold less than four months later
for $255,000, a magnitude of return rarely seen on Wall
Street. For each dollar that silver prices rose, the two groups
received $200 million in nightly margin payments on sil-
ver futures contracts, a massive wealth grab from other
market participants.

The abrupt price spike inflicted suffering across the economy. Many ordinary traders incurred debilitating losses. The headlines shrieked of brokerage houses, banks, and major metals dealers teetering on the edge of bankruptcy. Commercial silver users, like film and medical equipment manufacturers, struggled to contain costs. High silver prices even touched households. Police statistics showed a marked increase in burglaries for silver, 30 percent involving violence. When silver was not stolen, families sold silverware, jewelry, and irreplaceable silver artifacts to be melted down into bullion, lost to history, but exchanged for extra vacations, new cars, or extensions on their homes.

Minpeco, Peru's state-owned minerals dealer, was one of many on the wrong side of the wealth transfer when it lost $80 million in ten days as silver futures prices surged in early December 1979. Minpeco could no longer pay its margin calls when its chief lender, Peru's national bank, ran out of money, a stark display of the impoverished of the country as it transferred its limited capital to oil billionaires. The one life tied most directly to Bunker's at this trial, Ismael Fonseca, Minpeco's hedging chief, was fired and walked out of the rundown converted mansion that served as Minpeco's headquarters into a shattered, haunted life.

When the price bubble burst in late January 1980, money that came in so quickly went out quickly. Bunker Hunt's silver lost value daily, prompting a steady series of multimillion-dollar margin calls. For two months, Bunker struggled with a variety of schemes to steady deflating prices. He traveled the Middle East and Europe looking for financing, determined to maintain his crown as king of silver. No one would help him. On Silver Thursday, March 27, 1980, silver prices crashed back to $10.80, down from $51 just two months before. That night, the wealthy Hunt family was humiliated to announce they could not pay margin calls due to brokerage houses, banks, and others.

Newspapers blared panicky headlines. The US economy hovered on the brink of collapse from the escapade of a single family. Although "too big to fail" had not yet entered our collective vocabulary, Federal Reserve Chairman Paul A. Volcker, Jr. feared a Hunt default would bankrupt the venerable brokerage house, Bache, Halsey, Stuart, Shields Inc., and perhaps the country's largest, Merrill Lynch Pierce Fenner & Smith Co. A chain reaction of failures could crash the US economy, Volcker worried. Volcker fostered a secret bailout of the Hunts and, in turn, their irresponsible brokers and lenders.

Congress investigated. Politicians grandstanded with lofty speeches. "The futures markets," warned the formidable Senate Banking Committee Chairman William Proxmire, had "become the Indianapolis 500 for individuals hoping to strike it rich in the high risk, highly leveraged, and fast-moving marketplace." Causing it, he added, to "more closely resembled a demolition derby."

Gloomily tramping from Congressional committee room to committee room, Bunker Hunt failed to display any remorse or even awareness of the havoc he had wrought. He railed at commodity regulators for imposing market restrictions that had halted his accumulation of silver, breaking the price spiral. They "changed the rules in the middle of the game," Hunt blustered, perhaps revealing more than he intended by labeling the disaster a game. Really, what did he expect to do with a crown of silver? He was left to churlish lamenting: "A billion dollars isn't what it used to be" was his explanation for his family's inability to pay margin calls. Like Bunker, his father H.L. Hunt, the world's richest man, was good for a quote: "Money is just a way of keeping score," H.L. reputedly said. Bunker was losing the game at that moment.

The Hunt bailout was the first in a series of controversial bailouts that provoked intense debate over the ensuing thirty years. During the Congressional hearings, Paul Volcker was much criticized for not allowing Bunker to feel the full pain of his folly. But years later he told me, "I don't remember losing much sleep over it." Twenty-eight years later, he was proven right when the bankruptcy of the brokerage house Lehman Brothers triggered the worst recession since the Great Depression. This was the prequel.

Bunker and his fellow perpetrators were not prosecuted; the case supposedly was too complicated, I was told by one regulator. Thousands of victims were left on their own to unravel Bunker's vast scheme in order to recoup their losses. Cole Corette & Abrutyn, a small Washington, DC law firm, filed a civil lawsuit in Manhattan federal court for Minpeco, the single largest plaintiff in the many lawsuits filed. The lawsuits might do what the Government was unwilling to: provide some measure of relief for the victims and inflict some measure of retribution upon the Hunts, their cohorts, and the reckless brokerage firms that enabled them.

A phalanx of prestigious trial lawyers signed up for the defense. Cole Corette & Abrutyn did not even have a litigation department; it was a law firm of international business and tax lawyers that advised Minpeco in its regular business dealings. The firm recruited the deputy chief of enforcement at the Securities and Exchange Commission to file the complaint and fight the early skirmishes, but he did not want to focus his entire practice on a single case.

He found me to take over.

When Ted Sonde called, I was sitting in my office at the Justice Department coincidentally contemplating my future. The prospect of a trial against a notorious family that created a worldwide financial crisis was irresistible. I did not hesitate.

I assumed I was prepared. I had no concept of what awaited me.

Bunker Hunt on the stand; Lamar Hunt watching

Part One

The Opening

Chapter One

The trial began on a cold, winter morning, February 18, 1988, almost eight years after the silver markets crashed. The sun was bright, air was crisp, and a gentle breeze was pushing a few puffs of white clouds through a clear sky. On my way to the courthouse, I paused, inhaled deeply, exhaled the stress of opening day, and pulled my scarf closer around my neck, invigorated. It was a glorious New York day. I wished the weather would repeat, just fifty degrees warmer and when I could stay out to enjoy it. But I knew that would not happen anytime soon. Funny what you will remember three decades later.

On that frigid February morning, we were sitting in a packed courtroom watching US District Judge Morris E. Lasker patiently explain the outlines of the case and the applicable law to the jury. He was leaning toward the jurors on his green leather swivel chair, a calm grandfatherly figure in the tense courtroom. He had a slight build and curly brown hair. He did not look his seventy years. He was sitting, as usual, without black robes in a conservative business suit. A quiet, formal man, he had an informal style. Judicial robes were only for criminal proceedings. Lawyer conferences were more comfortably held in chambers, and he came down from the bench to conduct oral arguments from the jury box with his law clerks sitting next to him. Lawyers were always treated politely. Witnesses were never ravaged on cross-examination. Embarrassing someone in his courtroom was simply unnecessary and unwelcome it seemed.

Judge Lasker's initial instructions to the jury were quite simple: he explained the laws that prohibit price manipulation and fraud. The essence of his instruction was that we had to prove that the defendants had intentionally increased silver prices to levels higher than they would have been under normal market forces—that is resulting from the forces of supply and demand. Buying large quantities of silver is legal, Judge Lasker told the jurors, but buying it with the intent and in a manner that intentionally raises prices is illegal. We would have to teach the jurors to discern the difference.

Judge Lasker's courtroom was a large Classical Revival-style expanse with marble floors and high wood-paneled walls that reached to a twenty-foot high ceiling. Our team was spread out at a beat up wood table just below the judge's raised bench. The jury box was close on my left. My colleagues, Tom Gorman was next to me; Scott Andersen sat further down the table scribbling notes; and Raoul Gonzalez, looking pained and nervous was at the end of the table.

The famous defense lawyers had split among three smaller tables behind us. The Hunts' lead lawyer Paul J. Curran, "a lawyer's lawyer" according to *The New York Times*, was sitting behind me, closest to the jury, stony faced and glowering. Paul Perito, one of Washington's premier lawyers, representing the Hunt partnership with two Saudi sheikhs, International Metals Investment Company (IMIC), was sitting at a separate table facing the jury looking like a fighter poised to pounce, befitting his personality. Peter Fleming, the legendary trial lawyer who led the legal team of Mahmoud Fustok, brother-in-law to Saudi Crown Prince Abdullah bin Abdulaziz Al Saud, was sitting against the sidewall hunched in a chair too small for his 6'6" frame, looking relaxed and focused. Behind the jury were the heating vents that rattled from time to time and tall windows that let in what light could squeeze past an adjacent government building.

I glanced over at our opponents. They were the adults; I was a youngster trying to act like an adult. We were gathered in the same Foley Square courthouse in which I had earlier played a minor role in two historic cases: *United States v. The New York Times* (*The Pentagon Papers* case), the Nixon Administration's effort to enjoin publication of a Vietnam War history leaked by Daniel Ellsberg, and *Ronald Galella v. Jacqueline Kennedy Onassis*, in which an obsessed paparazzi was enjoined from harassing the former First Lady and her children. After making the unorthodox decision to turn down an offer from a major New

York law firm, a decision that had my father quietly shaking his head, I tried civil fraud and corruption cases around the country for the Justice Department, separated by a two-year stint at Consumers Union doing public interest lawsuits. After nine years, I had risen to a senior position in the department—Special Litigation Counsel—lead lawyer for the government on stimulating and important cases. When I joined Cole Corette & Abrutyn, the lead role for Minpeco was turned over to me.

Trials can be compared to impressionist paintings or perhaps jigsaw puzzles. Each witness adds a dab of knowledge here or a nugget there. The story is not necessarily presented in chronological order; it can be a blur until enough pieces fit together for a picture to emerge. The lawyers' opening statements give the jurors a guide by describing the conflicting themes of the plaintiff and defense. Our goal for this opening was daunting. We had to introduce our jury—a transit inspector, a teacher, a retired policeman, a young salesman, a nurse, and a college professor—to an array of eccentric characters, the obscure mechanics of the world silver futures markets, and a complex story of secret meetings and coordinated trading that had unlawfully raised silver prices. After rising to the podium, with the judge, jurors, and our three opponents staring at me, I described their scheme in stark terms: "We're not talking about large corporations. We're not talking about a small country. We are talking about a group of privileged men who used their power and influence to push up the price of silver illegally . . .

We will show they did this using their incredible fortunes with an utter contempt for the very legal and economic systems that were so very good to them." Although Bunker denied he was trading in concert with his brothers, IMIC, and the Conti Group, his path intersected regularly with the Brazilian billionaire Naji Nahas, Mahmoud Fustok, broker Norton Waltuch, and IMIC partner, Sheikh Ali bin Mussalem, at racetracks, five-star hotels, and lavish restaurants. Aided by three unprecedented rulings piecing Swiss secrecy laws, we had unearthed the Hunt and Conti Groups' silver trading through forty-eight companies and individuals operating in ninety-eight separate accounts at nineteen brokerage houses and Swiss banks. Our breakthrough in piercing Swiss secrecy also disclosed joint transactions that Bunker never expected the public to see. Our theme, that we repeated throughout the trial, was that their pattern of silver futures trading and bullion demands were coordinated during these encounters and caused the extraordinary price rise in the fall of 1979.

Simple economics dictated the scheme, I continued. Silver futures contracts are bought and sold on commodity exchanges, principally at the time, the Commodity Exchange, Inc. (COMEX) in New York, Chicago Board of Trade (CBOT), and London Metals Exchange (LME). A futures contract is a commitment to buy or sell 5,000 ounces of .999 pure silver bullion at a specified month in the future. The bullion that backs these contracts was kept in certified warehouses for each exchange. Although the world has almost limitless supplies of silver, these ware-houses have relatively small quantities, but those quantities are the basis for worldwide prices. The two groups bought extraordinary quantities of silver futures contracts that would mature in September and December 1979 and early 1980, and, at maturity, they took delivery of the bullion backing these contracts from exchange warehouses, which was unusual. "Basically what we are saying," I told the jury, "is that the scheme was to buy the silver bullion in exchange warehouses, constrict the supply . . . and by reducing the supply the price will go up." From their numerous accounts, the two groups had amassed control of 371 million ounces of silver bullion worth $16.4 billion ($50 billion today), at least 75 percent of the visible world supply. As their moun-tain of silver grew, the normally sleepy silver markets went into orbit from $9 in August 1979 to $51 on January 21, 1980. The December 1979 price surge inflicted $80 million in damages on Minpeco within ten days.

The formidable defense counsel followed with openings that ridiculed our circumstantial evidence. Paul Curran, a couple of inches short of six feet tall, with broad shoulders, bushy eyebrows, and a soft pudgy face, rose first. He was a celebrity in his own right; he had been the chief federal prosecutor in Manhattan, the bane of Mafia bosses, crooked cops, and a congressman. He later ran as Republi-can candidate for Governor. As a special prosecutor appointed by the Attorney General, he was the first lawyer to examine a sitting President—Jimmy Carter—under oath. At the age of fifty-five years, he was at the height of his career. Befitting his resume, he had a strong demeanor; his voice was quiet and understated, projecting strength but not warmth to the jury. To my surprise, he stayed behind the podium during his opening statement and stuck more closely to a written text than the other lead lawyers. He came late to the case when the trial was on the horizon. He used one of his young partners as a buffer to ensure that we rarely had to talk. His partner generally was open and friendly. Curran and I never warmed up to each other.

Curran sarcastically labeled our scheme "a broad daylight conspiracy." The Hunt silver trading made the newspapers in 1979 and they were meeting with other collaborators in public restaurants, hotels, and racetracks in Paris, London, New York, Geneva, Zurich, and Kentucky. "Some conspiracy!" Curran sneered, "Do your bad business in plain view of newspaper reporters, the public at racetracks, and in public restaurants where people know you? Would you do it that way, using your common sense?"

Curran introduced Bunker Hunt "as a believer in buying and selling hard assets." Buying silver is legal, even buying in large quantities, Curran stressed, reminding the jurors of Judge Lasker's initial outline of the law. Curran had an answer to our argument that the conspirator's unusually large silver bullion deliveries had intentionally driven up prices. Bunker had a legitimate reason for investing in large quantities of silver, Curran said; he viewed silver as a good investment, a hard asset that in 1979 was undervalued in his view. As for the price spike in the fall of 1979, that was caused by political and economic events, including the fall of the Shah of Iran, the Iranian hostage crisis, and 12 percent hyperinflation in the United States.

Curran's defense colleagues, Fleming and Perito, also attacked our conspiracy theory. Perito described it as a "cropped photograph," which omitted key facts to make IMIC, a legitimate business, appear as a "veritable Darth Vader of this creative alleged scheme." Fleming took another angle, saying: "the bright line that I heard was the Hunts are rich and powerful and Mr. Fustok is rich and, therefore, punish them. I think Mr. Cymrot is talking to the wrong people when he does that."

The three defense lawyers also attacked Minpeco's complaint as sour grapes of bad trading decisions rather than the legitimate grievance of a deceived trader. They suggested that the Peru government had made a lot of money when silver prices went up, so the jurors should reduce Minpeco's losses by the gains Peruvian mines had netted from higher silver prices. However, in a key pretrial ruling, Judge Lasker had barred the defense from making the "single entity" argument, which led to my first donnybrook with Fleming when he explicitly put the banned theory to the jury in his opening.

The jurors listened intently to the openings, but they swore to decide the case based on the evidence that would come in from witnesses and documents. We, as the plaintiff, had called our witnesses first in what is called our direct case or case in chief, which took seventeen weeks. That was a long time for any trial. With the Hunts and other key characters staying away, we had to play video clips of their pretrial depositions to the jury, a generally emotionless, listless presentation. When the trial moved to the defense case and Bunker appeared, the tenor changed. From the moment he walked into the courtroom, the trial became more the dramatic battle that we had imagined. In many ways, the trial began for real; we had just been waiting for Bunker to arrive.

That is how we will tell the story—through the competing versions of events told through our presentation, Curran's direct examination of Bunker, and my cross-examination, along with a description of other key witnesses.

Chapter Two

Once Bunker Hunt settled into the witness chair, Paul Curran began by asking him questions to create a sympathetic portrait of the oldest son of one of Texas' legendary families. The jury had heard one view from us—Bunker the manipulator. Curran wanted to give the jury a different perspective, Bunker the nice guy, family man, and businessman with many interests beyond silver.

Bunker started slowly in response to Curran's questions: he was married for thirty-seven years, had four children and fourteen grandchildren. Curran had him name his children. I was impressed that Bunker could remember their names under the stress of the witness stand. Bunker acknowledged that he was a wealthy man from a substantial inheritance. He described his father as "a farm boy . . . I think he only went to school one year, but that's a little misleading, because he was a very bright progeny, prodigy," Bunker stumbled briefly. "He could read and write before he was old enough to go to school, I think at the age of four or five, his mother was a teacher and so she didn't send him to school, they lived in the country."

When he moved off the farm, H.L. Hunt became a wild-catter, "that means one who explores for oil and gas in areas that—where there is none and, shall I say, virgin areas or undrilled areas," Bunker said haltingly, displaying his nervousness. Curran decided to help him along, asking in a low tone: "Mr. Hunt, would it be fair to describe your father as probably the most successful wildcatter and independent oil man in the history of the oil business in the United States?"

I had expected more fire from a burly Irishman, but Curran was soft-spoken and Bunker was speaking a slow Texas drawl, frequently dotting his answers with a deferential "Yes, sir." Bunker, responding to Curran's question, started haltingly: "I, I think that's a fair explanation. I think—I don't want to give him more credit than he was entitled to. He is deceased now some 14 or 15 years. But I think he was considered certainly one of the most successful if not the most successful." And then he added proudly in a stronger voice: "I do remember one thing. During World War II my father produced more oil for the Allied war effort than Nazi Germany had in production for itself."

H.L. Hunt became *Fortune's* richest men from the deals he cut. According to legend, he traded poker winnings for oil rights. After developing the idea of buying mineral rights surrounding successful wells, he secured title to much of the East Texas Oil Field, one of the world's largest oil deposits, and then expanded his holdings beyond. He built a fortune estimated at $3 billion, the equivalent of about $50 billion in 2017.

Curran sidestepped H.L. Hunt's less admirable qualities. Some on our team wanted to spend time exploring H.L.'s seamier side. He was a colorful, controversial character with three families simultaneous, including fourteen children, living across Texas and Louisiana, and a brash personality that reportedly was the chief inspiration for J.R. Ewing, the lead character in the popular TV soap opera, *Dallas*. He supported an ultra-right wing, bigoted, and anti-Semitic political agenda that he disseminated through radio and television programs and books by ultraconservative political figures, including, the infamous red-baiter, Senator Joe McCarthy. I found all that a distraction and potentially off-putting to some jurors looking for evidence of a conspiracy; I kept our preparation focused on silver.

When Curran asked about his upbringing, Bunker explained that he briefly went to college, was drafted into the Navy, and served on a battleship in the Pacific during the air battles in Okinawa, Iwo Jima, and over Japan.

"An enlisted man?" Curran asked.

"Yes, I was, sir," came Bunker's clipped response.

He came away with a mild hearing problem, "that's what my wife tells me and friends." His hearing problem was to come up later in the story when he supposedly didn't hear Mahmoud Fustok make a large silver order, but now he moved on. When Bunker returned to Dallas, he went to college briefly, but "I decided I want to get into business and I really wasn't that much of a student," he continued with a folksy smile; he was becoming more relaxed and settling into his story. The courtroom was silent. The jurors had not moved; they sat with stony faces.

Curran transitioned into Bunker's business career, which, according to the *Dallas Morning News*, "outdid his father in creating and losing fortunes through titanic plays in oil, silver, soybeans, sugar beets, cattle and thoroughbred horses, his passion." Bunker continued more smoothly now, "I had worked in the oil fields as a boy in the labor gangs and rough-necked on drilling rigs. So, I was pretty familiar with the business and so it was natural for me." He worked with his father and had his own independent operation in his father's office. Hunt Oil, their flagship company, stuck to exploration within the United States. Starting in 1955, Bunker began exploring for oil in new areas. Pakistan was an expensive bust, but Libya was a spectacular success. Partnering with British Petroleum, he discovered the largest oil field ever found in Africa. His operation was producing 475,000 barrels per day when the coup came; a young colonel Muammar Gaddafi overthrew King Idris. That event played a big role in Bunker's defense—his obsession for hard assets like silver bullion—but, again, Curran avoided the subject of silver and moved on.

When his father died in 1974, the management of Hunt Oil went to Bunker's half-brother, Ray Hunt, which must have been a stinging rebuke for Bunker and his brother

Herbert who did not even know about their father's secret second family for many years. The brothers negotiated a deal that left Ray with Hunt Oil, while Bunker and Herbert received two of his father's jewels: Placid Oil was one of the largest independent oil producing companies in the United States, and Penrod Drilling was the world's largest drilling company. They also took certain oil properties, including the untested but later very valuable leases on the Beaufort Sea on the Alaska North Slope, which Bunker would lose in the later parts of his story.

As Bunker rambled into a long explanation of the family oil businesses, he tried to make himself look like the victim, rather than the perpetrator of the silver debacle: "Unfortunately, right now, things aren't going so well. Placid Oil is in bankruptcy, and Penrod Drilling and the trusts that own Penrod are in bankruptcy." Then his voice dropped, "It, it isn't like it was," reflecting perhaps a genuine sense of loss.

I jumped up to interrupt, "Objection!" I shouted, probably too loudly, "may we approach the bench?"

Chapter Three

When I objected, Judge Lasker looked over at me with a scowl. He apparently did not like the interruption. Bunker's answer had touched on one of the themes Paul Curran had laid out in his opening statement: Bunker and his family should be given sympathy because the silver crash had wreaked havoc on the Hunt family finances. Our lawsuit could make things worse; it was the largest single claim coming out of the silver price spike and crash, but larger class action lawsuits—by people who had lost as prices rose and those who had lost when prices crashed—were waiting to be resolved once our trial ended. The Commodity Futures Trading Commission (CFTC), the small government regulator, had also started a proceeding against Bunker and Herbert that could result in a substantial fine and a lifetime ban on futures markets trading. Those cases dwarfed Minpeco's, but our trial would effectively decide them all.

If we had to argue the point we would say that Bunker was deserving of scorn, not sympathy, for causing the economic wreckage that resulted from his scheme. But we thought it best to keep the argument out of the case entirely. Now Bunker had interjected it into an answer that had not asked for it. Perhaps that was a setup; Curran may have feared this part of the story was inadmissible, as I was about to argue. The judge, however, was unwilling to interrupt the flow of Bunker's story. He postponed the argument until a recess. I was disappointed but returned to my seat trying, almost certainly unsuccessfully, to look unconcerned before the jury.

When he resumed, Bunker continued explaining his many business interests in cattle, agriculture, and thoroughbred horses, which were also liquidated due to "the press of business." After this one more shot about his troubles, he turned to an aspect of his business empire that touched on a relevant theme, his thoroughbred horses. Many of the key meetings took place at thoroughbred sales or races. He boasted, "I had one of the best racing stables in America, if not the best overall in the world." The discussion of his horses prompted Bunker to straighten up and become animated. He owned two training facilities in Chantilly, France, the major training center in Europe, and one in Lexington, Kentucky, the heart of horse country in the United States. He used public and private trainers.

While I was getting impatient to hear about silver, Judge Lasker seemed absorbed with horses, interrupting Curran to ask:

"Public means simply available to more than one person?"

"That's right. Available to the public," Bunker responded after turning toward the judge.

"It doesn't mean the government pays for them?" the judge continued.

"No. The government hasn't gotten into that yet," Bunker scoffed.

"Give it time," the judge retorted, which got a snicker in the jittery courtroom.

"Except as a tax collector I should say," Bunker quickly rejoined.

Was the judge star-struck, charmed by a celebrity in his courtroom? I was not sure. And what about the jury?

One of Bunker's public trainers was Maurice Zilber, a name that would come up later when Bunker finally got around to talking about silver. Zilber, also the trainer for Naji Nahas, introduced them. Nahas was the Brazilian billionaire who became Bunker's chief collaborator in manipulating silver prices. However, Curran again avoided the subject of silver and led Bunker on a tangent through more details of public trainers in France. Curran was suggesting that Bunker's many meetings with Nahas and Mahmoud Fustok at horseracing events were in pursuit of his passion for horses and not his passion for conspiratorial intrigue.

However, Bunker could not avoid the subject of silver forever. When Curran moved on to Bunker's relationship with his brothers, he asked Bunker whether he, Herbert, and Lamar had ever traded silver together, a key element of our proof. Bunker recoiled, "No, never jointly," he huffed as if the thought were offensive. He mentioned the idea to his brothers Herbert and Lamar. Herbert was interested; Lamar was not. He shared silver investment opportunities with Herbert, but he never invested "jointly." He never knew how much silver Herbert had. "I knew he was long in silver and had silver. I mean we talked about it. But as far as knowing what his position was specifically I really didn't care."

I was surprised Curran had gone back to the subject of joint trading so explicitly. Curran's question was a response to one of our more notable successes during Bunker's pretrial video deposition that the jury had already seen before Bunker arrived in court. After we established the close proximity of Bunker and Herbert's offices, reliance on the same senior staff, and their frequent conversations, I offered Bunker the logical conclusion of his argument: his similar trades with his brother must have been a *coincidence*. As soon as Bunker agreed, Paul Clayman—who had come up with the idea—dropped a stack of files on the table, and I began asking Bunker about similar or identical trades by Bunker, Herbert, and their international company, IMIC. After a time, Bunker's shoulders had slumped and his tone turned petulant; his lawyers were objecting and a chorus of objections came from the back of the room where the lawyers for the brokerage houses sat in two rows like a Greek chorus. I ignored their objections. Once the pattern of questions was established, Bunker's answers became almost irrelevant. The questions identifying identical transactions were the focus of attention. Whenever I tried to use the word *coincidence* in a question during trial, the defense table would ring out objections that Judge Lasker would sustain. Throughout the trial, I would use coincidence occasionally just to remind the jurors of Bunker's fumbled answers—or sometimes, just like a teenage terror—to annoy our illustrious opponents.

Curran concluded this family introduction with an invitation for Bunker to explain the common man in him:

"How, Mr. Hunt, would you tell us briefly, please, a little bit about your interests and your lifestyle over the last number of years?"

"Well, I've always considered myself pretty much an ordinary kind of guy," Bunker sat back, a little more relaxed, "I enjoy sports and sports events and go to them and got a big family now with 14 grandchildren and four children, enjoy them, I go to church occasionally. I'm a life-long Presbyterian, an elder in the Presbyterian Church and just sort of an ordinary fellow." And then he added a story he was well known for: "One thing I do, I always ride tourist on the airplanes. A fellow asked me why once and I said I found the tourist section and the first class get there at the same time. You might as well make it economical."

That story probably got a laugh from most audiences. Two jurors smiled but the others sat stony faced. They seemed too absorbed and infused with their serious assignment to laugh. I did not know how the jury was reacting to this series of well-rehearsed folksy yarns, but I was ready to hear about silver.

Judge Lasker called a lunch break.

Once the jurors had walked out, the judge directed us to the robing room to discuss "an important issue," Bunker's answer about the post crash bankruptcies of Hunt finances. The judge immediately started, asking, "Why is it relevant to the case?" Curran was ready with a response: "I think the jury should be able to see the entire picture of what happened with that market and what happened to them as a result of their investments; otherwise, you would be shutting off from the jury a major part of what happened in this case." "That argument seems to be as impermissible," the judge interjected before I could continue the argument I had started during the sidebar, "as it would be for a co-conspirator in a criminal case to say how could I possibly have done this when I'm facing 20 years of jail as a result of the claim . . . I'm sympathetic to the Hunts. You know I've gotten to really sort of like them personally. It's just not part of the case . . . I want you to stay away from the subject of hardship, let's call it, caused by the crash."

The jury had already heard the testimony that the judge labeled impermissible. What we had accomplished with the objection was to cut off a repetition of the "Poor Hunt" and "Poor Fustok" themes throughout the case; I suppose that was something. The judge's comments about liking the

Hunts were more interesting than his ruling. I gathered Bunker was coming off well during his direct testimony.

I pondered the judge's reaction as I went out for a quick, forgettable lunch and came back to scan my cross-examination notes. Not that I necessarily objected to the quality of the food near the courthouse; it is just that in the midst of trial, food gets reduced to its basic purpose—energy.

Chapter Four

With his sympathetic family history complete, Bunker Hunt and Paul Curran were forced to start his version of the silver story. In his opening statement, Curran had described Bunker "as a believer in buying and selling hard assets." Curran asked Bunker about the story that led him to this investment philosophy and his preoccupation with silver.

"Did there come a time in 1970 or 1971," Curran asked, "when something happened in Libya that shut you down?"

"Yes, unfortunately, we had a military coup in Libya that occurred and the king was overthrown, the king who had been a pretty nice kind of fellow and reasonable to deal with, was overthrown by a military dictator, Muammar Gaddafi," Bunker said, as if talking to heads of state came naturally to him. "I didn't last very long with Mr. Gaddafi," he added satisfied.

Gaddafi was one of the many colorful characters that the jury heard about during the trial. The son of a Bedouin goat herder, Gaddafi, as a young and charismatic army captain, led a bloodless coup removing the king, abolished the monarchy, and established what he called a republic. According to *BBC New* for the next four decades, Gaddafi "paraded on the world stage with a style so unique and unpredictable that the words *maverick* or *eccentric* scarcely did him justice." While surrounding himself with female bodyguards in high heels and dressed in bizarre costumes, Gaddafi had his brutal side at home and was one of the first state sponsors of terrorism abroad. At the time of trial, he was still a regular fixture on the international stage. Several of the jurors probably had read news stories about Gaddafi and cringed, a point of sympathy for Bunker. His most sinister act, the bombing of Pan Am 103 over Lockerbie, Scotland, came only months after the trial ended.

After first closing foreign military bases, Gaddafi challenged the foreign oil companies—including Bunker's—with the threat "people who have lived without oil for 5,000 years can live without it again for a few years in order to attain their legitimate rights." His gambit worked. Many of the companies renegotiated their contracts, a move soon followed by other Arab countries, which led to the 1970s Arab oil boom and a historic transfer of economic and political power to the Middle East.

Although the major oil companies were more adept or willing to sidestep trouble, Bunker stubbornly refused to renegotiate his contract, which prompted Gaddafi to expropriate his oil fields. Bunker got little compensation. Bunker supposedly was buying large quantities of silver bullion in 1979 because he did not want his wealth at risk to the vagaries of fickle governments, including the US government we would later learn. He wanted to invest in a hard asset he could keep his hands on.

In response to Curran's questions, Bunker readily admitted that by 1973, he and Herbert had decided a fortune could be made in silver. Frustrated by inflation's toll on their fortunes and fearing unpredictable governments like Libya's Gaddafi, the Hunts became silver bugs, advocating the virtues of silver investments to anyone who would listen. I was a "believer in hard assets," Bunker mimicked Curran's opening, "things like real estate, oil, gas wells, silver, cattle, horses . . . rather than stocks and bonds, somebody else's business." After Gaddafi expropriated his oil fields, "I wanted to buy something—invest in something that I could keep my hands on."

In around 1972 or 1973, he read a book by Jerome Smith, "Silver Profits in the 1970s" that argued silver "was going to make a very large move, many times its value." The reason principally was industrial use far exceeded the annual mine production. Bunker discussed the idea with several brokers and became "very bullish on silver," a phrase he repeated often. His philosophy "has always been strictly long term," implying he was not interested in a short-term bonanza from a silver squeeze. He was a wealthy person looking for a safe haven in midst of a storm of political and economic events—"some very disquieting situations"—that were causing inflation. Investing in millions of ounces of silver futures and bullion was a good investment.

Following their new investment passion, Bunker and Herbert purchased silver futures contracts representing a combined 41 million ounces of bullion worth more than $100 million and took delivery of the physical silver as their futures contracts expired in 1973 and 1974, an unusual move in the futures markets. They left the silver bullion in the exchange warehouses, but their control over it effectively reduced the supply of bullion backing silver futures contracts. Silver prices responded to the reduced supply by ascending from $2.80 to $6.00 per ounce.

At his pretrial deposition (that we had played to the jury), Bunker had difficulty providing an innocent explanation for the unusual move of taking bullion deliveries through a commodities exchange. He gave a series of confusing and contradictory answers, starting with he did not want to deal with the paperwork of the exchange.

"That was the only reason?" I asked giving Bunker several opportunities to come up with a better answer.

"That's the only reason I could think of." He responded. But later he amended his answer:

"Are you now saying that paperwork wasn't the only reason why you took deliveries in the early 1970s?"

"Yes. If the answer sounds like that, that wasn't what I meant to say at all. I mean, you know, the tax considerations are a much bigger factor than the paperwork, but just lack of confidence in the paperwork exchange . . ."

Tax considerations became Bunker's justification for his unusual conduct. After a further give-and-take, he dropped his original answer: "Paperwork, I'll scratch that."

At trial, Bunker leaned in toward the microphone to answer Curran's questions about his early silver purchases. He began by buying perhaps 20 million ounces, "a very substantial amount." The "paperwork, scratch that" story was replaced with a new one. He explained a more rational story for buying futures contracts as a source of bullion: "Well, I checked to see if silver was available and could be bought in substantial amounts and I found out pretty negatively that the production was well accounted for. A lot of it did go into the COMEX, from the various mines in this country, Mexico and Peru and whatnot and so it was hard to buy the physical silver at that time. If you wanted physical silver the simplest thing was to buy the futures contracts and take delivery."

Bunker recounted buying 2 to 3,000 futures contracts, or maybe it was 2 to 4,000 contracts—commitments for 10 to 20 million ounces of silver. "I mercifully don't remember all these things. If I did, I wouldn't have time to sleep," he chuckled, now more relaxed as he was into the midst of his story.

Futures contracts were also attractive because they leveraged his investment, he added; he only had to make a 5 percent down payment. He maintained a 20 to 40 million ounce investment through 1978 and began proselytizing the virtues of silver to others, including at seminars.

Bunker's trio of explanations—silver as a good investment, tax considerations, and simplicity of purchases—was his response for his demand for large bullion deliveries in 1979–1980. I did not recognize at the time that Bunker had unconsciously doubled the amount of silver he held. By referring to 20 to 40 million ounces, he had included Herbert's silver. That would have been a telling point for cross-examination, but I missed.

Alone the Hunts could not sustain the price; it dropped back from $6 into the $2 to $3 range. After sidestepping a 1974 congressional investigation, the brothers began looking for partners in the Middle East to give them greater financial firepower. The 1970s was the heyday of OPEC. That was where the money was. Once the Hunts got prices moving upward, they could add financial wherewithal and an element of panic to the silver markets with the threat that Arab petrodollars were buying up the world silver supplies. The panic would accentuate the upward price movement by encouraging others to buy silver.

Chapter Five

The brothers turned first to Persia. At the time, the Shah of Iran was at the height of his powers. Iran had not participated in the OPEC oil embargo of December 1973, but, instead, the Shah had increased oil production to take advantage of higher prices. Iran's gross domestic product (GDP) had jumped by 50 percent, which had fueled an economic boom and westernization of a growing middle class. The Shah, a close ally of the United States, had recently spent a reported $100 million for a celebration of 2,500 years of Persian monarchy, which had fueled the stirrings of dissent within the populace. Local discontent was of little concern to the Hunts; they were drawn to the money and perhaps the autocracy too.

Herbert Hunt flew to Tehran first. At a meeting with the Shah's finance minister in 1974, Herbert Hunt proposed that they jointly create a silver broker-dealer, which became the Hunt format for a silver partnership for the next five years. Herbert found no interest. He flew back to Dallas disappointed.

In March 1975, Bunker tried his hand in Iran. Bunker described a call to his friend, Prince Gholam Reza Pahlavi, the Shah's brother: "He is a nice fellow, very shall I say westernized. I think he's a graduate of the University of Michigan and, sort of a prince of a fellow," Bunker mused, "I think that's a good description of him."

After the prince set up a meeting with the finance minister, Bunker flew to Tehran with his special assistant, Bill Bledsoe. Bunker gave what became a well-rehearsed speech about silver as a good investment. The finance minister disappointed him again by saying Iran was not interested in buying nonproductive assets, like silver. "They wanted to invest in buildings and industrial plants such as steel mills and that type of things."

Within four years, the Shah had fallen, the victim of his own arrogance, extravagance, and autocratic rule. Bunker's take was different: "I guess the Shah's people got in trouble [when] the more old-time Muslims objected to all the development. They got in trouble for doing too much instead of too little."

There was nothing new in that story from the one we had presented during our direct case other than folksy details.

On his return from Teheran, Bunker stopped in Zurich and instructed Bledsoe to remain and visit banks. Bledsoe's March 21, 1975 report on his visits to three of the largest Swiss banks, UBS, Swiss Bank Corporation, and Credité Suisse, all had a similar theme: "He does not see the Arabs investing in the silver market," which supported our theory that the Hunts were looking for oil-rich Arab partners who would, just five years after the OPEC oil embargo, panic the silver markets. During our direct case, the jury had heard an excerpt from Bunker's deposition in which I had walked Bunker through the three references to Arab interest; Bunker had feigned ignorance:

"And was part of Mr. Bledsoe's instructions to ask the banks whether they knew of any Arabs who had interest in the silver market."

". . . I don't know what you are referring to," was Bunker's testy response.

When Curran returned to Bledsoe's report, Bunker told a new story that surprised us; he was trying to find Arabs who would buy some of his silver. "My wife asked me to get my debt down," Bunker continued his family man theme, "as well as I knew I needed business funds." He embraced the Arab world at the time: "Well, that's where the money was and that was the source of big supplies of money from people that were precious metals minded . . ." Bunker, as the modern man with his wife participating in business decisions, seemed implausible. I glanced at the jury; they were watching intently but expressionless. Bunker repeated the line twice; it probably had been rehearsed and tested with mock jurors.

I scribbled an illegible note to myself, as Curran transitioned to his next point.

Chapter Six

Bunker Hunt and Paul Curran took another day to finish the direct examination before I rose to cross-examine. But the story is best understood by following the events chronologically, contrasting the two competing storylines for each stage of the conspiracy. So I will interrupt Paul Curran's direct examination to relate what happened when I finally got my turn to cross-examine Bunker at trial.

Bunker watched me walk to the small podium positioned close to the jury box, just beyond the last juror. The annoying heater behind the jury box—that had sporadically clanged during opened statements, as we had played videotaped depositions, or listened to collateral witnesses—was quiet now in early summer. The air conditioning was hissing softly in the silent courtroom. The jurors were looking expectantly at me. I put down my notebook on the small podium. This was the place I never thought I would be. I stared at Bunker across the well of the courtroom. He frowned back. We had done this before, for fourteen days spread over many months in pretrial deposition, battling in a law firm conference room where his lawyers were free to interrupt because there was no judge to control them.

But this was different. We were in a packed courtroom before a jury that would decide the case. Bunker wanted to come across as the hapless, misunderstood billionaire who just wanted to invest in a lot of silver and hang around thoroughbred horses. I wanted to expose him as a clever, lying manipulator who stole from a poverty-stricken country, thousands of other traders, and almost crashed the US economy. I did not want the jury to hear more long speeches or down-home, folksy stories. In a staccato style, I wanted to control the exchange, have Bunker repeat our timeline, admit to inconsistencies, and impeach his innocent-sounding explanations for talking to wealthy Arabs and later buying most of the exchange warehouse silver. That might be second nature for Curran, Perito and Fleming with their experience and aura of authority. But for a young man to control a prominent businessman on a public stage would be a challenge.

After scoring quick points about Bunker's last answers (which I will relate later in the story), I doubled back to the competing versions of Bill Bledsoe's visit to Zurich. Moving to Bill Bledsoe's report on his Zurich trip, I asked:

"And was part of Mr. Bledsoe's instructions to ask the banks whether they knew of any Arabs who had interest in the silver market?"

"No, I don't recall that," Bunker stammered, "I, I, I don't know what you are referring to." Bunker had forgot his lines again, his direct testimony that the Arab world was where the money was. Bunker reverted to his deposition answer: he did not know what I was referring to.

I pulled out Bledsoe's memo from my notebook and walked rapidly across the well of the courtroom. When I handed it to him, I asked whether it refreshed his memory about his instructions to Bledsoe, prepared to score a telling point. Bunker stared blankly at the paper unread and got testy: "The memo does not say that!" he blurted without reading the memo, "I don't want to criticize you because I know you are trying to do a good job and doing a good job, but it is a two-page long memo, it gives about three or four peoples opinion what is going to happen to silver."

That stung. Describing me as a sincere but misguided youngster was condescending. I turned testy. I too rapidly read Bledsoe's three references to conversations with Swiss bankers, each reporting a lack of "Arab interest" in silver. I snarled a question that I knew would bolt Curran to his feet objecting:

"Now, Mr. Hunt *is it just a coincidence*," emphasizing the offensive language, "that Mr. Bledsoe would comment at each bank about Arab interest in silver or the lack of it without any instructions?"

Curran obliged me, bounding up incensed: *"Objection, your Honor!"*

And Judge Lasker obliged him calmly, "Sustained as to the form of the question."

I shrugged and turned back toward the podium. After I asked a proper question—didn't the memo refer repeatedly to Arab interests? Bunker huffed, "You will have to ask Bledsoe that." Bunker did not remember his innocent explanation; I moved on.

From Iran, the story turned to questions about a Hunt broker, Scott McFarland, who was to provide one of the more dramatic moments in the trial before Bunker arrived.

Part Two

Searching for Oil-Rich Partners

Chapter Seven

Starting in the summer of 1975, Scott McFarland, a broker at Drexel Burnham Lambert, became a front man for Bunker Hunt. McFarland's engagement marked the next step in Bunker's quest for partners in the Middle East with the financial wherewithal and interest to create an OPEC-styled monopoly over world silver supplies. Bunker first met Scott McFarland in the early 1970s and found him knowledgeable about silver. He came to consider him a friend. McFarland moved around from Drexel Burnham to Shearson, Lehman, to E.F. Hutton, and then to Bache for a period of six or seven years, "so it seemed like I always gave him some business wherever he ended up," Bunker testified. In the summer of 1975, Bunker told McFarland he had to sell 15 to 20 million ounces of silver, his ploy for probing for those interested in silver. McFarland came back several weeks later, reporting he could not find anyone interested in the United States; he would have to go to Europe. That trip proved fruitful. McFarland later introduced Bunker separately to Mohammed Affara and Haji Ashraf Amin.

While in London in 1976, McFarland met Affara, a
Yemeni-born investment adviser to prominent Saudis. During his opening statement, IMIC's lawyer, Paul Perito,
introduced Affara as, "a true Horatio Alger story from Saudi
Arabia. From very humble beginnings in South Aden, this
man picked himself up by his bootstraps, got an education,
went into the civil service, started at the bottom and in a
few years he became the equivalent to our secretary of health
and human services and then the first secretary of state of
this small country. After studying at Cambridge University in England, one of the world's great universities, Affara
seized the opportunity, putting together a very flourish-
ing business by in effect being the middleman, the catalyst
to bring people together . . . He brought Saudi's together
with Americans and he earned a commission for that and
that's not illegal, unethical in any country of the world."
Perito went in great detail about Affara's relationship with
various brokerage firms and clients, suggesting that Affara
sought out Bunker Hunt and not, as I had supposedly suggested, vice versa.

The fifty-year-old Perito, short, intense, with black hair
and dapper in a double-breasted blue suit, was the junior in
the defense trio but nonetheless a formidable figure. After
graduating Harvard Law with honors in 1964, he had suc-
cessfully prosecuted thirty-five cases in the US Attorney's
Office. He stayed in public service appointed by President
Richard Nixon as Chief Counsel of the White House Special Action Office on Drug Abuse Prevention, and later he

became Chief Counsel to the US House of Representatives Select Committee on Crime. For two decades, he was a prominent fixture in the Washington, DC trial bar where I practice law. Unlike Paul Curran, Perito was always outgoing and friendly even when he was needling me. Perito would serve as my English instructor, insisting on precise language. When I would ask a witness:

"Did he *indicate* [something or other]?"

I came to expect Perito's interjection mockingly: "Do you mean did he *say* it?"

I now scold young lawyers with the same objection but without Perito's thick Boston accent. However, I never developed Perito's ability to lighten the mood. During his opening, Perito distracted the jury with a self-deprecating joke: "You might wonder how I got to be chosen to speak last," he began. "You heard yesterday that this case is about longs and about shorts and you saw Mr. Fleming and Mr. Curran. I'm the shortest of the long defense lawyers," he chuckled as he spoke breathlessly. "I have some solace in that. Talk about unrealistic expectations. When I, as a youngster, wanted to be a basketball player, an unattainable objective, my dad gave me an assurance; he said, son we're from a family that measures height from the neck up. I'm going to let you ladies and gentlemen of the jury decide that." It was a funny line, I thought.

McFarland introduced Affara to Bunker who offered Affara a 3 percent commission like McFarland's for introductions to prominent Arabs. Affara's first introduction was prominent Saudi banker Khalid bin Mahfouz, the billionaire chairman of the National Commercial Bank, the first private bank in Saudi Arabia. Mahfouz maintained opulent homes around the world and traveled in his own jet with gold-plated bathroom fixtures. At one time, he was ranked twenty-fourth in a list of the fifty richest Arabs, with a fortune estimated at $3.35 billion. Mahfouz flew to Dallas and later met Bunker in London, according to Bunker, negotiating to buy Bunker's silver.

The more important aspects of the encounter were described in memos prepared by Bunker's friend and lawyer, Walter Spradley, who confirmed our version of those meetings. His notes from the London trip say "Interesting Arabs in silver," which mimicked Bill Bledsoe's memo and a phrase Spradley reluctantly admitted he heard from Bunker. That contradicted Bunker's earlier denial that he had sent Bledsoe looking for Arab partners. According to Spradley, Bunker and Mahfouz were not discussing a sale of silver to pay off Bunker's debts, but *a joint venture to buy large quantities of silver*—another version of the Iranian broker-dealer proposal—and another contradiction of Bunker's testimony.

A real bonus from Spradley was his warning that if Bunker went through the Mahfouz deal, he would be subject to investigation by the Commodity Futures Trading Commission (CFTC), the government commodity regulator, for manipulation, which was important evidence that Bunker knew a scheme to hoard silver was unlawful.

During our case, the jury had heard Bunker's deposition testimony when Bunker was dismissive of Spradley's opinion, he did not recall it; "sometimes I don't pay much attention to what lawyers say and what Mr. Spradley says." He did not deny the Mahfouz meeting or the Spradley's percipient warning. Although it was certainly believable that Bunker did not put much stock in lawyers or feel constrained by governments, he was now living the consequences of those conceits.

When Curran turned to the Mahfouz meeting, he broke up events so the chronology was less obvious to the jury. Bunker gave a rather bland explanation for the meeting: "I talked to him about it at some length, thought he was somewhat interested, but later he notified Affara that he did not want to buy any silver." Curran did not remind the jury of Spradley's warning about a CFTC manipulation investigation, but he invited Bunker to deny its import, asking:

"Did you ever discuss with him a plan where you and he would each buy silver and agree not to sell it?"

Bunker quickly countered: "No, absolutely not, not with him or anyone else," once again sounding like he was offended by the thought.

However, additional Spradley memos—presented to the jury during our direct case—provided evidence that Bunker knew exactly what he was doing in 1979 when he and his cohorts took delivery of large quantities of silver bullion. A Walter Spradley memo from February 1976 warned about the potential illegal impact of large bullion deliveries. After their frustrations with Iran and Sheikh Mahfouz, Bunker and Herbert tried to create their own silver-hoarding vehicle at home by acquiring a controlling interest in Great Western United. The company bought large silver futures positions and took delivery of 20 million ounces of bullion. Spradley testified to a conversation with Bunker these large bullion deliveries: "I recall general conversations . . . that if [Great Western] stood for delivery on futures contracts that it might have an effect on the shorts."

In technical jargon, Spradley was saying that Great Western's unusually large bullion demands were creating the risk of a "squeeze" or "corner" of the traders holding short positions. At maturity of a futures contract, most traders will close their short or long contracts by buying offsetting contracts. If a single dominant long trader is standing for delivery and unwilling to offset short positions, the shorts who do not have silver bullion to deliver against their contracts have to bid up future prices until they found a trader willing to offset their positions. As a result, prices would rise artificially.

As Spradley predicted, Great Western's large bullion deliveries prompted a warning telegram from the CFTC, stating: "It appears . . . an orderly liquidation of the Chicago Board of Trade June 1976 contract is dependent on your trading activities . . . [Y]ou are required by law to avoid any *artificial price* in either futures or cash markets . . . Price manipulation is a violation of the Commodity Exchange Act." Herbert Hunt wrote back, denying Great Western was engaged in manipulation; it was just trying to acquire a large bullion position.

After Great Western took 20 million ounces in bullion deliveries, the CFTC did not pursue the matter. The Spradley warning and the CFTC letter, however, were additional proofs that Bunker and Herbert knew that large bullion deliveries on the commodity exchanges could result in price manipulation. But they did it anyway. Large bullion deliveries became a key element of Bunker's scheme in 1979.

Great Western adopted another bizarre strategy to gain control over worldwide bullion supplies. The company approached the strongmen of Panama, Philippines, and Nicaragua proposing a plan to barter a minimum of 10 million ounces of silver for sugar cane it needed for its operations. According to an internal memo, the bullion would be "moved to Switzerland, stored, and placed in escrow," thus, effectively removing silver bullion from visible world supply, another element of price manipulation that foretold the Hunts' 1979 activities. A common theme to the Hunt scheme was developing.

In response to Curran's questions, Bunker said that he was not involved in the Great Western's silver trading; he was nominal chairman. But it turned out that he was sufficiently involved to scope out the largest silver mine in the United States owned by Sunshine Mining Company. Great Western bought a 30 percent interest, as Bunker explained. It seemed that Bunker and Herbert were not just interested in monopolizing exchange warehouse silver but also were

looking to take control over the ultimate silver supplies
in the mines of Mexico, Peru, and elsewhere. After two
years, however, the Hunt-installed management objected
to their plan for the company and brought a lawsuit, which
prompted Bunker and Herbert to sell their interest in Sunshine Mining. At that point, Judge Lasker interjected a
lighthearted comment into the tense courtroom:

"It was all gloom after that, no more sunshine."

Bunker looked up at the judge nodding: "As far as we
were concerned, it was quite gloomy."

Owning a public company proved to be too fraught with
regulations and too public. The brothers sold their shares
in Great Western and moved on. This history depicted a
picture of Bunker and Herbert experimenting with ways to
take control over world silver inventories but running into
legal barriers that they would later know about but ignore.

And Curran moved on. He did not touch the other
Spradley memos, perhaps calculating that the jury had
heard them weeks before and they were too technical to
understand or remember. Curran was now approaching
one of the more dramatic exchanges during our direct case,
a fight over the testimony of Max van Til, a McFarland
friend and the broker for Ashraf Amin, who had an important meeting with Bunker.

Chapter Eight

Max van Til's story was an intriguing insight into the world of Bunker Hunt. Van Til, one of Scott McFarland "drinking buddies" in London, told him about Haji Ashraf Amin, a bullion dealer from Dubai who would buy silver in Pakistan, Iran, and India and swap it for gold in London. Amin was another likely candidate for the Hunts. He was a wealthy businessman, knowledgeable about silver. Van Til was Amin's commodities broker.

In 1976, Scott McFarland arranged through van Til a dinner for Bunker Hunt and Amin. They met in a private suite in Claridge's Hotel, a five-star London hotel that promoted itself as "rich with glamor and timeless elegance." After dinner, Bunker drew Amin to the terrace for a private chat. Left behind on the sofa, McFarland explained to van Til why Bunker had sought the meeting. Bunker, according to McFarland, was going to make a proposal to Amin *to drive silver prices up.*

Herbert Deutsch, the colorful counsel in one of the related class action lawsuit, took van Til's deposition in

London several months before trial. Deutsch was almost the perfect counterpart for me, a straight-laced, Justice Department-trained lawyer. He wore plaid suits to my pinstripes, a ready joke to my low-key serious persona, and a common sense aggressive style. We worked together well during most of the pretrial stage. While we would think about formal discovery requests to obtain information, Herb would hop on a plane and knock on Mahmoud Fustok's front door at his Chantilly horse farm outside of Paris. And to my surprise, Fustok answered the door and talked to him. From then on, I started picking up the phone or making a visit as my first strategic choice to get information from a witness, instead of writing out a subpoena.

In response to Herb's questions van Til described his introduction of McFarland to Ashraf Amin. After several meetings, McFarland set up the Claridge's dinner. Van Til confirmed that when he, Bunker, Amin, and McFarland were present, silver was the topic of conversation. As van Til described it, "They were talking generally about silver production in India, silver stocks. Hunt asked how Ashraf saw the silver price moving, and Ashraf asked the same thing to Hunt." That testimony was not particularly significant. Hunt was bullish on silver; the whole world knew it. Van Til's description of his conversation with McFarland on the sofa was the important breakthrough.

Deutsch asked: "And what did McFarland say to you?"

Van Til responded: "McFarland told me that Bunker Hunt was going to give a proposal to Ashraf Amin *whereby the price of silver would increase a lot.*"

This hit the essence of the case: Hunt did not want just a hard asset, a hedge against inflation, or a good investment—as he was claiming—he wanted to drive up worldwide silver prices.

Van Til's testimony did not end with the Claridge's dinner. Apparently no deal was struck between Bunker and Amin on the terrace, but McFarland and van Til continued to meet. McFarland returned to London in 1978 and had a series of encounters with van Til during which they discussed a silver squeeze, a form of illegal price manipulation. Van Til related the substance of those conversations:

"What did Mr. McFarland tell you?" Deutsch asked.

". . . He was in London trying to set up a syndicate to buy silver."

"What was the purpose? *Was it to squeeze the market, the silver market?*"

"*Yes.*"

"How did that subject come up where McFarland told you that he was in London on behalf of Hunt and his purpose was to set up a squeeze for N.B. Hunt?"

"I can't pinpoint a specific meeting that this was said to me. It came during the course of several meetings as McFarland was . . . a contact who was working temporarily in the London office."

In testimony about a breakfast with McFarland in a brasserie on Fulham Road, van Til gave the jury an insight into McFarland's recruiting technique, testifying:

"Did Mr. McFarland ever show you a document that he told you that he was sending to wealthy Arabs describing the silver market?"

"Yes."

"What did he tell you it was?"

"He told me that this was a proposal to—of course, Arab wealthy individuals and to move the price—*how to move the prices higher.*" Unfortunately, we never found a copy of this document but McFarland's description served our purpose well.

"Did he tell you in words or substance that he was sending this document on behalf of Hunt to the Arab[s]?"

"Whatever Scott McFarland did in London or anything he did in London was basically on behalf of Hunt."

McFarland told van Til how the squeeze would work, and van Til told the jury. McFarland said they would take delivery of silver at the maturity of silver futures contracts and ship it overseas, which is exactly what Bunker and his cohorts did in 1979. And Deutsch asked:

". . . Did McFarland tell you why people wanted to do that?"

"*It's quite obvious. The price would go higher.*"

"Why is that . . . ?" Deutsch quickly asked.

"Silver stocks would decline, therefore . . . it would be made very difficult for the short sellers to find silver.

Therefore, they would continue to buy or cover their shorts in the COMEX market, and *the result of that would be that the price would be higher."*

Van Til's testimony was powerful evidence. It supported many of the elements of our circumstantial case. It confirmed what Bunker was up to—driving silver prices higher—who he was talking to, and how he proposed to accomplish his goal. It provided a believable picture of Bunker preparing over an extended period of time to manipulate silver prices.

Although powerful, van Til's testimony first had to be admitted in evidence before the jury would hear it. That proved no easy task. The testimony could provide perhaps the most direct link to Bunker's state of mind of any evidence introduced at trial. But the evidentiary issues raised were complex. Van Til was relating an out-of-court statement by McFarland, who in turn was reporting conversations with Bunker Hunt. This type of testimony is often considered unreliable hearsay and not admitted in evidence. Judge Lasker was troubled, as he explained: "Normally situations that one is considering that fall under that rule involve what I will call first-degree hearsay, that is to say, the agent himself quotes his principal, and people are generally satisfied that's a trustworthy enough situation so that it should be admitted. What we are dealing with here, though it falls under the same rule, is second-degree hearsay. We have Mr. van Til quoting Mr. McFarland, who is quoting Mr. Hunt, and that makes me a little less satisfied than I would otherwise be. Therefore, I feel that if Mr. McFarland is going to be here as a witness and he could be cross-examined about whether he did say what Mr. van Til says that he said, I would have no concern, so I will leave it to you to let me know."

In other words, the judge wanted us to call McFarland, a hostile and unpredictable witness, in order to present van Til's videotaped deposition to the jury. However, he did not make a final ruling. As he left it, he said, "I won't say I won't consider the matter otherwise, but I am saying that I am prepared to rule in your favor if you are prepared [to call McFarland]."

The judge's order presented a significant strategic dilemma. Van Til's testimony might be very helpful, but the risks of calling McFarland were substantial. Van Til had been a hostile witness presented on videotape rather than live. He had resisted testifying to the point of defying a subpoena; he appeared only after being threatened with arrest. As a result of his attitude and the circumstances of the deposition, the testimony was disjointed. The jury might not grasp the significance of the statements. Van Til's testimony could also be substantially diluted or negated if McFarland proved to be a good witness for the Hunts. A strong denial from a live witness could prove more persuasive than the videotape. The credibility of our circumstantial case could be severely damaged. And I had made reference to van Til's testimony in my opening statement when I did not anticipate the judge's ruling. If we did not play van Til's deposition, Paul Curran would remind the jury during closing. A failed effort to make a major point often can change the jury's perception of an entire case. If McFarland's appearance were a flop for us, it could be a crippling blow. We concluded van Til's testimony was too powerful to pass up, even if it meant calling McFarland.

We played the van Til videotape, watching the jury intently, but they gave nary a clue about their reaction. I went home wondering whether we had made the right decision. Did we have the ammunition to undermine McFarland hostile testimony? Would I use it effectively?

Chapter Nine

Scott McFarland, tall, blond, and well dressed in a gray, double-breasted suit and conservative tie, entered with long strides into the courtroom, took the oath, and sat down. As he settled into the witness stand, he looked pasty and nervous. The judge spoke first, telling the jury that he had required Minpeco to call McFarland in order to present other evidence. He then nodded to me. I was standing at the podium close to the jury looking at McFarland about fifteen feet away. The courtroom was silent.

Max van Til's testimony was not the first place to turn. McFarland could be made to be helpful—albeit reluctantly—even if he was going to deny van Til's statements. I asked about background first. McFarland told how he had met Bunker Hunt through a "cold contact" in about 1975 and how Bunker had quickly become 90 percent of his business. He confirmed that he had been the commodities broker for Bunker Hunt and his children for several years.

He conceded that in 1977 he had entered orders for more than three million bushels of soybean futures for Bunker,

Herbert, and other family members. Those trades collectively were in excess of the amount CFTC regulations permitted, which led the CFTC to sanction the Hunts after finding they were trading in concert. That finding was a good parallel for the Hunt's silver trading in the face of the Bunker and Herbert Hunt's repeated denials that they ever traded together. In upholding the CFTC's action, the US Court of Appeals had said: "This misconduct was *systematic and carefully preconceived.*" I had borrowed that phraseology in my opening statement to refer to the Hunt silver trading.

In early 1979, McFarland's trading suggested he knew a move was about to be made on silver prices. In February 1979, McFarland, who made about $100,000 annually, borrowed $2,500,000 from Bunker Hunt to buy silver futures. He later took delivery of the silver bullion, mimicking on a small scale the trading of the other conspirators. In the midst of the price rise, McFarland sold this silver to Bunker Hunt at a substantial profit, which arguably paralleled Affara's million-dollar commission. However, McFarland suffered a hard landing when silver prices crashed. He became *persona non grata* at his brokerage firm—then Bache—and soon became unemployed. Bunker loaned him money for a time but then repossessed his home, an interesting insight into Bunker's personality.

After making these helpful points, I turned to the key issue of van Til's testimony. McFarland confirmed that, in return for the promise of a substantial commission, probably more than $1 million, he had spent several years introducing Bunker Hunt to wealthy Arabs to find a buyer for 20 million ounces of silver. He testified to a series of meetings over a four-year period that he had arranged for Bunker with wealthy Arabs. McFarland also confirmed the Claridge's dinner with Amin and van Til, and Bunker's trip to the terrace with Amin. But on his critical conversation with van Til on the sofa, McFarland gave the predicted denial when I asked:

"In that conversation, isn't it a fact that you told Max van Til that Bunker Hunt was going to give a proposal to Ashraf Amin whereby the price of silver would increase a lot?"

"Did I make that statement to Max van Til?"

"Yes."

"No, I do not believe I did." I accepted his anticipated denial, hoping I had sufficiently masked it with good points to diminish its impact.

During cross-examination, however, Paul Curran methodically walked McFarland through each element of van Til's testimony and elicited a long string of additional denials: He did not tell van Til that Bunker Hunt was going to give Amin a proposal to increase silver prices; he did not show van Til a document to induce wealthy Arabs to move the price of silver higher; Bunker never attempted to set up a silver squeeze; and so on.

It was a strong performance as feared; it required an effort at redirect. I returned to the podium anxiously calculating where to attack. McFarland had presented confident denials that he had undoubtedly rehearsed with the Hunt lawyers. I did not want to invite him to repeat those denials in answering my questions. However, in prior statements, McFarland had admitted to memory lapses due to his past drug and alcohol problems. I asked McFarland about his drug problem, which promptly brought a rebuke from Judge Lasker. He curtly told me to ask another question; that was too impolite a subject for his courtroom, I suppose. But I continued by taking a jab at McFarland's memory:

"And are you saying that no, when Mr. Amin and Mr. Hunt went out of the room in Claridge's, that you never said to Mr. van Til that Bunker Hunt was going to give a proposal under which the price of silver would go up a lot? You are saying no to that and you are not saying you don't recall."

"*Well, I'll back up if you will.* I don't remember ever having that conversation with Mr. van Til. I do not—I cannot recall what conversation, if any, we had while Mr. Hunt and Mr. Amin were not in our presence."

With this opening, I pressed further: "So it is that you don't recall whether you said that Mr. Hunt was going to give a proposal to Mr. Amin that the price of silver was going to go up a lot, is that your testimony?"

"*I don't recall any conversation* like that at all."

"You feel your recollection of events in the period 1976 to 1980 is pretty good?"

"Not particularly."

"So it may be that you just don't remember this conversation? That's right, isn't it?"

"Oh, that's possible."

"The conversation may very well have occurred?"

"*That's possible.*"

I sucked in a breath, blinked, and looked at the judge; he looked at me pokerfaced. Now, there was a surprise ending! The predictable result would have been conflicting testimony between van Til and McFarland, leaving the jury to sort out the truth. Now McFarland had admitted that van Til might have had it right; the conflict evaporated.

Pleased with the risk we had taken, I quickly announced "No further questions" and strode back to my seat. Judge Lasker later said he was pleased with his unusual ruling. He undoubtedly was thinking that admitting or rejecting van Til's testimony without McFarland's would have been a close call that the disappointed side could have challenged on appeal. He was now immune from second-guessing by those troublesome appellate judges.

When Bunker came to court, he admitted the dinner but Curran had him denied the import of the conversation. Bunker testified: "we talked at length about silver and had a nice, pleasant dinner I thought, sat around and talked for two or three hours, had dinner ordered up to the room . . . I pretty quickly got the impression that he wasn't really in the market for anything . . . He just wanted to meet me." He also denied they talked about driving up silver prices, but I did not think the denial carried much force.

With his last answer, Scott McFarland's role in the trial ended, and Max van Til's testimony was left intact for me to read to the jury during closing argument, and I was saved from having been too aggressive in my opening statement. I was growing up as a trial lawyer right in the midst of the trial.

After these intense moments, the trial approached Bunker's final preparations for the key 1979 period of his conspiracy.

Chapter Ten

Although Haji Ashraf Amin did not sign onto his plan, Bunker Hunt was not discouraged; he continued to look elsewhere for partners for his silver escapade. The story is finally approaching the critical year of 1979. Bunker's credit card receipts revealed his next move, a meeting with the flamboyant Dubai tycoon, Abdul Wahab Galadari. On January 31, 1979, Bunker had a breakfast with his brother Herbert and Scott McFarland at the Fairmont Hotel in Dallas. Two days later, Bunker's made a call to Galadari. On February 5 and 6, 1979, Bunker and his son-in-law traveled to Dubai on their way to inspect Bunker's drilling rigs in Abu Dhabi.

Abdul Wahab was the risk taker among three Galadari brothers who had made millions trading gold. After splitting with his brothers, Abdul Wahab built the Hyatt Regency Hotel and Galleria, opened the Union Bank of the Middle East (under a special decree issued by the ruler, Sheikh Rashid), started a Citroen car dealership, published a daily English Language Newspaper—the Gulf News— started a string of construction, engineering, and trading companies. Several years later, he was to be the first Dubai bankruptcy, briefly imprisoned before his brothers bailed him out. But in 1979, he was a good candidate for Bunker.

Bunker's visit to Dubai came at a transformative moment in history, which supported the Hunt defense that political and economic events drove up silver prices in 1979. Iran returned to center stage in Bunker's story. Four days before Bunker reached Dubai, Ruhollah Khomeini, the charismatic cleric, returned to Tehran from Paris after fourteen years in exile. Joyous crowds estimated at five million people greeted him. The Shah, one of the United States' most loyal allies in the Middle East, had fled two weeks before. His efforts to modernize Iran curbed the power of the ancient elite and challenged the power of the clerics, had led to religious discontent. And his increasing autocratic rule, brutality, corruption, and extravagance led to widespread demonstrations and rioting that forced him to abdicate his throne and flee to Egypt.

Within the next two weeks, Khomeini had overwhelmed the interim government and taken control of the country. He named himself Grand Ayatollah and Supreme Leader of the newly established Islamic Republic of Iran. The Middle East was dramatically destabilized. Eight months later, on November 4, 1979, Khomeini's followers stormed the US Embassy in Tehran and took fifty-eight US diplomats and citizens hostages, enraged that President Jimmy Carter had allowed the Shah to enter the United States for humanitarian reasons—cancer surgery. The standoff led to a 444-day hostage crisis and later to the reelection defeat of President Jimmy Carter to the more aggressive Ronald Reagan.

The Shia and Sunni divide also came to the forefront, when, in September 1980, Saddam Hussein's Sunni-led Iraq invaded Shia Iran in an effort to become the dominant Persian Gulf power. That war, which had been a frequent subject on the nightly news, was just coming to an end in the summer of 1988 in the middle of the trial.

With his fierce, public persona, Khomeini was also a frequent subject of the nightly news. His image still sent shutters through many US audiences and perhaps the jury, which could have given credibility to the Hunt defense. At the time of Bunker's visit to Dubai, Khomeini was making headlines in every newspaper around the world, and those in the Middle East who knew him best could anticipate the disorder that was about to come. Khomeini and what he represented for future events in the Middle East must have been in the forefront of the minds of Bunker's Dubai audience of businessmen. It is not hard to imagine that when Bunker gave his stock silver speech about Jerome Smith's book and the shortfall of industrial demand over silver supplies, his audience would respond with a frenzy of speculation about what the upcoming disorder would do to precious metals prices—drive them sky high.

When Paul Curran turned his attention to Bunker's trip to Dubai in February 1979, he had to confront a major

inconsistency in Bunker's story—Bunker said he was trying to sell silver to reduce his debt, but his trade book
showed that from Dubai he had placed an order with Scott
McFarland to buy 500 February silver futures contracts
(2.5 million ounces) on the Chicago Board of Trade
(CBOT), and he took bullion deliveries when those contracts expired. What happened to his burdensome debts?

Curran started walking Bunker through the story.
Galadari bought and sold silver and had other businesses,
including a real estate development with combination,
hotel, apartment building, shopping center and ice rink. "I
thought it was pretty good in an Arab country, in the middle
of the desert, to have an ice skating rink." They talked
about silver at considerable length. Although Galadari was
interested up to a point in buying silver, he "didn't think
right now that he want to put that much money out."

Bunker met eight or ten friends or acquaintances of
Galadari in Dubai, including again Ashraf Amin, who he
did not immediately recognize, and then drove two and
a half hours to Abu Dhabi to inspect his oilrigs. However, those conversations left an impression, according to
Bunker: "I found them extremely bullish on the silver market and the most optimistic bullish people that I had ever
encountered and a lot of it was tied to the ascension of power
in Iran of Khomeini . . . a very un-stabilizing influence
had arrived in the Middle East and the Shah, a stabilizing
influence had been deposed."

Curran directly confronted the inconsistency of Bunker, who had been supposedly selling silver for five years, placing a buy order for silver futures from Dubai. During our direct case, the jury heard Bunker fumble an explanation for these purchases when I had asked:

"Can you give us any information at all as to why, when you were in Dubai offering to sell silver, that you bought $18 million worth of silver. Any information at all on that point?"

"No, I have no recollection."

However, Bunker now had a ready explanation when Curran asked whether "anything out of the ordinary" in the political sense had occurred in the Middle East. "I mentioned just about the time the Shah had left Iran, Tehran, in fact, was being kicked out and being replaced by Khomeini. It may have been something else that I overlooked right now." It seems Bunker had forgotten a prepared speech to justify the inconsistency. Curran prompted him to recall that Ayatollah Khomeini flew back to Iran on February 1, 1979. That would have been a good time for me to interrupt to object to Curran's leading question, break their pace or even push them to move on, but I missed my cue.

With Curran's prompting, Bunker remembered his lines: "I do recall something now. You prompted my memory a little bit. He was a rather elderly fellow at that time, I guess he's a lot older now than he was then; people weren't sure just what he was going to do. The first thing he did was he found the wildest militant that he could find and made him prime minister."

The judge was absorbed with Bunker's story and interjected: "Are you talking about Khomeini?"

"Khomeini did, yes," Bunker responded, "So to all of these Dubai people that I was speaking with, they knew this guy and said there was going to be a lot of trouble with that fellow in there and less than a year later there was a war started between Iran and Iraq and they have already killed over a million people and are still going strong. So, they were not too far wrong."

"And in connection with the Dubai trip," Curran continued, "instead of selling some silver when you were there, you ended up buying some for the reasons you have given, is that it?"

"Yes, that's right." Through that stretch of story, Bunker had a bumpy ride, stumbling with some of his answers. But Curran wanted to put the best face on the story before I could cross-examine. Whether he immunized Bunker from my cross-examination, only the jury could say, and they were not talking. But each time I took a look, they were paying close attention.

Chapter Eleven

For four years Bunker was talking to wealthy Arabs about selling 20 million ounces of silver while supposedly carrying the same excessive debt burden, according to his wife. His story was implausible, which I tried to demonstrate with my questioning:

"And you didn't sell any silver to Mr. Galadari, is that correct?" I asked.

"No."

"Isn't it true, Mr. Hunt, that you could sell silver futures contracts and deliver your silver bullion to the market to sell that silver?" I asked.

"I could. But that, that, that," he stumbled, "causes a lot of problems. That's not easy to do at times. The market won't take much short selling . . ."

Bunker's answer about the impact of large sales gave me an opening to make a point about the power of large bullion deliveries on price.

"You mean by selling 20 million ounces into the market all at once, you might depress the price?"

"That's right; and there might not be enough shorts there to buy it."

"Now, if you sell silver into the market over a four or five year period, you probably wouldn't depress the price?"

"That's right, if you sold a little bit every day for four, five years, I don't guess you would bother the market."

That was an important admission: Bunker knew large bullion deliveries could move the market, a tactic he and his cohorts used during the critical period in late 1979. He also knew ways to sell silver, reduce his debt, and not affect prices.

I moved to another inconsistency: Bunker's purported effort to sell to wealthy Arabs while offering 3 percent commissions to Scott McFarland and Mohammed Affara was not economical; he would end up receiving less. Conduct that is uneconomic, except if prices are being manipulated, is evidence of intent to manipulate. After we fenced for a time with the logic of Bunker's plan, Bunker retreated into not recalling; he did not remember whether a 3 percent commission to McFarland or Affara was more than the broker's commission for selling silver into the futures exchanges.

Then I got to a key point: Bunker did not have to find individual buyers of his silver; he had already sold silver by delivering bullion into the futures market without the difficulties he was now using as an excuse.

"Now, Mr. Hunt, you say throughout this period you were trying to sell silver, but you were unsuccessful. Isn't it true in 1975 that you sold about 10 million ounces of silver into the market and you didn't have any trouble doing that?"

"I took—I did make a delivery into the market at some time," Bunker responded while gazing into space as if he were trying to remember. "I don't remember when, but I took less than I thought it was worth." I had hit a nerve. Bunker's voice got so low that Paul Curran had to help the court reporter—who was stationed ten feet from Bunker near the jury—by repeating his answer: "I think I took less, I believe," Curran repeated.

I continued: "Mr. Hunt, your records show that . . . you sold about 16 million ounces of silver into the market."

"Yes. I hope that was all right. Yes, I did," Bunker responded, trying to sound cooperative and nonchalant.

With that answer, I could have moved on. He had a clear way to solve his wife's debt issue; he was up to something else. But I did not want to leave the jury with any doubt about our point. If I had asked Bunker whether he intended to manipulate silver prices, he would have responded with an emphatic denial. I used his friend and lawyer to make our point. I reminded Bunker and the jury of Walter Spradley's testimony that Bunker's meeting with Saudi banker, Khalid Mahfouz, was not about selling silver, but Spradley said they discussed a program to buy silver. And Spradley had warned about the legality of the proposed joint venture, which I highlighted by asking:

"Mr. Spradley has testified that he told you that if you carried out the proposed transaction with Sheikh Mahfouz, that, 'I thought there was a possibility that you would be subject to investigation by the CFTC for manipulation.'"

"I don't recall him saying that," Bunker said defiantly, "I think he is making that statement 12, 14 years after the fact and I think I don't recall it. That's my memory."

"You are not contesting Mr. Spradley's testimony that he made that statement are you?"

"I have, I have no recollection. He didn't know much about silver and so he could have gotten mixed up, I'll say that. I didn't use him any more after that . . . although we are still good friends because I really didn't think he had an understanding of the business."

"It is clear you don't contest his testimony?"

"Yes, I don't recall that at all."

That exchange left Spradley's testimony warning Bunker against manipulating prices uncontradicted. The fact that he did not use Spradley thereafter was an added bonus. The jury was free to reach the conclusion that Spradley was not sufficiently flexible to be involved in unlawful activity.

I had a final point about the new details Bunker was jovially adding during his direct examination. When I had asked Bunker during his pretrial deposition why he bought silver futures during his trip to Dubai, he could give no explanation; he simply did not recall he said. During his direct examination, his memory had been reawakened; he testified that he became bullish while listening to Dubai businessmen talk about the radical views of Ayatollah Khomeini. So, I asked:

"Sitting with your lawyers refreshed your recollection about something that happened back in 1979, but sitting with me didn't refresh your recollection?"

Curran quickly bound to his feet: "Objection, your Honor!"

"He has a right to ask him that," the judge responded turning quickly back to Bunker to hear his answer.

"I went over the records, that's right," Bunker shot back.

"With your lawyers?" I countered.

"That's correct."

That sounded like he had made up a story with the help of his lawyers. I felt the jury got it, but perhaps that was just my ego in the glow of the moment. I moved to my next topic.

After the telling of the Dubai meetings, the story was about to transition from a search for partners to the implementation of the Hunt strategy for an assault on world silver supplies. As that was occurring, Minpeco was preparing for its fateful decision to enter the futures markets on the urging of its US brokers.

Chapter Twelve

Two weeks before Bunker Hunt made his dramatic entrance to a packed courtroom, another short pudgy man came through the double doors. The visitor gallery was half empty; our team and Minpeco executives were the nervous observers. For the reporters and spectators following the trial, this day did not seem important. I did not agree; it was one of the most intense two days of the trial for me. Dressed in a brown tweed suit with a vest and a simple tie, Minpeco's disgraced futures trader, Ismael Fonseca, seemed uncertain walking down the center aisle. When he reached the divider separating the well of the courtroom, he opened the gate, stopped, and looked around, bewildered. Four teams of lawyers, six jurors, and an alternate stared back at him.

As Bunker Hunt was gearing up for an assault on world silver supplies, Minpeco's Board of Directors was taking its first steps to learn about the use of futures trading. Minpeco had been created in 1973 as the exclusive agent to sell Peru's minerals, including its 45 million ounces of silver extracted annually from mines high in the Andes Mountains. For years, US brokers and dealers had traipsed to Lima, which was a small, drab town in those days, shilling the benefits of the futures markets. In mid-1979, the Minpeco's Board of Directors—meeting in a bare room in a rundown colonial mansion in Lima—appointed Fonseca, one of its members, to create a new hedging department.

Judge Lasker stood from his stuffed leather chair, welcomed Fonseca, and pointed him toward the witness chair where an interpreter was waiting for him. When he turned with a furrowed brow, the judge asked his name for the record; Ismael Alfredo Fonseca Montoya came the quiet response. The clerk read the oath, the interpreter translated, Fonseca responded with a barely audible "si," the interpreter echoed "yes" as Fonseca sat down. Standing by the podium, I began the laborious process of asking questions through an interpreter. Fonseca was there to explain how a major international metals dealer could end up with $80 million loss in the silver futures markets.

The decision to call Fonseca was the most disputed one within our team. He had been tricked by the defendants, blamed and fired by Minpeco, and subjected to a criminal investigation for three years. He was hostile to both sides, unpredictable, and often unpleasant. His initial demeanor when entering the courtroom surprised me; he was usually full of bluster and anger. He was not strictly needed to present Minpeco's case. Several company executives had explained its silver trading activity and damages. Fonseca presented a target for the defendants' skilled cross-examiners who were ready to make their case that Minpeco was just a sore loser, at fault for its own losses.

But to me, Fonseca embodied the damage inflicted by the conspiracy, the wreckage that it made of his life and many others. He was as much an exhibit as a witness. He was a silent, honest, and hardworking victim of the Bunker's self-absorbed folly. When the jurors heard his story, I felt they would intuitively understand how Minpeco had been taken in by surging, historically unprecedented prices manipulated by the billionaire Bunker Hunt, his family, and Saudi cohorts. Fonseca gave the cold complexities of longs, shorts, tax straddles, and bullion deliveries a human face. I decided to call him despite our internal dissents.

I started by asking Fonseca about his successful rise through a stratified society that made upward advancement difficult. Before joining Minpeco, Fonseca had worked in sales positions for a fishing company and textiles manufacturer, two of Peru's main industries, and then moved up to a position at Peru's central bank. For ten years, he rose from an assistant in the commercial area to a supervisor of three bank regulatory areas. He joined Minpeco, shortly after it was created in 1973, as an advisor in the finance department. He again rose through the ranks to be assistant to the general manager, and then assistant to the president, concentrating his advice on finance issues. He had a populist streak that made him well liked among the workers. They voted him their representative on the board of directors, and he organized and was president of a fund to support workers. The other members of the Minpeco board were patricians in Peruvian society; Fonseca had more the background and manner of the common man.

In 1976, he was assigned by the board of directors to organize a hedging department. "Hedging operations had always been of concern to the board," Fonseca began slowly, but "there was practically no literature on futures operations in Spanish in Peru."

"So, what did you do to get information about future markets?" I asked.

"I began, for example, to go through brochures issued by Merrill Lynch. I read loose reports on hedging operations, obtained also from E.F. Hutton and Merrill Lynch and other companies like Mocatta that had at one time submitted something on hedging, but with such scarce information, I mainly took this brochure from Merrill Lynch as the basis."

In the mid-1970s, US brokers began showing up in Peru. Jim Ferro and a colleague from E.F. Hutton would come three or four times a year.

"Did they say anything about their own sophistication and expertise in the futures markets?" I asked.

"They introduced themselves as having many years of experience," Fonseca continued in a low quiet voice. "Their hedging area was extremely well-organized. It had great prestige worldwide and all that experience and all that knowledge was at our service for the success of our operation."

Merrill Lynch brokers started coming to Lima and giving lectures to groups of Minpeco officials about hedging, Fonseca continued. "For example, I remembered that on one occasion with the support of visual aids, one of Merrill Lynch's representatives lectured a group of Minpeco officials and workers, among them myself, pointing out what happens when you hedge, what happens when you don't hedge. And, finally, the second part of his lecture had to do with the way Merrill Lynch would help us to overcome the problems that he had mentioned in his lecture." The Merrill Lynch brokers came back for a three-day lecture to a larger group that included senior executives from sales, finance, and the Board of Directors.

"Can you be a little more specific about what advantages they talked about for Minpeco?" I asked.

"Basically, the advantage for Minpeco concretely was that it could make sure of prices for itself covering its costs and profit expectations in a physical operation, whatever it might be."

Other major metal dealers paraded to Lima, including the venerable Henry Jarecki from Mocatta Metals, one of the major New York metals dealers and a prestigious COMEX board member; he would play a key role in the fall of 1979 during the heat of Bunker's intrigues. Jarecki made a written proposal to take over Minpeco's physical silver sales operations and combine it with a hedging operation. "He also explained about hedging operations," Fonseca continued, more animated now. "I remember one thing that he mentioned, that there were at least two or three thousand reasons for prices to move, and that if one had those two or three thousand reasons in one's computer right away, there would be two or three thousand new reasons. Anyone trading, in this case silver, would never know where he stood, which justified the hedging system."

"And why did that justify the hedging system?" I asked.

"Because the holder of the silver, whether miner, trader, or middleman, was not exposed to this gamble of prices rising and falling."

Many businesses want to enhance their planning by eliminating the risk of price movements, which is one function of the futures markets. These markets are made up of speculators and hedgers. Speculators take the risk on price movements, while hedgers use futures contracts to remove price risk—which makes for more predictable business planning. Both are necessary to a properly functioning market and both are entitled to a fair market. So, for instance, a miner or a dealer like Minpeco has physical silver or commitments to buy physical silver, which will decrease in value as prices drop or increase in value as prices rise. In order to know what its revenues will be three or six months hence, it could offset its long physical position by selling a futures contract. A short futures contract (a commitment to sell) will increase in value when prices drop. Thus, in theory, as the dealer's physical inventory or commitments—its long positions—lose value with a price drop, it will make an equivalent amount from its short futures contract and vice versa. The overall value of its position stays steady. Prices of future sales of silver are locked in at the time the futures contract is acquired.

At the time, Minpeco was not that sophisticated; it did not even have a price monitor from the exchanges, and the newspapers in Lima did not report COMEX prices; Minpeco would have to wait several days for reports from its New York office to know about price movements and other market news. That left it helpless to the vagaries of price movements.

The periodic broker visits continued until February 1979 when Jim Ferro of E.F. Hutton made a proposal. "We went out to lunch after a meeting in the office," Fonseca said. "In the course of lunch, the idea came up that since we knew these operations in theory but had never seen them in practice—none of us had ever set foot in an exchange of whatever kind—it was time to go from theory to a visit that would give us a better idea of practice."

Minpeco's Board of Directors liked the idea. From May through August 1979, Fonseca and two colleagues went to Chicago, New York, and London for futures markets training. Unbeknownst to the Minpeco board, some of the wealthiest in the world were preparing to make their new hedging department an unmitigated disaster. As Fonseca was learning his new skill, Bunker Hunt was gathering forces for an assault on silver prices, a scheme for which no amount of training could have prepared Fonseca.

Part Three

Gathering Forces

Chapter Thirteen

Minpeco's decision to explore the silver futures markets could not have come at a worst time. Upon his return from Dubai, Bunker Hunt sounded the call to arms within his family. The time seemed right to drive up silver prices: the Iranian Revolution and a recession with hyperinflation held the promise of worldwide instability that would fuel a rush to the perceived safety of precious metals. On the same day in February 1979, Bunker's children—Houston, Mary, Elizabeth, and Ellen—opened commodity accounts and bought silver futures contracts—using Scott McFarland as their broker. Bunker's brother Lamar started building a relatively small silver position (300 contracts). Herbert Hunt's children followed shortly thereafter. When Bunker took delivery of silver from Dubai, the family silver futures positions almost doubled in a matter of months from a net 6,082 to 11,164 long contracts (commitments for a whopping 55.8 million ounces), plus Bunker and Herbert already owned a combined 40 million ounces of silver bullion stored in exchange warehouses. Even before the price surge, the combined family stash was worth about $575 million that represented a substantial percentage of the visible supply of bullion in exchange warehouses.

The Hunt family trades in February 1979 looked systematic and preconceived, but Bunker denied that he ever traded silver jointly with his brothers and children. To rebut our point, Paul Curran invited Bunker to distinguish the brothers' business interests to suggest they did not do things together, which gave Bunker the opportunity to tell more homespun tales. For instance, Herbert did not share Bunker's interest in cattle and agriculture: "No. Herbert, as a little fellow, I remember he had a bunch of turkeys and he was looking after the turkeys and they had some kind of a disease, the turkeys, when he was about eight or nine years old and inside of about two days he had 250 turkeys die to the last turkey that he had and I think it sort of broke his spirit and he decided he didn't want anything to do with something that was involved in farming and ranching and so since then he has avoided it." Herbert's primary interest beyond oil and gas exploration was real estate development.

Lamar favored professional sports. Frustrated in his effort to buy a National Football League (NFL) franchise, Lamar thought big like his father and brothers. He helped organize the American Football League (AFL), created the Kansas City Chiefs, and engineered the AFL's merger with the NFL. Lamar also had an interest in the Chicago Bulls basketball team and was an organizer of World Team Tennis. Bunker summarized Lamar's exploits but did not mention that Lamar has been credited with naming the "Super Bowl." Perhaps that would have been too immodest. Asked whether he was involved in Lamar's sports investments, Bunker sounded like a typical big brother: "No, I was not. I'm a big football fan, basketball, and baseball. I see a lot of games and enjoy them very much. I volunteered to go into the football with [Lamar] when he first started the league. He was fairly young in his twenties and I think he decided that he would rather do it by himself without my help. I probably would have given him too much advice."

And neither brother shared his interest in thoroughbreds, Bunker testified in the self-deprecating style he feigned well: "A fellow asked me once why my brothers didn't have some horses. I said to him, I guess they are smarter than I am. It's a tough business."

When my time came, I preferred facts to folksy stories. I went back to the formula that had worked earlier; I spent my time asking Bunker about forty-five identical or nearly identical transactions that he, Herbert, and IMIC undertook. Each time Bunker denied that he was acting under an agreement or understanding with Herbert or IMIC. For example, I asked:

"Now, between December of 1976 and January of 1979 your total of silver bullion owned stayed the same at 19.8 million ounces and your brother's only changed slightly to from 18.4 to 18.5 million ounces. Were you and he acting under an agreement or understanding at that time?"

"No." Bunker responded simply.

"In June of 1979 you and your brother Herbert changed your trading patterns in silver futures . . . you started trading in straddles. Did you and your brother have a formal agreement or understanding that you would change your patterns at that time?"

"I had no agreement with Herbert . . ."

"Is it your testimony that your brother acted in the same way at the same time for totally independent reasons?"

"Well, you can ask him."

"I'm asking whether you had an understanding about what actions he would take."

"I didn't have an understanding with him. He's very independent. He's liable to do the opposite. You never know."

I did not try to go back to repeating *"coincidence"* each time; the judge would have certainly cut me off. But the sheer number of common transactions told the story. When I tried a bit of sarcasm, the judge reined me in:

"So, these contracts just kind of happened to happen at the same time in the same amount?"

Both Paul Curran and Paul Perito shot up to object.

"Sustained," snapped the judge, "That's for the jury to decide."

As I continued to ask Bunker whether his litany of parallel trades were made in agreement with Herbert, he got testy: "You'll have to ask Herbert," he said.

With the Hunt family arrayed in the silver markets, the Conti Group began coalescing. The shadowy figure of Naji Nahas was the first to come onto the stage. He also began buying silver futures in February 1979 through his broker, Norton Waltuch at ContiCommodity. Nahas was thirty-five years old in 1979, a Lebanese born in Egypt, who had built a business empire in Brazil. He ran two-dozen businesses including a large insurance group, the world's largest rabbit farm, a construction company, a grain operation, and a property developer. He speculated in stock options and commodities, and was reputed to have made millions speculating in coffee futures. Nahas boasted friendships throughout the Middle East, and he loved gambling on thoroughbred horses, which is how he met Mahmoud Fustok and later Bunker Hunt.

Nahas had wrangled an introduction to Bunker through Maurice Zilber, the horse trainer they had in common, at a dinner in a public dining room at the Hotel George V in Paris. Located just steps from the Champs-Elysées, the hotel, according to its own advertising, has "private terraces that command all of Paris, lovingly restored 18th-century tapestries, and a defining spirit of elegance and charm [that] redefines luxury in the City of Light," a locale that fit Paul Curran's "broad daylight conspiracy" argument. Bunker recalled five or six people at the dinner: "It was more of a social occasion than anything else, just a bunch of people—mostly all of them were interested in horses, had horses and Mr. Zilber was a trainer and we spent most of the time talking about horses. I believe Nahas made a comment to me that he had been in the silver market. He had previously been in the coffee market I recall he volunteered."

Nahas said he had a broker—Norton Waltuch—who was bullish on silver.

Nahas and Bunker developed an unusually close relationship that lasted beyond the silver crash—at least for a time. Even at trial, Bunker's affection for Nahas came through when Curran asked about him. Bunker responded: "Well, he's a Brazilian of Lebanese descent and he's about six feet, I guess, two or three inches tall, tall and slender, about in his early forties, . . . a very interesting fellow, very knowledgeable on world affairs. He spoke about every language a person would hear. He could speak I'd say eight or nine languages at least, great linguistic ability. Just a very nice fellow, very entertaining, good storyteller . . . Very knowledgeable about international politics and that type of thing."

They became "good friends," Bunker recalled. Nahas spent time at the Bristol Hotel in Paris. When Bunker would come to Paris several times a year, "[Nahas] would usually hear that I was in town and give me a call or vice versa." As Curran walked Bunker through their 1979 encounters, he emphasized their common interest in horseracing, vague conversations about silver, usually at the race events or dinner at public restaurants. Curran and Bunker went into a long, distracting discussion of the racetracks around Paris and in Kentucky, the racing seasons, and the annual horse sales. Bunker related proudly that he had "one of the leading stables in Europe" with seventy-five to one hundred horses. He would spend July each year at the thoroughbred yearling sales in Kentucky. He could not be conspiring to manipulate silver prices if he was so busy doing other things, I suppose was his point. I was getting antsy with all this horse talk, but there was not much I could do except watch the jury and look exasperated.

Curran moved on to confront our long list of telephone calls Bunker had with Nahas over the fall and winter of 1979-1980. Our team had spent many months patiently going through telephone bills from Hunt Energy and hotels picking out telephone numbers associated with the conspirators. Bunker was again breezy: "Yes. Mr. Nahas—I don't know how best to describe it other than to say he's a *'telephoniac.'* He constantly is on the telephone. I've never seen a person that could talk on the telephone as much as he does. And he would call me very frequently." They would talk about horses, the weather, business, international affairs, but never the details of their silver investments, according to Bunker. "No, I never related anything specific, but you have to realize that it was in the newspapers constantly that I was long in silver and had a very sizable position in the silver market, so anybody that would read the papers would know that"—yet another reference to Curran's theme of a "broad daylight conspiracy." Bunker supposedly never told Nahas how many silver contracts he had, the contract months he held, or his trading intentions. "No, no, no, not at all," Bunker repeated firmly. Nor did Nahas relate his either. "He talked a lot but not that much about himself."

Bunker placed his first meeting with Nahas in April 1979, after Nahas had started buying silver futures, but the earlier testimony of the bald, dapper Norton Waltuch pushed the meeting back a year into 1978. Waltuch, who was the only central character to appear in person during our direct case, seemed relaxed as he walked into the courtroom. His firm, ContiCommodity, had paid a total of $35 million settling with us, settling with other plaintiffs, and settling its claim against him. Waltuch had walked away "gratis" from the many lawsuits his trading had wrought. He then sued Conti and won indemnification of $2.2 million in personal legal fees he had spent defending himself. Under the particular wording of the indemnification law, the Court of Appeals ruled: "Waltuch's settlement, thus, *vindicated* him," which must have been stinging words to Conti officials. Waltuch reportedly had walked away from his silver escapades with a personal fortune of $10 million. He no longer had a personal stake in the outcome of our case. He was puffed up and full of himself.

And he had no plans of being a cooperative witness. After some fencing, Waltuch finally told of his first meeting with Nahas in January 1979, testifying: "I was discussing silver and I told him what my views were at the time. Nahas said, 'You know, I know Bunker Hunt—I know him from horseracing, he is involved in silver . . .' He says, 'I know him well, I think I'll give him a call,' which he did." Impressed, Waltuch effused: "Everyone knows that Bunker Hunt is involved in silver. He's been in the press since the early 1970s as probably the primary silver bull in the world."

Nahas later reported back that indeed Bunker was bullish on silver. In addition to his account at Conti, Nahas also opened futures trading accounts at two other brokers about this same time, which suggested that his partnership with Bunker was already well into the planning stages.

Mahmoud Fustok, who knew Nahas from the horseracing circuit, also began trading silver in February 1979. He bought silver futures contracts through an omnibus account at Banque Populaire Suisse managed by Advicorp Advisory and Financial Corporation, S.A. (Advicorp), an investment advisory firm in Geneva with wealthy Arab clients. Both Fustok and Nahas had ownership interests in Advicorp.

In May 1979, just as Ismael Fonseca was heading to Chicago and New York for futures market training, Waltuch headed to Geneva where Nahas introduced him to the Advicorp crowd, including Jean-Jacque Bally one of the directors. Not much happened according to Waltuch; they shared their backgrounds for two hours and went to dinner. That was soon to change. Advicorp opened an account with Waltuch at ContiCommodity, and Nahas and Advicorp, investing for its Middle East clients, soon put money into Waltuch's new investment vehicle, Conti Capital Limited.

As the Conti Group was getting to know each other, the second prong of Bunker's plan was coming together.

Chapter Fourteen

In late 1978 or early 1979, Mohammed Affara was still looking to earn his commission by hooking up Bunker Hunt with wealthy Arabs. He arranged a meeting for Bunker with Sheikh Ali bin Mussalem at the Dorchester Hotel, a five-star hotel just east of Hyde Park in London that describes itself as "a favourite choice of celebrities, world leaders, royalty, and high society." Mussalem was wealthy Saudi banker close to the Saudi royal family, a perfect target for Bunker. They discussed, not Bunker's sale of silver to pay the debts that so worried his wife, but, according to Affara: "the idea of forming a joint venture to purchase precious metals in order to protect cash investment against inflation." Mussalem told Bunker, "I want to do a joint venture with you because you are in the market. You know it better than me," said Affara. The conversation sounded much like the ones Bunker and Herbert had been having for the past five years in Iran, their brief foray into Great Western United, and Bunker's conversations with Wahab Galadari and Sheikh Mahfouz, another Saudi banker from

Jeddah. Walter Spradley, Bunker's friend and lawyer, had warned Bunker that a joint venture to purchase silver could bring government scrutiny, but he was no longer invited to repeat his ominous warning.

Bunker, Mussalem, and Affara met again at Le Meurice Hotel located between Place de la Concorde and the Louvre in Paris, another luxury locale. According to Le Meurice, it "is ideally situated for visiting the finest art that Paris has to offer. Salvador Dalí was a regular visitor and today the hotel still enjoys a close relationship with many artists." Nobody mentioned art during the trial. Affara testified that Bunker and Mussalem again "discussed the idea of forming a company that would deal in commodities and other worldwide investments."

When he described the meeting at trial, Bunker kept to his storyline: "I think I was interested in selling some silver at around that time." Mussalem said that with the perilous state of the Middle East, he thought precious metals were an excellent investment. Bunker described vaguely the transition from an effort to sell silver to a partnership.

"And what was the outcome of those meetings that you had with [Sheikh Mussalem]?" Paul Curran asked.

"Well, I found that I had a lot of respect for Sheikh Mussalem, a very intelligent man and he suggested—we sort of mutually suggested," Bunker stumbled through his important change in purpose from silver seller to buyer, "and came to the formation or discussions of the formation of a company to operate there in the Middle East, in general."

The conversation reached a point at which Bunker wanted to consult with his brother Herbert. On June 8, 1979, Bunker and Herbert Hunt met with Mussalem and Affara in Hamburg, Germany. Mussalem introduced the name of his partner Sheikh Mohammed Aboud Al-Amoudi, "a tricky name," according to Bunker. Sheikh Al-Amoudi who was born in Ethiopia, lived in Jeddah, and had developed a fortune in Saudi Arabia in construction and real estate, branching out to oil refineries in Sweden and Morocco. *Forbes* listed Al-Amoudi among the world's wealthiest billionaires. After further negotiating, they reached a preliminary agreement to form a joint venture, and Herbert Hunt wrote an outline of an agreement to form IMIC, which the two Hunts and Mussalem signed.

During his opening statement, Paul Perito, IMIC's lawyer, had given a spirited response to our skepticism that IMIC was ever intended as anything more than a huge hoarder of silver. While Paul Curran was strong and quiet, and Peter Fleming, Fustok's lawyer, was comfortable but combative, Perito was like a spark plug about to ignite. Perito marched quickly in front of the jurors and, waving his arms for emphasis, he denied IMIC had committed any wrongdoing. "IMIC was created as a legitimate, corporate business," he declared, repeating the phrase twice for emphasis; IMIC wanted to become an international bullion dealer. Perito continued by expressing the frustration of defense counsel who must sit quietly and listen to "Mr. Cymrot's interpretation of the evidence." With a backhanded slap, he attacked my opening: "It was all nice and neat. Mr. Cymrot, we respect him greatly, he is an exceeding able fellow. As a matter of fact, yesterday, I found that he was exceedingly creative and resourceful because all the evidence that is unhelpful to him hasn't been alluded to. It has been kind of tucked away . . . A cropped photograph." I was surprised he was attacking me personally; it is good to strike a chord, I thought—better than being ignored.

In his testimony, Bunker kept to Perito's themes. IMIC was a "normal corporate set up," Bunker insisted. He and Herbert each owned 25 percent, and two Saudis each owned 25 percent through a shell company called Profit Investment. His brother Lamar had no interest in IMIC. The agreement provided that IMIC would be located in Bermuda, so the Sheikhs would not have to pay US income taxes; they insisted it would be a non-US company supposedly doing business outside of the United States, which ignored its extensive trading in US futures markets.

Each side would contribute a managing director, Mohammed Affara for the Sheikhs and Bob Guinn, a trusted employee, for the Hunts. Bunker expanded that picture: "We had known him since he was a young boy, his father before him had been one of our top people and we had a lot of confidence in him."

Each side would invest $15 million in IMIC, Bunker continued, but the Sheikhs would get the first $10 million in profits, which sounded to us like anything but a normal corporate setup. During his opening, Perito, in seeking to increase our burden in the eyes of the jurors, had accused us of suggesting the $10 million was a bribe, which was not our point; it exposed the Hunts' expectations that the company would not make ordinary business profits—what's a few million when you are planning to make billions. But that was not Bunker's explanation:

"Why did you agree with that?" Curran asked.

"Dealing with Saudi Arabians or any Middle Easterners is very difficult, very tough and they insisted on it, as a condition to making the deal," Bunker explained. "And since it would be out of profits I thought they were worth it." He answered as if it was the most natural partnership in the world.

Bunker and Herbert also agreed to pay Affara a $1 million commission, to which the Sheikhs did not contribute. "Well, they thought we should pay it and we agreed." The commission was for putting the company together, Bunker explained, as he breezily skimmed over prickly points suggesting he and brother Herbert expected extraordinary profits that would dwarf the extra money they were paying; he had done nothing wrong, his confident tone and appearance implied.

Bunker explained that he and his brother Herbert wanted to do various businesses in the Middle East with highly regarded Saudi Arabian, a different story than the selling silver version he had told just a few minutes before. His wife's concern for his debts went unmentioned, as Bunker tried to expand IMIC's concept beyond buying and hoarding silver bullion: "Well, it would do potentially various types of business, such as oil concessions, mining concessions, some silver investments perhaps, precious metal investments. We considered a large number of other things, any attractive Middle Eastern situation that might come along." They might eventually start a broker-dealer in precious metals, which was an idea they had tried to sell to the Iranian government four years earlier.

Bunker and Herbert left Hamburg with the elements of a deal with Sheikh Mussalem to form IMIC. They flew in different directions. What happened next, however, was no ordinary business transaction.

Chapter Fifteen

Immediately from his Hamburg meeting with Sheikh Mussalem, Bunker Hunt flew to Paris to huddle with Naji Nahas at the Bristol Hotel, which would be their meeting spot for the next year. Herbert Hunt, Mussalem, and Mohammed Affara flew to London to hammer out with their solicitors a written partnership agreement for IMIC. The two arms of Bunker's conspiracy plan were coming together: the now expanded resources of the Hunt Group with the addition of IMIC, and the Conti Group led by Naji Nahas. The Hamburg and Paris meetings marked a critical transition point from the prior five formative years of the conspiracy to the execution phase of Bunker's plan.

Leslie Jordan, our commodities expert, who had spent years analyzing the Hunts and Conti Group silver positions, testified to the dramatic change in the Hunt trading followed the Hamburg and Paris meetings on June 19 to 21, 1979. As of June 18, 1979, the Hunt family owned a gross long 15,396 silver contracts (77 million ounces), and Bunker and Herbert owned an additional 40 million ounces of bullion in exchange warehouses. From his London meeting with Mussalem, Herbert Hunt began the implementation of the plan. He called his Merrill Lynch broker to close his nearby silver positions—particularly July 1979—and to expand his silver futures holdings in early 1980 maturities—February, March, and May 1980. Bunker made a similar change over the next several weeks—closing July, August, and September positions and building a position of 70 million ounces in February and March 1980 contracts. The Hunts almost doubled their gross long positions to 28,851 contracts (144 million ounces), mostly maturing in early 1980 contracts. They also had short contracts that matured further in the future that were largely irrelevant to their scheme.

After June 18, 1979, Bunker and Herbert not only expanded their silver positions, but also changed their pattern of silver futures trading of many years. Ever since they had begun investing in silver in the early 1970s, Bunker and Herbert had held long futures contracts in nearby maturities that they had "rolled forward" when they were about to expire. That meant, for instance, if they held a long futures contract that expired in March, they would close that contract and buy the next available contract, May or July. But after the June 1979 meetings, they started buying "straddles," which is a package of two silver futures contracts bought at the same time, one a commitment to buy (a long contract) and the other a commitment to sell (a short contract). The change in trading pattern, particularly coming after a series of key meetings with coconspirators, was evidence the Hunts were up to something—with enormous silver futures positions in early 1980s maturities, they had put into position the second prong of an attack on silver prices. The first prong was yet to come.

At trial, theories are good but confessions are not easily extracted from wealthy confident businessmen. Although the participants gave bland descriptions of their encounters with no hint of conspiracy, their actions spoke louder, we hoped. Paul Curran would wander from subject to subject, confusing the time frames, but our team was insistent on keeping the chronology before the jury in order to emphasize the connections between the events. I first wanted to connect the Hamburg meeting to Bunker's meeting with Nahas in Paris. I asked Bunker:

"On direct examination you talked about a meeting [with the IMIC Sheikhs] in Hamburg, Germany. Do you recall that?"

"I believe so, yes."

Curran interrupted: "Your Honor, as I recall, the testimony was Germany. I don't think Mr. Hunt testified on direct to the word Hamburg."

Curran wanted to blur the details, but after three months of testimony, we had credibility on points in the timeline. Judge Lasker did not want to waste time, saying: "Everybody agrees that it was Hamburg. It was Hamburg, wasn't it, Mr. Hunt?"

"That's my recollection. I could be wrong. It was in Germany."

I would have preferred the judge let Bunker resist. I was about to extract the same admission with documents, a more powerful way to undermine his credibility. After establishing in quick order that his brother Herbert and the Sheikhs Mussalem were present at the Hamburg meeting, I continued:

"And the result of that meeting was a handshake agreement that a company would be formed with the sheikhs?"

"I don't recall that it was handshake agreement. But I think that was an agreement we work to form a company, until the company was formed there was nothing absolute set in concrete."

Bunker was prepared for the question. The IMIC agreement was not formally signed until July 25, 1979. Supposedly nothing significant happened in June 1979 was the impression Bunker had conveyed in response to Curran's questions. Bunker was trying to diminish the importance of the relationship between the June 1979 agreement to form IMIC and his change in trading pattern—the purchase of large straddle positions—almost immediately after those meetings. I pressed on to see how much of the story he would resist before I would confront him with documents.

"There had been a general agreement that you ought to go ahead and try to put it on paper, right?"

"I believe that's correct."

"Was that approximately in June of 1979?"

"You know, I wouldn't remember the date." Curran had fuzzed up the chronology by saying May or June in his direct question, but the precise date was important in order to line up the meeting with the Hunt trading.

"And after leaving Hamburg, did you fly to Paris and see Mr. Nahas?"

"No. I have no recollection of that. It's possible that I might have gone to Paris. I don't have a recollection."

I asked whether he generally saw Mr. Nahas while in Paris, but he continued to resist, saying: "No, I didn't always see him . . ." Nahas quite often stayed at the Bristol Hotel, he acknowledged.

After these exchanges, I turned to the documents, which told an unimpeachable story meticulously pieced together by Scott Andersen and other members of our team. I flourished a bill from Hill World Travel while walking across the well of the courtroom to hand it to him:

"Do you recognize your signature on it?"

"Yes."

"It says 'Okay, N.B. Hunt,' correct?"

"That's right."

"It's a bill for a trip on June 7, 1979 from Dallas, Ft. Worth, to Frankfurt and the 8th Frankfurt to Hamburg and then on the 9th Hamburg to Paris and an open return from Paris to Dallas. Is that what it says?"

"I guess, yes, as far as I knew. Yes, I think you called it right," he said.

"Is that the time when you had your meeting with Sheikh Mussalem in Hamburg?"

"I believe so."

"And then you went to Paris afterwards; is that correct?"

"Yes. It shows to Paris," Bunker acknowledged, but he wanted to put doubt in our story by adding, "I am not sure I went there. Quite often I changed planes to go somewhere else. I won't argue whether I went or not because I don't recall."

I was prepared for this equivocation. While walking the ten feet back across the well of the courtroom again, I waved an American Express receipt (something like a bloody knife in a murder case) and asked if he again could identify his signature. Bunker and I had spent days in a similar routine during his deposition; he now seemed resigned, his shoulders slumped, his head dropped, he was returning to the Buddha pose he had so often assumed: "Yes, that's my signature."

"Does that refresh your recollection that after you met with Sheikh Mussalem and reached a general agreement to go ahead and try to form a company that you went to Paris and stayed at the Bristol Hotel?"

"I think I did."

These details may seem tedious to present, but they are essential in telling a coordinated story. Once I had reestablished the timeline, I wanted to put Nahas at the Bristol Hotel, but I did not have a hotel bill for him. Bunker testified that he did not recall whether he saw Nahas on this occasion. That left a hole in our story. But I found a way to fill the hole. I pulled out Bunker's deposition in which he testified that from the time he met Nahas until July 1979, they had met "five, six, seven maybe . . . It might have been a few more." After suggesting that was a lot of meetings for a two-month period, I drew Bunker back to the critical June 1979 time frame, asking:

"You were in Paris in June. I showed you those records yesterday."

"Yes, I was there . . . I was there at that time. That's the big French Derby and French Oaks period of time." He was returning to his horseracing theme, but it gave me the opening to ask:

"You saw him at that time?"

"Yes, I recall I did."

That put in place the last piece of the June 1979 chronology: the IMIC Sheikhs and the Hunts reached an agreement in principle in Hamburg, the IMIC negotiations for a formal agreement were ongoing in London, while Bunker with Naji Nahas got together in Paris, and the Hunts' change in trading pattern followed. With the Hunt positions in place, Bunker mobilized the first prong of his attack plan with IMIC and the Conti Group.

Chapter Sixteen

With Bunker and Herbert Hunt now holding enormous silver futures positions in early 1980 maturities, the first prong of the attack by IMIC and the Conti Group was implemented on July 25, 1979. On that day, Herbert Hunt and Sheikh Mussalem were meeting again in Hamilton, Bermuda to complete the formal steps necessary to create IMIC, while Bunker Hunt was having breakfast in Lexington, Kentucky, with Naji Nahas and Norton Waltuch. Silver prices were at $9.36. They had had a strong run for the year up from $6.08 at the beginning of the year, which was in its range for several years.

Bob Guinn and Mohammed Affara told most of the story about the Bermuda meeting. IMIC was formally incorporated and the Board of Directors, consisting of Herbert Hunt and Sheikh Mussalem (with Bunker and Sheikh Al-Amoudi absent) established a 10,000 futures contract trading limit representing a breathtaking 50 million ounces of silver.

Shortly after the Bermuda meeting, Herbert Hunt began implementing IMIC's trading plan. When he met with senior Merrill Lynch officials, Herbert told them IMIC would be taking delivery of 50 million ounces of silver, a commitment for close to half the total supply of silver bullion in the COMEX and Chicago warehouses. Merrill Lynch apparently did not hesitate. They saw no problem with such larger deliveries, an obvious indication of monopoly; it never looked beyond the large commissions it would earn from the trading.

Although Guinn and Affara considered many options, conspicuously absent from Bunker's recitation was any suggestion that IMIC actually did anything other than purchase silver futures contracts and take delivery of bullion. Tom Gorman had already made that point in cross-examining Bob Guinn who was more directly involved in those events. IMIC never got into the mining business, Guinn admitted, never reached any agreement to sell silver from Mexico, was not acting like a bullion dealer, never had any customers, and its only activity was to accumulate an inventory of 30 million ounces of silver. Herbert Hunt was more explicit: "It was felt that if a company was going to be formed that it should have a silver inventory to trade."

For all his distracting wandering among subjects, Curran could not avoid IMIC's silver trading, asking Bunker:

"Do you know whether IMIC opened long future contracts on the United States exchanges?"

"I believe it did," Bunker said vaguely, as if it were a distant memory rather than a well-rehearsed history.

Bunker maintained that he was not involved in the day-to-day operations of the company; he was just a member of the Board of Directors, which set general policy. Guinn and Affara made trading decisions, although Bunker admitted his brother Herbert had oversight of the company.

Bunker's focus was on the Conti Group. While Herbert was meeting with Sheikh Mussalem in Bermuda, the silver crowd in Kentucky was only tending to their thoroughbred horse businesses, according to Bunker. Curran and Bunker entertained the courtroom with a lengthy dialogue about the July Selected Yearling Sale at Keeneland, which was considered the largest and most prestigious thoroughbred sale in the world. For instance in 1979, Spectacular Bid became one of the nineteen Kentucky Derby winners sold at Keeneland.

Interesting, but more to our point, Naji Nahas invited Norton Waltuch to join him at the Keeneland Sales and they stayed at the same hotel. While at a dinner before the sales, Mahmoud Fustok happened by and Waltuch testified sounding awed: "Nahas introduced me to Mr. Fustok, which was the first time I met Mr. Fustok, and he introduced me as an expert on silver. Mr. Fustok asked me about silver and I expressed my opinion and that was it."

The next day Bunker ran a competing thoroughbred horse sale at his 8,000-acre Bluegrass Farms, just down the road, he told us. He did not like the snobby Keeneland crowd. Again, interesting, but we were focused on Nahas who took Waltuch to breakfast with Bunker Hunt at the Hyatt Regency Hotel in Lexington, another public locale, fitting Paul Curran's theme of a "broad daylight conspiracy." "Mr. Nahas told me he was going to arrange for me to meet Bunker Hunt and we would have breakfast," Waltuch testified, again sounding awed. "At that time I was very anxious to meet Mr. Hunt because I was hopeful of getting some business from Mr. Hunt."

When I asked Waltuch about that breakfast, I got little of substance out of him. He started with more horse talk; Bunker had told the story about how he had started his own yearling sale the prior year to circumvent the Kentucky blue blood attitude that was at Keeneland, Waltuch went on, but I interrupted:

"Mr. Waltuch, this case is about silver."

"You asked me what went on at breakfast," came Waltuch's sarcastic retort.

The judge interjected: "I think it's interesting."

"Oh, okay," I responded quizzically. "Then go ahead, Mr. Waltuch."

"Irrelevant but interesting," the judge rejoined. After Waltuch finished the story of Bunker's decision to start his own yearling sale, the judge interrupted again: "I guess we had better go back to silver."

"It was nice to have a break," I observed with my own touch of sarcasm, something I would never have dared in a courtroom before this trial began.

Waltuch shot back a wisecrack: "There is more than silver in the world, Mr. Cymrot."

"I hope to get back to it someday," I concluded, while the unrelenting five years of grueling work flashed through my mind.

Waltuch had little more to say about the breakfast. And, in response to Curran's questions, Bunker did not add much more. Bunker acknowledged that Nahas had introduced him to Waltuch at breakfast in a public dining room at the Hyatt Regency Hotel. Although Bunker had a house down the road, Nahas and Waltuch did not stay with him, Bunker volunteered in his friendly, I'm-just-a-normal-guy way: "I would have been glad to have them," and then he rambled on, "I'm very democratic, practically everybody else stayed with me at one time or another, but I didn't invite them and they didn't stay with me . . . They may have preferred the hotel, but I didn't invite them."

The discussion at breakfast was not memorable, according to Bunker, continuing another defense theme that any talk about silver was incidental and nonsubstantive. "I don't have any recollection of anything. Mr. Waltuch is not that much of a talker. Of all the people I've met that were commodity brokers, I think he is one of the less talkative that I have met around, not that he is not eloquent, but he just didn't have much to say and we just did sort of an ordinary breakfast." That was a different image from the Waltuch who showed up at trial. Although he knew Waltuch was a silver broker, Bunker denied they had gotten together to talk about the silver market. "Well, I got the impression he was sort of in horses. I think he did buy a few horses." No one ever told Bunker anything; he often got the "impression," according to his version.

Curran quickly moved on to the horses that Bunker and Nahas bought together, even presenting as evidence the Bluegrass Farms catalog for Bunker's annual sale on July 25, 1979. Nahas paid $703,000 for a partial interest in eleven horses; Bunker explained, and he kept a 25 percent interest in these horses, a deal he offered everyone purchasing at his sales. As Curran took the time to display the invoice to the jury, I let out a deep breath and wondered whether the jury could be distracted by all this horse babble. Bunker Hunt continued with his folksy tales, confusing the timeline and giving facile explanations for his actions.

Toward the end of the direct examination, Curran asked Bunker whether he had ever disclosed to Nahas, Fustok, or Waltuch the size of his silver positions, the contract months in which he held silver positions, or his plans to take bullion deliveries. Bunker responded with a huff: "No. That was my own private business. That's like asking you, Mr. Curran, how much money are you going to make this year. I mean I'd like to know . . . [but] I consider that bad taste."

"Bad taste!" I marveled to myself.

When my turn came, I tried to summarize what Bunker and his "good friend" Nahas had done together, but stumbled, showing my inexperience with a speech rather than a question:

"After the meetings in July of 1979," I began, "the one in Bermuda, and the occasion of your horse sale in Kentucky, IMIC began trading, Nahas began increasing his trading, Waltuch began increasing his trading, Banque Populaire Suisse which had an account at ACLI International opened an account with Waltuch, a company by the name of Gilion opened an account with Mr. Waltuch, ContiCapital Limited which was a fund that was run by Mr. Waltuch and others began trading in silver futures . . ."

That drew the three defense lawyers bouncing to their feet, shouting objections.

"I have not asked a question, yet," I protested.

"That's just the problem," Judge Lasker rejoined in a monotone.

"Well, there's a lot of things that happened," I pleaded.

"The objection is sustained," the judge sternly concluded the exchange.

This was an important transition point. I tried to mask my confusion with a quick question off point. Then I recovered. I broke down the events into their component parts for the jury. Bunker, as anticipated, responded with a series of denials, but my questions placed the overlapping events together for the jury.

"Did you know that Mr. Nahas increased his trading in silver futures after this meeting in Kentucky?"

"No, I did not."

"Did you know that Mr. Waltuch increased his trading in silver futures after this meeting in Kentucky?"

"I don't know what Waltuch did. His firm used to run full-page ads soliciting people to invest in commodities."

I ignore Bunker's addition and continued the same exchange asking about Waltuch's customers, Banque Populaire Suisse, and Gilion Financial and Litardex Traders, both companies we had associated with Nahas. I was not concerned about Bunker's denials; I wanted to put the timeline and the conspirators' trading pattern together for the jury. By the conclusion of this segment of the examination, I felt I had reassembled a timeline that Curran had confused and demonstrated the close relationship of the key meetings and trading decisions at the start of the conspiracy.

Fortunately, the trading records told a more dramatic story of IMIC and the Conti Group's entrance into the silver markets after the July meetings. For all his vagueness, Bunker could not avoid the obvious. After IMIC was created on July 25, 1979, it immediately began trading not like a dealer, but, by buying long silver futures contracts, concentrated in the September and December 1979 maturities. Within weeks it held more than 8,000 contracts (40 million ounces). By June 18, 1979, the Conti Group had liquidated the few silver contracts they held earlier in the year. After the July 25, 1979 meetings, the Conti Group mimicked IMIC's trading, buying more than 9,200 (46 million ounces) long positions concentrated in the same maturities, September and December 1979. As the newcomers in the markets, IMIC and the Conti Group were in a position to take delivery on large quantities of silver bullion before anyone could figure out what they were up to. With their enormous positions in early 1980 maturities, Bunker and Herbert could take possession of the remaining visible supplies of silver bullion.

Did they have sufficient resources to pull it off? The last part of Bunker's plan needed to fall into place—directly accessing the wealth of the Saudi royal family.

Cast of Characters

Hunt Group

Nelson Bunker Hunt

William Herbert Hunt

Lamar Hunt

Hunt children

International Metal
Investment Corp. (IMIC)

- Sheikh Ali bin Mussalem

- Sheikh Mohammed
  Aboud Al-Amoudi

- Robert Guinn

- Mohammed Affara

Conti Group

Naji Robert Nahas

Mahmoud Fustok

ContiCommodity Services, Inc.

- Norton Waltuch

Banque Populaire Suisse

Advicorp Advisory and Financial
Corporation S.A.

- Jean-Jacque Bally

- Pierre Hirschey

- Antoine Asfour

Chapter Seventeen

Following the Keeneland, Kentucky, yearling sales, the horse crowd moved on in August 1979 to Deauville, France, where Bunker Hunt and Naji Nahas sought to enlist additional firepower from Mahmoud Fustok and the Saudi royal family. In his opening statement, Peter Fleming had introduced Fustok to the jury. Tall, lanky, and exuding confidence, Fleming was like an actor playing a lawyer; Jimmy Stewart might have been imitating his posture and gait. Robert Morgenthau, the fabled NY District Attorney, described Fleming as "one of the best around." Starting in 1961, Fleming won forty-nine of fifty trials as a prosecutor and then won many high visibility acquittals as a defense lawyer, including for John Mitchell, Richard Nixon's Attorney General, Don King, the infamous boxing promoter, and John J. Rigas, the founder of the sixth largest cable company.

Fleming awed even Judge Lasker. The year before our trial, Fleming and Arthur Liman, the lawyer for Conti-Commodity, squared off in a related case: Fustok was trying to blame his broker, ContiCommodity, for his silver losses. Shortly before that trial, Judge Lasker surprised me one day, exclaiming: "Do you know who is going to try a case before me? Fleming and Liman!" He was like a kid going to his first World Series game. Liman, also tall and angular, was another illustrious member of the defense team until he engineered ContiCommodity's pretrial settlement with Minpeco. *The New York Times* described Arthur Liman as "a masterly legal strategist." He represented blue chip corporations like Time Warner, Weyerhaeuser, Pennzoil, Heinz, and CBS, as well as notorious Wall Street characters like Robert Vesco, Dennis Levine, and Michael Milken. I too was awed. I took a day to watch the two giants stalking the courtroom, hoping to absorb a tip or two. Unfortunately, not much happened that day. And Judge Lasker never got to watch past the third inning; the case settled after a few days of trial.

Fleming described Fustok as the head of a large family. He was born in Lebanon, came to the United States in the 1950s for high school, and graduated from University of Oklahoma with a degree in petrochemical engineering. He moved to Saudi Arabia where he worked as a petroleum engineer until his father died, at which time he took over his father's many businesses along with his brothers. He "engaged in certain businesses and earned some money," Fleming continued. Once he became wealthy, he supported his mother, sisters, and brothers and enjoyed his thoroughbred horses.

Fustok developed a business empire that included auto dealerships (Dodge, Land Rover), jewelry (Cartier), perfume (Christian Dior), real estate, construction, and oil-related industries, and he married the sister of Saudi Crown Prince (later King) Abdullah. According to Norton Waltuch, aircraft, weapons, or whatever—including the telephone system—were sold to the Saudis through Fustok for a commission. Fustok was also a partner of Nahas in projects in Brazil, including a Volkswagen factory and real estate.

Fustok had homes in Saudi Arabia, London, and Long Island, as well as in locales close to the thoroughbred horseracing scene—the 465-acre Buckram Oak Farm outside Lexington, Kentucky; another estate in Chantilly, the site of a famous chateau and racetrack outside of Paris; and a third in Florida near the horse tracks there. A local lawyer who showed me the Kentucky farm said Fustok did not like the roll of the hills so he redirected them in the opposite direction. His vast pastures were better manicured than my tiny patch of front lawn.

Fustok never appeared at trial; we presented his testimony to the jury through various pretrial depositions in our case and others. Some were on videotape, but some portions were read incongruously by our paralegal, Raoul Gonzalez, who would exaggerate an important answer with a Cuban-accented, "Oh, yes!"

Fustok first had a casual encounter with Bunker Hunt in 1977 or 1978 during the July yearling sales in Kentucky, I asked:

"You went to visit where he was selling his consign-
ment [of yearlings]?"

"Yes. He said, I am Bunker Hunt. I said, I am
Fustok."

"And he seemed to know who you were, your
reputation?"

"Yes."

They met for an ice cream and talked about horses, nothing
else. That was an image I had trouble conjuring: two billionaires walking out of an ice cream shop chitchatting and
licking ice cream. Did they order a single or double scoop?
They shared the same public trainer, Maurice Zilber, who
also worked for Nahas. Zilber was always praising Bunker,
Fustok said.

Our collection of receipts showed the next key meetings
took place during the Deauville race season. Bunker and
Nahas were at the Bristol Hotel in Paris in early August
1979 before traveling to Deauville, a quaint fishing village
by the sea in Normandy where the thoroughbred horse season resides for the last two weeks of August. Bunker stayed
at the Hotel Normandy from about August 19 to 27, 1979.
The Normandy has been described as a "stately hotel"
where the "classy rooms and suites have warm tones" and
terraces have a sea view.

Fustok described the scene when he invited Nahas and
Bunker Hunt for a key dinner: "I was in the race in Deauville, and as I was passing by from one race to another, there

was a restaurant. Mr. Nahas had taken some people and Mr. Hunt. So he waved hello. I came in and said hello. And he was going to introduce me to Mr. Hunt. I said I know Mr. Hunt." And Fustok continued, "They invited me for dinner . . . So I said, why go to your place? Why don't you come to my mother's place? They agreed. They came over to my mother's place for dinner." He and his mother had homes within the same Chantilly estate.

Fustok continued by describing the conversation at dinner: "Actually, the whole dinner we didn't speak about silver, except at the end they were speaking about—we were speaking about horses, mares. At around the end, Nahas told me that silver was a good buy. I asked why. And they explained to me why." As they were walking out, Nahas asked Bunker to explain, which he did with his well-practiced speech about silver's use in industry and the annual gap between silver production and consumption—only 150 million ounces produced but 200 million consumed. As a result, "the price of silver is very low," Fustok continued. "It should be, in reality silver should be more than this. It's underpriced or whatever."

Nahas joined in saying that he and Bunker had large silver investments; Fustok did not ask how big, he said, but testified: "I mean he was talking big. When he talks and he has got Mr. Hunt with him, he is big in horses, so I expect him to be big as well." Nahas predicted silver prices would "double or triple." And Nahas foretold how it would happen, according to Fustok's testimony:

"Did Mr. Nahas say anything about what the effect might be if several people bought silver together, large amounts of silver?"

"I don't recall, but he said *the price is going to go up very much.*"

This testimony was more revealing than Fustok may have intended. His description of the conversation contains the admission that Bunker and Nahas knew the other had large silver investments and expected prices to rise substantially. Although they would respond that they were talking about supply and demand, the jury could equally conclude that silver prices would increase from their new, large, coordinated silver purchases.

That was the message Fustok got, whether it was delivered indirectly as he described or more directly did not really matter. Hunt and Nahas were going to push silver prices upward, and he wanted to be part of it. Fustok turned to his Advicorp banker, Antoine Asfour, who were walking with them on his left and ordered him to buy $30 to $40 million in silver, as large an investment as he had ever made, other than his investment in thoroughbred horses, which was "much bigger." Fustok was in a hurry; he wanted the order entered "tomorrow."

Fustok continued in response to my question:

"You didn't feel that you needed an advisor to confirm the statements that were made about silver?"

"I had my consultant. I had Mr. Hunt, who was the king of silver. I had Mr. Nahas, who is the specialist, a very wealthy man, in gold and silver. What more consultant could I need?"

Fustok spoke loud enough for Bunker and Nahas walking on his right to hear, Fustok opined but Bunker later contested, relying on his hearing problems that Paul Curran had raised during Bunker's direct examination.

Recruiting Fustok and the Saudi royal family was an enormous coup for Bunker, but the story sounded very different when he told it at trial. During his direct examination about the Deauville racing season, Paul Curran kept the focus on horses. Bunker told about his purchase of a 50 percent interest in five horses for $500,000 with Naji Nahas buying the other half-interest. As I fidgeted, Bunker went into a long discussion of joint ownership of racehorses. Maurice Zilber, their horse trainer, selected the horses. "None of them covered themselves with appreciable glory," Bunker continued, "they were just moderate horses and we dispose of them."

Not to leave a heartless image of the glue factory, Curran jumped in: "In time they were sold?"

"Yes they were."

Curran jumped away to other subjects, but he finally came back to Fustok. "I knew him socially and we were friendly, that's all," Bunker reflected, adding, "but, you know, I know probably a couple hundred people over there in the same fashion so I can't say it was any special relationship."

"Did you participate in any conspiracy or agreement with Mr. Fustok to raise the price of silver?"

Sounding offended by our accusation, Bunker huffed: "I have never participated in any conspiracy with anybody at any time . . . I'm an upfront open guy and I don't get involved in any conspiracies."

Curran continued jumping to other topics, but later in the examination, Curran asked Bunker whether he had ever told Fustok the details of his silver positions. "No," Bunker responded emphatically and speaking rapidly, continued: "I never spoke with Mr. Fustok about it. As a matter of fact, from the few times I met Mr. Fustok, I didn't consider him very knowledgeable about the business and he really—as we speak of a businessman in the United States, he's not a businessman."

Again out of chronological order, Curran asked about the dinner at Fustok's home; Bunker responded with another drawn out story: "There was a good big crowd there. As I recall, his house was pretty small and the house got very crowded. There wasn't a place to sit down. So I'd say 35 or 40 people . . . They seemed to be a multinational group from all over and were speaking many languages, pretty much an international crowd." Bunker knew only Fustok, his mother and sister, Nahas, and one or two others. Bunker continued with a description of an awkward billionaire standing among the horseracing aficionados at a crowded buffet dinner: "You had to balance your plate. That's not easy . . . And so that's how formal it was and that it wasn't possible to have any conversation, not that I wanted one. But if anybody came and talked to me I might have talked about silver. I just don't recall."

When Curran sought to elicit a denial about silver conversations, Bunker added: "you know, there were a lot of people there speaking four, five, six languages. I only speak English," said Bunker, reverting to his familiar gee-whiz attitude, "so all I heard was what someone might say in English, but it was sort of a, you know, a buffet party or cocktail party kind of thing. It was pretty noisy."

Although they were sticking to the notion that conversations about silver were nebulous, Curran had to confront Bunker with Fustok's admission, asking:

"Did you hear Mr. Fustok say he wanted to buy $30–40 million in silver?"

Bunker went into one of his long, rambling, self-deprecating answers: "No, Mr. Curran, I didn't hear it, and he could have said it, but I don't always catch everything that's said, but usually I'm not listening that close. I mean, I'm not the kind of person that over—I'm just not a curious, overly curious kind of person—I probably would not have paid attention if I had heard him say it."

Curran had Bunker repeat the denial to be sure he had not left any ambiguity. "Fustok speaks English rather well," Bunker testified, "although he's very soft-spoken, has a rather high-pitched voice and you have to concentrate when you are talking to him to make sure you understand him." Curran connected this answer to Bunker's hearing problems from his war service, later solved by his wife's insisting on hearing aids. Then Curran returned to his theme of a broad daylight conspiracy:

"Mr. Hunt, if you were—I want you to assume something. You have described this dinner party. If you were involved in a conspiracy to fix the price of silver, do you think that dinner party would have been a good place to have conspiracy meetings?"

This time it was my turn to jump up objecting.

"Sustained," the judge said. "That is a pretty good argument. It is for the jury to decide, not for Mr. Hunt."

When I reached the same point, I was not going to let Bunker get away with a folksy, evasive answer. I confronted him with Fustok's version of the same dinner by quoting Fustok's testimony:

Q. Who explained to you why silver was a good investment?

A. I think Mr. Nahas asked Mr. Hunt would you explain to Mr. Fustok why and they told me it is needed in the industry and there is a shortage of silver every year because industry consumes more than the mines produce and the price of silver is not the right price and the world is always in need of silver even though there is production, but the production is less than that consumption is, while gold is only jewelry.

That was a familiar speech by Bunker to anyone who would listen, but Bunker still said he did not recall the conversation but added defiantly: "If somebody asked me what my opinion was I would have told him and perhaps he did ask me. I wasn't walking around refusing to talk to people."

"So you wouldn't contest Mr. Fustok's testimony that that took place?"

"I wouldn't contest it. I don't recall it."

He was equally adamant that he did not hear Fustok order his Advicorp bankers to purchase $30 to $40 million in silver. "I didn't hear him say that," Bunker insisted, "He could have told anybody anything," Bunker huffed.

Bunker also denied knowing that Fustok's silver futures trading increased very substantially after the dinner. "No, I never knew what he did," he insisted again. Nor did he know that Fustok's futures positions lined up with IMIC's.

Despite his many denials, the basic story was uncontested. Bunker went to dinner at the home of Fustok's mother with Nahas and the Advicorp advisors, and he talked about the benefits of investing in silver when the price was about to go up substantially. Fustok's testimony suggested the discussion was a lot more in depth than Bunker would admit. But the trading records would tell the rest of the story. Bunker's plan to manipulate silver prices was now in place and would begin within days.

Chapter Eighteen

Following Mahmoud Fustok's instructions to Advicorp, the Advicorp account at Banque Populaire Suisse expanded dramatically. Its investments in long September 1979 and December 1979 silver futures contracts expanded from 1,173 to more than 4,500 contracts (5.8 to 22.5 million ounces). The trades paralleled those of Naji Nahas, other Conti Group members, and IMIC. Fustok's sense of urgency—"buy tomorrow"—was telling. At the time of the dinner, the September 1979 silver futures contract was about to expire and the other members of the Conti Group were about to take surprise deliveries on their contracts, which, they hoped, would cause the first big silver price jump. Fustok must have known more than he and Bunker were letting on.

The total Advicorp trades were well more than the $40 million Fustok ordered, which suggested he had let the word out that a squeeze was about to begin. Fustok's Advicorp advisers confirmed that supposition in written testimony from Switzerland. They said Fustok recommended others to them in August 1979 to invest in silver futures. One of them was Crown Prince Abdullah. It seemed strange to me that the US Government never made an issue publicly of the Saudi royal family disrupting US markets. That says something about how weak US officials felt about our energy future when faced with the rising power of OPEC.

By the end of August 1979, IMIC held commitments to 45 million ounces while the Conti Group—including Fustok—held a similar amount. The long futures positions of the Hunt Group (including IMIC) and Conti Group combined had increased from 83 million ounces of silver to 254 million ounces, commitments for more than twice the 110 million ounces of silver bullion in the certified warehouses of the COMEX and Chicago Board of Trade. And the Hunts already owned about 40 million ounces of bullion in those warehouses as the year began. Taking control of the rest must have seemed so easy.

Silver prices reacted to the new demand by climbing to $10.32 on August 31, 1979, making the combined Hunt and Conti silver stash worth more than $2.6 billion.

As we hoped the jury saw, the newcomers to the market—IMIC and the Conti Group—were in position to surprise silver traders by taking large silver bullion deliveries as their long futures contracts matured in September and December 1979. Bunker and Herbert would sweep up the remaining silver bullion by taking deliveries on enormous long positions they had establish in early 1980 maturities. Together, the Hunts and Conti Group could buy the entire bullion supplies in the exchange warehouses and additional amounts that would normally enter those warehouses from known sources.

We displayed the dramatic change in the Hunts and Conti Group silver positions graphically on two charts that showed their positions in May 1979—before the Hamburg and Paris meetings—and in mid-September 1979 after IMIC and the Conti Group had arrayed their positions following the July 25, 1979, meetings in Bermuda and in Lexington, Kentucky.

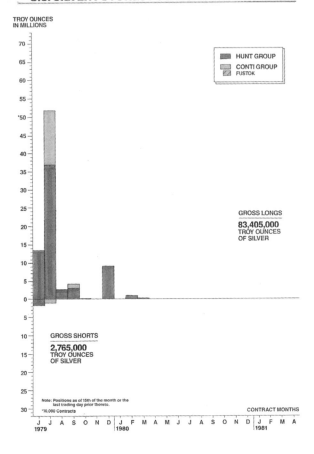

U.S. SILVER FUTURES POSITIONS MID-MAY 1979

TROY OUNCES
IN MILLIONS

HUNT GROUP
CONTI GROUP
FUSTOK

GROSS LONGS

83,405,000
TROY OUNCES
OF SILVER

GROSS SHORTS

2,765,000
TROY OUNCES
OF SILVER

Note: Positions as of 15th of the month or the
last trading day prior thereto.

*10,000 Contracts

CONTRACT MONTHS

J   J   A   S   O   N   D   J   F   M   A   M   J   J   A   S   O   N   D   J   F   M   A
1979   1980   1981

U.S. SILVER FUTURES POSITIONS MID-SEPT. 1979

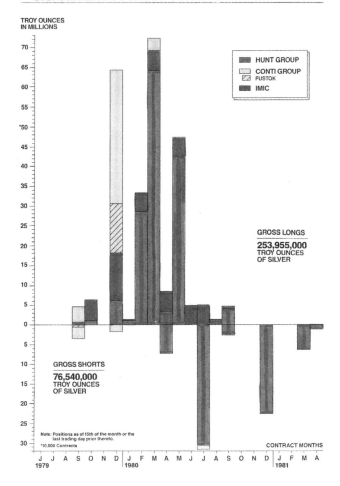

TROY OUNCES
IN MILLIONS

HUNT GROUP
CONTI GROUP
FUSTOK
IMIC

GROSS LONGS

253,955,000
TROY OUNCES
OF SILVER

GROSS SHORTS

76,540,000
TROY OUNCES
OF SILVER

Note: Positions as of 15th of the month or the
last trading day prior thereto.
*10,000 Contracts

CONTRACT MONTHS

J J A S O N D | J F M A M J J A S O N D | J F M A
1979   1980   1981

Chapter Nineteen

While the Hunt and Conti Groups were preparing to squeeze the silver futures markets, Minpeco was just learning the basics. Based on the suggestion of E.F. Hutton's Jim Ferro, the Minpeco Board of Directors authorized Ismael Fonseca and two colleagues to travel abroad for futures training in May 1979. The trio spent two weeks at E.F. Hutton's offices in Chicago, receiving instruction and visiting the Chicago Board of Trade. On the stand, Fonseca quietly described their rudimentary training: "They were working and we were by their side watching everything they did, and we, in turn, carried out imaginary hedging operations to see what the results would show in comparison with the reality on the market."

They moved on to E.F. Hutton's New York offices for more training. While in New York, they visited Merrill Lynch and several other brokers. I started moving into the heart of the case, asking:

"Would you tell us how you described the company to the Merrill Lynch people?"

"Minpeco was a very important enterprise, very well run, organized, with strong idealism among the workers of the company," Fonseca stated proudly, "which had enabled Minpeco to overcome a period of evolution faster than other companies; it had matured in many important aspects, but we were trying to learn more as in the case of hedging, which in spite of the fact that we had studied it, was an unknown because of the degree of sophistication it required."

We moved into a discussion of the unique role Minpeco played in the sale of Peru's minerals. Before I had gotten involved in the case, I had not realized the extent to which many developing countries during the 1960s and 1970s had converted to state-run economies, similar to the Soviet style. In Peru's case, a left-wing military dictatorship had taken over in the late 1960s, nationalizing many private properties, and organized state-owned companies to run key segments of the economy. In the mining area, many of the private mines had been confiscated. Minpeco was created in 1973 to be the exclusive agent for Peru's mineral sales abroad. Democracy was restored in 1980 and the state-run system began collapsing. However, in 1979 Minpeco had the monopoly on selling Peru's annual production of minerals, including 45 million ounces of silver, which Fonseca slowly explained through the interpreter, along with the complexities of selling physical silver on the world stage. Since silver was reaching price levels it had never before reached, it was given preferential treatment in the conversations with the brokers.

"In a general way, how did you describe Minpeco?"

"Not long before this Minpeco had been considered as one of the 500 most important business concerns in the world by a business publication," Fonseca continued. "I had taken a copy of that magazine. With that as a starting point, we would talk about the different things that Peru produces, which is copper, silver, lead, zinc mainly. These are our minerals that can be hedged. Plus additional materials for which there are no exchanges, such as cadmium. I would give them the whole framework of production and marketing. We talked about financial matters. We talked about foreign exchange controls in Peru, which had made it impossible to hedge before."

With Minpeco's responsibility for selling Peru's entire metals output, hedging was an important tool, according to the New York brokers. Minpeco was responsible for obtaining the best possible prices for Peru's minerals, which benefited not only the producer but also the whole country.

"With hedging, Minpeco could lock in the current high world prices for silver that would be sold over the next year to 18 months," Fonseca explained, which was a key point we wanted to make. Minpeco's trading strategy came from its brokers; it was not the fantasy of a rogue trader.

"Did the brokers say anything about their research capabilities?" I continued.

"Yes."

"What did they say on that subject?"

"They said that they had experts in every area, that these experts were permanently studying the market and that this information would be given to us."

"Did Minpeco already have this capability?"

"To my understanding, no, because Minpeco was very far from the nerve centers of the markets. Whatever was studied by the corresponding areas of Minpeco was out of phase between what already happened and what might happen next."

Fonseca discussed with the brokers the mechanics of trading in silver futures. The brokers recommended that he "hedge between 30 and 35 percent [of our annual sales] and the percentage could increase depending on how the market moved."

"How would you hedge your company's physical operations?"

"I would summarize it as daily communication in which they told us about markets and we would hedge on the basis of that information. Then they would provide us with the results of each of our operations. For instance, among such events, I now remember the problem of Iran, the hostages, that at that time there was talk that there was the possibility of a recession here in the United States, that interest rates had climbed considerably. These were all factors that that the brokers supplied to us."

I moved into an area that responded to Paul Curran's "broad daylight conspiracy" argument; I asked Fonseca to describe what the brokers told him about increasing silver prices in mid-1979. Even before Bunker's assault on prices in September 1979 when silver prices took their first spike from $9 to $18 per ounce, they were already at historic highs, starting at $6 in January 1979 and moving upward. So I asked:

"And did the brokers express an opinion as to why silver prices were going up at that time?"

"They stated approximately the following: There were usually an undefined number of people that devote themselves to hedging exchange, but because of these political/economic events every dentist and housewife was speculating, trying to make a little money on the exchange. These people were pushing prices up."

"Now, in the same period, May to August of 1979, did the Merrill Lynch people express an opinion as to how long they expected this upward price trend to last?"

"They were pessimistic. They thought that this period of price expansion could be over any time and prices would go back to their original levels. In other words, they thought prices would go down."

During his trip to New York, Fonseca visited Mocatta Metal's Henry Jarecki who shared the thought that prices would move downward; $10 to $12 silver in August 1979 was a level that he had never seen before. That opinion may have been the source of Jarecki's upcoming problems in September 1979 when his company, one of the world's largest silver dealers, almost went bankrupt. Fonseca also talked many times to Jim Ferro of E.F. Hutton who had a similar view. "'Someone had to put a stop to this increase because it was hurting the trade in silver,' Ferro said. He could give no other explanation for it but collective movement."

"What do you mean by collective movement?"

"That many people had become interested in silver, many people had begun to buy and this is what causes prices to go up."

When Fonseca returned to Peru in August 1979, the Minpeco Board of Directors authorized him to open commodity accounts with E.F. Hutton and Merrill Lynch. Minpeco was barreling toward disaster without a clue what Bunker Hunt was brewing with his cohorts on the thoroughbred horse circuit.

Part Four

September 1979 Trap Is Sprung

Chapter Twenty

Then came September 1979. The Conti Group—Naji Nahas, Mahmoud Fustok, Banque Populaire Suisse—and IMIC delivered the first blows to the silver markets by demand-. ing delivery on 7.4 million ounces of bullion during the first trading days. Fustok's share was 3.7 million ounces from 740 futures contracts hurriedly purchased the prior week. That suggests his conversation with Bunker Hunt and Nahas was a lot more explicit than the participants let on. Rather than leave the bullion in COMEX warehouses, Fustok sent Brinks trucks to collect it, loaded Boeing 747s, and flew 6.2 million ounces to Switzerland.

It was a brash and unprecedented assault on silver inventories. Silver prices reacted by jumping to $2.50 in a matter of days. The financial shock wobbled many of the usual market participants for whom 10 cents was a big price move in prior years. Both the COMEX and Chicago Board of Trade (CBOT) responded to this unusual activity by increasing initial margins substantially; COMEX margins went from $1,500 to $5,000, the largest they had ever been.

The move was designed to make futures contracts more expensive and dampen demand. But the Conti Group and IMIC continued to take deliveries during the second week in September.

The impact of dwindling bullion supplies, fueled by an active rumor mill, continued to drive silver prices upward from $10.32 at the end of August to $13.40 per ounce by September 17. The silver futures markets were in such chaos that normal trading was not possible on many days. When price movements hit their daily limits, the "lock limit," trading was halted. The futures markets were becoming inoperative for their usual purposes as price discovery and hedging tools. The extraordinary price movements locked the futures markets on 102 of the next 140 days.

The impact on businesses could be read in the financial pages. Some businessmen were bewildered and concerned. Kodak, perhaps the largest user of silver for film and photo paper products, was hit hard. "The real problem for Kodak watchers," the *Wall Street Journal* wrote, "is that they haven't any better idea than anyone else where the spurt in silver prices will stop. Every $1-an-ounce change in the price of silver if it continued for a year can change bottom-line earnings 15 cents to 17 cents a share, analysts estimate." The next day the *Journal* quoted nervous executives from Zales, Tiffany, and Cartier trying to sound nonchalant about the impact of the silver price rise on jewelry sales. Where some executives saw trouble, others saw opportunity—Gulf Resources & Chemical Corporation announced that it was spending $1.6 million to expand a silver mine near Kellogg, Idaho.

Our team's endless hours of studying telephone bills and hotel receipts told the behind-the-scenes story. Bunker Hunt and his friend, the "telephonaic" Naji Nahas, were having daily telephone calls. And a hotel receipt put Nahas and Advicorp's Jean-Jacques Bally at the Berkshire Hotel in New York from September 10 to 12, 1979. Norton Waltuch testified what was on Nahas's mind—beyond the obvious excitement that the scheme was working. "Both of them really were inexperienced in the procedure [for taking delivery] and there was a significant amount of money that was going to be required to be placed on deposit with Conti . . ." Futures contracts could be bought on margin—a small percentage of the total price—but bullion deliveries required full payment. They had to deposit an estimated $70 million at ContiCommodity to pay for their silver bullion deliveries, which they did leaving no doubt they were backed by vast wealth.

The September 12, 1979 minutes of the COMEX Board of Governors expressed apprehension about the unknown forces that had sudden hit the market. Who were these guys demanding bullion deliveries? And were silver bullion supplies sufficient should deliveries be demanded against the December 1979 contract, the next major COMEX contract?

The Chairman, Lee Berendt, reported that he had been in touch with the CFTC regarding December 1979 silver. The board authorized the Clearing Association to disclose the name of holders with positions in excess of 500 contracts and instructed the staff to begin discussions with the brokerage houses "for the purpose of formulating alternative method of dealing with a possible emergency situation in December 1979 silver."

IMIC delivered the second blow just as silver prices seemed to be settling down. On September 13 to 14, 1979, the IMIC Board of Directors—Bunker, Herbert, and Mussalem—reacted. While meeting at the luxurious Dolder Grand Hotel in Zurich, they decided to take delivery on IMIC's remaining September and October 1979 silver futures contracts, transport some of the bullion to Zurich, and increase IMIC's trading limit to 15,000 contracts (75 million ounces). That alone constituted a substantial percentage of the visible bullion supply in US certified warehouses. Historically, each exchange had between 50 and 60 million ounces of bullion in their warehouses.

After the board meeting, IMIC immediately demanded delivery of almost 5 million ounces of silver bullion. IMIC added fuel to the rampage by buying additional spot September 1979 contracts and immediately taking delivery.

When silver prices jumped $5.00 on September 18, the COMEX declared an emergency and increased initial margins to an astronomical level, $50,000 on spot contracts and $20,000 for future months. The exchanges, however, were dealing with the oil wealth of both the billionaire Hunt family and the Saudi royal family, perhaps the richest traders around. They did not blink; they paid their margins, kept their positions, and added to them.

By October 2, silver prices reached $18.1, a volcanic spike of almost $8.00 in one month when pennies were the normal moves. IMIC and the Conti Group had insisted on delivery of 13.3 million ounces of silver bullion, and on October 1, 1979, IMIC took delivery on another 6.7 million ounces. When shipped to Zurich, visible silver bullion supplies dwindled further. Lamar Hunt also jumped into the fray by opening a 1,000-contract bull straddle position similar to those Bunker and Herbert had put on in June 1979. Thus began a seesaw battle between the regulators and the traders that lasted for the next six months.

After recounting these numbers, Leslie Jordan, our commodity expert, explained the technical trading points to the jury. Although futures contracts are promises to buy or sell bullion, the futures markets are not normally used for bullion purchases. Futures contracts are most often closed before they mature, she explained. Acquiring offsetting positions, instead of taking delivery of bullion, was the usual method for closing futures contracts. For instance, a trader holding a long position would acquire an offsetting short position, which the exchange would match and close. At that time, silver futures contracts were backed by silver bullion of a specific amount and purity—specifically, 100-ounce silver bars of 99.9 percent pure silver—held in five warehouses. There was a limited supply, which was exactly the point of the conspiracy: buy up the warehouse silver.

Since the price spread between months was not at "full carry"—an interest factor between contract months—the deliveries were uneconomical, Jordan continued. Swapping warehouse receipts—COMEX receipts for Swiss receipts— would have been a "far less dramatic way" and more economical way to move silver bullion to Europe, Jordan explained. Exchanging warehouse receipts would also not have reduced the supply of bullion in the COMEX warehouses, while shipping the bullion to Switzerland reduced visible supplies at a time when demand was conspicuously increasing. Since businessmen usually act rationally, undertaking actions that appear uneconomical suggested they have another aim that would increase profits and thus make their conduct economical. An illegal price manipulation fits that description. The Hunt and Conti Group uneconomic conduct of taking deliveries and shipping bullion was proof that they intended to increase silver prices; their intent was a critical element of our case.

Through September 1979, IMIC and the Conti Group had just taken control over more than 20 percent of the COMEX warehouse stocks. Bunker and Herbert already had long-held holdings of 40 million ounces in New York and Chicago, which was as much as 30 percent of visible bullion supplies. The Hunt and Conti Group combined inventory of silver futures and bullion expanded from 221 million to 321 million ounces worth more than $5.78 billion, up more than

$3 billion in a month. Peru's gross domestic product (GDP) at the time was only about $12 billion.

As they watched silver prices surge, Bunker and Nahas were having daily conversations that must have turned ecstatic. Bunker and brother Herbert, we imagine, must have shared a quiet toast to their successful ambush of short investors.

Chapter Twenty-One

When asked to describe reasons for the "startling increase" in silver prices in late 1979, Bunker Hunt augmented his silver-as-a-good-investment theme with two more prongs of the defense: political events and inflation. Paul Curran had laid out in the theme in his opening: "The evidence as distinguished from conjecture will show," Curran dramatically intoned in his deep voice, "that the price rise was caused by events in the world, political, and economic scene, the same forces that have always affected the price of silver but were at this point in history more frequent, more powerful, more compressed than before or since."

Undoubtedly some on the jury remembered that the US economy was in turmoil in 1979. But Bunker's litany of key events did not coincide with the September 1979 price surge. In the wake of the Iranian Revolution, oil production dropped, which drove up prices, fueling already raging inflation. The appointment of Paul Volcker as head of the Federal Reserve Board in October 1979, brought on an aggressive plan to increase interest rates in order to curb inflation, which sent the US economy further into a downward spiral, but that did not happen immediately. And the Iranian hostage crisis was still a month away.

Bunker gave his version of the turmoil. "If you think back, it was very, very unsettling year politically, particularly if you had experience in the Middle East, which I had had." He recounted the US Embassy hostage crisis, which began on November 4, 1979 and continued the gloomy world picture by describing the seizure of the Grand Mosque in Mecca by a "bunch of radicals, guys with guns . . . In effect," he concluded, "it was an attempt to take over the Middle East where 80 percent of the world's petroleum is, so that was a factor." He was referring to a group of insurgents calling for the overthrow of the House of Saud, another US stalwart, who took hostages at the Masjid al Haram Mosque in Mecca, Islam's holiest site, shocking the Muslim world. That attack in late November 1979 led to two weeks of running battles between militants and Saudi security forces, supported by French Special Forces, before it was suppressed.

In the midst of the crisis, the United States pointed fingers at Ayatollah Khomeini, who did more than point fingers back. Within hours, a crowd gathered in front of the US Embassy in Islamabad, Pakistan, attacked and burned it down, killing American and Pakistani personnel. Bunker added that the Russians' invasion of Afghanistan was "the first time that the Russians had invaded a neutral country with their army and everybody thought they were going to keep going." On December 24, 1979, the Soviet Army invaded Afghanistan to support its puppet ruler, who had brutally suppressed traditional Muslim Afghans and were in open rebellion. They were on the verge of taking over the country before the Soviet Army invaded, leading to a ten-year war there.

Bunker did not give dates or try to associate the events with movements in silver prices, which would have been futile because the events did not coincide with Bunker's key straddle trades in June 1979 or the price surge in September 1979. Nonetheless, that is why Bunker supposedly increased his interest in silver, he said: "I think in hindsight it made me much more bullish and made me more confident that silver was an excellent investment than it was shown to be."

When Paul Curran asked Bunker about the IMIC bullion demands in September 1979, Bunker responded with a quizzical tone: "I think they did take some deliveries."

"What did you understand IMIC's purpose was in taking deliveries of physical silver?"

"*That was for the Sheikhs*," Bunker said, sounding more assured now. "They wanted to get into the bullion and wanted to own the actual metal."

Blaming the empty chairs—characters not at trial—continued as Bunker's theme throughout the remainder of his testimony. It was the Sheikhs who wanted silver bullion; the Hunts were "bullish" on silver, but Bunker never acknowledged that he and his brother wanted bullion too.

When Bunker related conversations with the Sheikhs, I was on my feet objecting regularly. Bunker's testimony about what the Sheikhs said was hearsay—statements made outside of court by persons we could not cross-examine. Judge Lasker kept overruling my objections on the grounds that Bunker's thought process—his intent to manipulate—was at issue, which might have been influenced by the Sheikh's statements.

After a series of objections, I asked for a bench conference to take advantage of an order the judge had entered during pretrial proceedings. After a brief sidebar with lawyers arguing in hushed tones while gathered around the judge, he gave an instruction to the jury that did not go quite as far as I would have liked: "Ladies and gentlemen, in regard to Mr. Hunt's testimony about what the Sheikhs said or insisted upon, you're entitled ultimately to consider all this. Just remember that the *Sheikhs have been ordered to appear* and decided not to do so. I am not suggesting that Mr. Hunt has them in his control."

The judge had ordered Sheikh Mussalem and Sheikh Al-Amoudi to appear as witnesses at trial, but they were ignoring his order and staying away. I felt the judge had softened up the instruction. But he had made our most important point: in response to his court order the IMIC Sheikhs were metaphorically thumbing their noses at our legal system. That seemed like an important reminder to the jurors, which I hoped would make the jurors question Bunker's story.

When my turn came, I wanted to tie Bunker directly to IMIC's decision to take September 1979 bullion deliveries. Bunker, however, lapsed into vagueness, denying he was involved: "I do recall [IMIC] took a delivery sometime there. I'm not just sure when." Bunker resisted my suggestion that he must have discussed these deliveries with his brother Herbert and Sheikh Mussalem. "I wouldn't argue that we didn't discuss it because I just don't recall."

"You were both on the Board of Directors of IMIC?"

"That's correct."

"And the Board of Directors authorized the taking of those deliveries, didn't it?"

"I would say so, yes."

When I reminded him and the jury that Bob Guinn had placed Bunker at the board meetings, he relapsed into his down-home affect: "I talked to Sheikh Mussalem always through an interpreter. But he was very easy to understand through an interpreter." However, Bunker would not argue with Guinn's testimony that he was there and joined in the decision to take deliveries: "Mr. Guinn has a much better knowledge of that than I and I would accept whatever he said in that respect." That answer put Bunker at the meeting and participating in the decision but without an innocent explanation for IMIC's unusual bullion demands.

I moved on to the Conti Group deliveries during September 1979, knowing Bunker would deny any knowledge of them. But my questions were intended to put our timeline before the jury. This time, I broke the questions down, having learned something from my earlier hiccup:

"Now, at the time that you participated in discussions about whether IMIC should take delivery, did you know that Mr. Nahas was taking delivery on September 1979 silver futures contracts?"

"No. I never knew what Nahas was doing."

I asked the same question for Fustok, Banque Populaire Suisse, and Waltuch's personal deliveries and got a similar expected answer, but I was putting the coordinated events before the jury. Bunker denied discussing the pros and cons of taking bullion deliveries with Nahas. I tried to suggest with prices shooting skyward, good friends would talk about a common investment. Bunker's denials seemed unnatural, at least to me; I hoped the jury felt the same. I pressed further with Bunker's prior admissions, which resulted in a quick banter:

"Now, you did discuss the silver market with him quite a bit, didn't you?"

"Yes, I did."

"You talked to him about three or four times a week?"

"Two, three, four times a week sometimes . . . He would call me and I would talk to him."

"Now, it's your testimony that during none of these conversations you discussed taking the delivery of silver futures contracts?"

"I don't have any specific recollection of discussing it with him. If he asked me, I would have told him what I thought about it. But I don't recall that he ever asked me."

That was not quite an admission but far less than a denial. I felt my more senior opponents—particularly Peter Fleming—might have thumped Bunker into more of a confession, but I moved on. Minpeco was bewildered by the price surge, an event unprecedented in any metal in the long careers of its senior officials. They were joined in their bafflement by the US commodities regulators, who were asking questions.

Chapter Twenty-Two

Even before IMIC and the Conti Group demanded bullion deliveries in September 1979, the CFTC had taken note of the new large traders on the COMEX and Chicago Board of Trade (CBOT). An important element of our story was about to begin. During our case in chief, a series of witnesses from the commodity exchanges and CFTC described a six-month running battle with the Hunts and Conti Group, as the regulators were grasping to understand what was happening in the silver markets and seemingly bewildered about what to do. Their groping was yet another response to Paul Curran's "broad daylight conspiracy" argument; the regulators, at least initially, could not see what was coming. And the evasive responses of the traders were further evidence they were hiding their wrongdoing.

From large trader reports filed by brokerage houses, the regulators viewed September and December 1979 long positions concentrated among new, unknown traders: a Bermuda company (IMIC); two other foreign companies,

Litardex and Gilion (Nahas companies); and a large Swiss bank, Banque Populaire Suisse. The newcomers had managed to array their large futures positions and take substantial bullion deliveries before the regulators had become fully aware of their activities. The infamous Bunker and Herbert Hunt—who had earlier received CFTC scrutiny over their silver and soybean trading—were sitting holding ominously large long positions in February, March, and May 1980 maturities. The regulators had no way to know whether the Hunt positions were related to the new traders at ContiCommodity and Merrill Lynch.

As they investigated further, the regulators realized that the Hunts and the mysterious new traders were holding silver futures positions that dwarfed the visible bullion supplies in exchange warehouses. This new demand, several regulators testified, created "congestion." That is like a serious cold threatening to turn into pneumonia. With large concentrated long positions, the holders of short positions might not have sufficient silver bullion to meet the long's demands for deliveries when their futures contracts expired. That could result in a "squeeze" when the shorts, who do not own silver bullion, must bid futures prices up to entice someone to sell them long positions to offset and close their short positions. Prices go higher and higher. Those traders holding the largest long positions might not be willing to sell futures; they might sit and demand delivery. In the worst-case scenario, shorts have to default on their futures contracts.

Fear of a squeeze kept the regulators investigating. But the Hunts and Conti Group were misleading them about their relationships and intentions for additional deliveries, discouraging the regulators from acting, which we argued was good evidence they were up to no good.

Although the white-haired Paul Volcker, the new Chairman of the Federal Reserve Board, was preoccupied with his hard-charging inflation fighting campaign, the thirty-six–year-old Lee Berendt, President of the COMEX, was assisted by his twenty-seven–year-old chief counsel, Alan J. Brody, with oversight provided by the thirty-three–year-old CFTC Chairman James M. Stone. Young regulators ruled the normally sleepy commodity exchanges. Only the CBOT, where Robert K. Wilmouth was President, had experienced leadership. It seemed like an unfair fight with the wily, egocentric, and wealthy Hunts treating the youngsters with arrogance and silent distain, an attitude the regulators may have earned after their ineffective responses to the Hunts' 1974 silver and 1976 soybean escapades.

At first, all the CFTC knew about IMIC was its post office address in Bermuda. On August 22, 1979, the CFTC sent a first class letter to IMIC (hard to imagine snail mail today), reminding it to file a large trader report, Form 40, identifying persons with an interest in its trading. Paul Perito, IMIC's counsel, had laid down a challenge to us during his opening statement about IMIC's response to this and subsequent CFTC requests. Perito had described Bob Guinn, IMIC's comanaging director, as an army

officer discharged as a captain, a forty-two–year-old corporate lawyer with Hunt Energy, a member of the bar with no
complaints against him. "This is the supposed liar who was
characterized by Minpeco yesterday!" Perito was describing our position in the extreme in order to increase our
burden in the eyes of the jury. Perito argued that Guinn
was open and honest with the government, a rebuttal to
our argument that the conspirators had delayed and misled the US commodities regulators at key times in the fall
of 1979.

Guinn responded to the CFTC's August 22 letter on September 5 by listing Mohammed Affara and himself as the
persons with interest in IMIC's trading. That, of course, was
incomplete, a point we attacked during our direct case by
having Guinn admit he had no trading experience before
joining IMIC, did not even know about Herbert Hunt's
meeting at Merrill Lynch to establish IMIC's account, and
did not know that Herbert could place orders for IMIC.

It seemed the CFTC also did not accept Guinn's representation that he and Affara controlled IMIC's trading. On
September 7, 1979, the CFTC issued a more formal "special
call" to IMIC, asking again who controlled IMIC's trading. Guinn claimed he did not receive it until September
19, which was four days after he returned from an IMIC
board meeting. He had been with Bunker, Herbert, and
Mussalem from September 13 to 14, 1979, at the Dolder
Grand Hotel in Zurich when they decided IMIC would
take delivery on its September and October 1979 silver

futures contracts. That is not what Guinn told the CFTC in response to its inquiry. On September 20, 1979, Guinn submitted the required CFTC report again with a key omission; he did not disclose the Hunts or Sheikh's shareholdings.

But, the CFTC now had an office telephone number. One day later—while IMIC's bullion demands were rocking the New York market—the CFTC's chief of market surveillance called Guinn asking for IMIC's shareholders and directors. Guinn was reluctant to give names over the phone, he countered; it was confidential information he said. We countered by showing that the information was a public record in Bermuda where IMIC was incorporated, so Guinn was caught in another evasion, but that did not help the CFTC at the time.

The CFTC's growing anxiety about the silver bullion supply could be seen through the chief's questions: Why did IMIC decide to buy silver through the futures market rather than other means? And did IMIC plan to take the silver out of the United States? Guinn told the CFTC that it was more economical to take delivery on futures contracts, an answer the surveillance chief likely found unconvincing. Guinn also said, "It is probable that some of the silver will be taken overseas." When asked about IMIC's trading intentions, Guinn responded that they are "entirely dependent on the direction the market takes . . ." Guinn did not disclose that the IMIC board had already authorized the company to demand bullion deliveries on its September and October 1979 futures contracts, yet one more evasion.

In response to the CFTC's demand, Guinn wrote to them on September 24, 1979, identifying Bunker and Herbert Hunt and Sheikhs Mussalem and Al-Amoudi as IMIC's directors. That letter, Guinn admitted, would take about a week to arrive in Washington from Bermuda—*after* IMIC had taken its September 1979 deliveries and started taking substantial October 1979 deliveries.

The letter must have sent alarm bells ringing through the halls of the CFTC, where the Hunts were already known as a threatening force. IMIC's bullion demands on 2,528 September and October 1979 contracts (12.6 million ounces) and total futures position of 3,800 contracts (19 million ounces) represented a substantial increase in the Hunts' historical overall silver position, and IMIC's delivery demands suggested the Hunts might again be interested in taking bullion deliveries on their 70 million ounces of silver futures with early 1980 maturities. The Hunt deliveries in 1974 had led to a jump in prices and a warning about their obligation not to manipulate prices. Were they at it again? That must have been the question worrying CFTC officials. And with the help of petrodollars? Even more worrying.

Guinn had hidden IMIC's ownership and intentions from the CFTC until IMIC had taken its September and October 1979 bullion deliveries. When I asked Guinn during his pretrial deposition about his representation that IMIC's trading intentions were not yet decided, he acknowledged that at the time he talked to the CFTC, "There was agreement by the board to continue the September deliveries that we had already begun, and an agreement by the directors to take delivery of the October position." When confronted with this inconsistency, Guinn claimed IMIC did not yet have financing. However, we showed that between September 19 and 25, 1979, IMIC purchased and took delivery of an additional 180 spot September contracts (an additional 900,000 ounces) and continued to take delivery as the October 1979 contracts matured. IMIC had no financing problems taking delivery of almost 13.5 million ounces of silver bullion costing $243 million.

Paul Perito must have thought that financing did not give Guinn a sufficient cover for his answer; he needed a better explanation for such large-scale bullion demands. During his opening statement, Perito had come up with an answer— the Koran. He attributed IMIC's bullion demands on the religious beliefs of Sheikh Mussalem and Mohammed Affara, telling the jury: "Mohammed Affara will tell you that he would not have participated in this company, nor his clients, if it simply was a speculator—if it simply took positions in the futures market, long positions, for the sake of rolling them over and taking a profit. Why? This man guides his life by religious principles and he interprets the Koran, as Sheik Ali does, as prohibiting gambling."

Surprised and annoyed, I immediately rose to object because religion had been the subject of a particularly contentious pretrial motion. Although we had not mentioned religion once during pretrial discovery, IMIC had filed a pretrial motion accusing us of a plan to prejudice the jury by referring to the Sheikh's Muslim religion. I imagine Perito's pretrial jury research must have shown him that the Muslim religion had negative associations for some segment of New Yorkers who might end up on the jury. The trial was well before September 11, 2001, and widespread terrorism, but the disruptions caused by the OPEC oil embargo in 1973 were still firmly etched in many memories. Despite our objection, the judge had ruled we could not refer to the Muslim religion.

Perito, however, along with Paul Curran, must have decided their best explanation for IMIC's large bullion demands was the Muslim religion—despite the potential negative reaction of some potential jurors. In my objection to Perito's opening, I reminded the judge of his earlier ruling. The judge did not agree that the situation was similar. "The jury may be entitled to consider these beliefs when the time comes to consider the state of mind of the defendants," he said. In other words, we could not mention it, but they could use religion to explain their conduct. I sat down frustrated.

Although he had not mentioned the Koran before trial, Guinn picked up on Perito's new story that the Koran, not financing, explained his slippery answers to the CFTC. Tom Gorman, who was cross-examining Guinn at trial, sought to demonstrate that the Muslim religion did not justify Guinn's answers, either, but Guinn dodged his question.

Judge Lasker, however, would not allow him of be evasive jumped in:

"You didn't talk to Mr. Horn [CFTC] about the Sheikhs' religious beliefs?"

"No, your honor, we did not get into a discussion of the Muslim religion," Guinn meekly responded.

Guinn's weak excuses—financing and religion—did not justify his failure to tell the CFTC about IMIC's September board decision to take large bullion deliveries. His slick answers were evasive, particularly when compared to IMIC's actions. I thought we had met Paul Perito's challenge; Guinn might not be a liar but he certainly was evasive with the regulatory authorities. As the regulator's questions continued, the responses of the Hunt and Conti Group became even more misleading.

The US Commodity Regulators

Commodity Futures Trading Commission (CFTC)
James M. Stone, Chairman
Read Dunn, Vice Chairman

Commodity Exchange, Inc. (COMEX)
Lee Berendt, President
Robert J. Brody, Chief Counsel

Chicago Board of Trade (CBOT)
Robert K. Wilmouth, President

Special Silver Committee
Dr. Andrew Brimmer, Chairman
Mark Buckstein, Counsel

Business Conduct Committee
Robert E. Goldberg, Chairman

Board Members
Herbert Coyne- J. Aron
Edward W. Hoffstatter – Sharps Pixley
Henry Jarecki – Mocatta
David T. Johnson – E.F. Hutton
Charles Mattey - Bache
Raymond Nessim – Phillips Bros (Engelhard)
Jerome M. Spielman – Merrill Lynch

Chapter Twenty-Three

As silver prices soared, the regulators must have had growing anxiety that they did not know what they were confronting. In addition to the CFTC inquiries of IMIC that Bob Guinn had deflected for weeks, the CFTC gave COMEX the names of new large traders in the Conti Group: Banque Populaire Suisse, Nahas, Gilion, and Litardex. When COMEX President Lee Berendt called Norton Waltuch about the new accounts, Waltuch told him that Banque Populaire Suisse and Gilion had the same investment advisor, but there was no relationship between those accounts and Naji Nahas. That statement may or may not have been literally true as far as Conti knew, but the jury had already heard considerable testimony showing that the real situation was quite different: Nahas had an office across the hall from Advicorp in Geneva, where Waltuch met Nahas and Jean-Jacques Bally and his colleagues; Nahas had enlisted Mahmoud Fustok, with Bunker's help, into their silver scheme and they both were shareholders in Advicorp; and Nahas, the owner of the Gilion and Litardex accounts, was coordinating his trading with Fustok and Bally. Fustok admitted he was trading through Banque Populaire Suisse, but we never identified the other traders in the bank's omnibus account—although some appeared to be associated with the Saudi royal family, including, Fustok admitted, his brother-in-law, Crown Prince Abdullah.

Just before Judge Lasker ruled on whether Banque Populaire Suisse had to disclose the names of its customers trading silver, the bank wrote a big check to settle with Minpeco. The judge then ruled—as a nonparty—that the bank did not have to violate Swiss law by disclosing the names of its customers. He implied that the ruling might have been different if the bank was still a party to the lawsuit. That is how he ruled when the issue came up for Bunker and Herbert and their accounts at Swiss Bank Corporation; he ordered them to disclose their transactions in Switzerland, which produced a bonanza of evidence.

On their call, Lee Berendt told Waltuch that COMEX was concerned that the silver bullion supply would be inadequate if his clients stood for delivery on their December 1979 contracts. After talking to Nahas and Bally, Waltuch responded with a September 17, 1979, letter assuring the exchange that "[The Conti Group] have authorized me to inform you that they are willing to switch forward a certain portion of their long positions in the December silver futures to March, or May, or possibly July." The COMEX board minutes of September 17, 1979, also reported that a Conti representative had said that no "squeeze" was intended with respect to December silver. But that did not calm everybody; some members expressed concern that "manipulation of the December silver market might be in progress." The Chairman, however, reported that the CFTC was opposed to any "harsh" action by the exchange.

The COMEX board instructed the staff to get more specifics. A COMEX representative had additional discussions with Waltuch's boss, which resulted in a specific schedule for reducing their silver futures positions to a maximum of 10 million ounces. That agreement was designed to relieve congestion—that is, to ensure that the long positions did not exceed the available supply of silver bullion when the December 1979 futures contracts expired.

When someone at COMEX leaked the agreement to the press, Waltuch and his clients were furious. The article on September 21, 1979, in the *Wall Street Journal,* with the headline "Silver Broker Reportedly Told by COMEX to Sell Some Holdings," attributed the statement to two board members and an unnamed industry source. "The board was very afraid that there's a squeeze on the market," the *Journal* reported. The market immediately went limit down (the daily maximum), dropping almost $2.50 in one day, from $16.50 to $14.04.

Waltuch described the reaction at Advicorp: "Mr. Bally was extremely upset that the COMEX board, who had been supposedly sworn to secrecy about this, and they, who were acting with the COMEX in good faith to move positions forward, had leaked this. It had a dramatic

effect on the spread differentials because the whole market knew that Conti's customers were going to be moving
positions forward." Waltuch and his boss at Conti were
also "very, very upset."

In a fit of anger, Bally ordered Waltuch to the trading floor
to increase his December 1979 positions by 131 contracts
(655,000 ounces), a very visible and provocative act. The
floor traders buzzed whenever Waltuch showed up to trade.
A later *Fortune* article described a typical scene on the trading floor during this period: "According to Waltuch's office
colleagues, it was his ceremonial custom, late in trading sessions, to don his yellow Conti jacket and strut confidently
into the COMEX silver pit, where his mere presence would
buoy the market. 'The major silver long is in the ring,' an
audio hotline would report to all Conti offices around the
world. 'Someday they'll make a movie about this,' Waltuch
announced to his coterie in the pit one day as silver continued to soar." Waltuch testified that his orders had "some
impact on the price of silver," which was a rather astonish-
ing admission in a price manipulation case.

The uproar led to scurrying at the exchange and additional conversations with Conti executives. On September
27, 1979, with silver prices approaching $17, the Conti Group
traders reaffirmed their commitments to move forward
their December 1979 positions into months beyond March
and May 1980 where the Hunts had their large positions.
According to the minutes of the COMEX board, these reaf-
firmations were repeated throughout the fall of 1979.

"And the purpose of moving forward these positions was to prevent any sort of squeeze?" I asked Waltuch.

"Well, to prevent a squeeze and to prevent the perception of a squeeze."

"And the clients were informed of that fact?"

"Yes, they were and they were very agreeable."

That testimony was a brief moment of help from the quirky Waltuch. A squeeze is exactly an illegal form of price manipulation that we had to prove.

The unspoken battle between the Hunts and Conti Group and the regulators continued into October and November 1979. But before that battle could fully materialize, the Hunts had to deal with one of the grave consequences of the September 1979 price surge—a consequence that threatened to undo their scheme—a major metals house faced bankruptcy. At the same time, Minpeco was making the fateful mistake of entering the silver futures markets.

Chapter Twenty-Four

With silver prices roaring toward $18 per ounce, three times their historic highs, Minpeco was beset by brokers. In 1979, Peru was the third largest silver producer in the world with an economy largely controlled by the government. All miners, whether state owned or private, were required by law to sell silver and other minerals through Minpeco. The brokers, particularly E.F. Hutton (Nahas's broker) and Merrill Lynch (IMIC's and Hunts' broker), warned Minpeco that it would lose a historic opportunity if it waited any longer to enter the futures markets. By selling silver futures contracts for deliveries in three to six months, Minpeco could lock in the current, extraordinary high prices for its future bullion sales, the brokers advised.

Minpeco's Board of Directors took their advice. It authorized its new hedging department, headed by Ismael Fonseca, to open accounts with Merrill Lynch and E.F. Hutton and begin hedging Minpeco's future sales of silver. It was a decision with catastrophic consequences for Minpeco only two months later.

Fonseca described the scene to the jury. E.F. Hutton's Jim Ferro came to Lima on September 17, 1979, to meet with Minpeco's senior management, along with Fonseca. With the first big price surge in progress, Ferro kept up the broker's drumbeat that prices were about to drop and Minpeco would lose an opportunity to lock in historic high prices. Ferro's market view gave the jury an insight into what market participants understood about the already historic price rise; he supposedly had no idea silver prices were surging due to extraordinary delivery demands by IMIC, his client Naji Nahas, and the other members of the Conti Group, which was another subtle response to Paul Curran's broad daylight conspiracy argument. Ferro said prices could be "coming down any moment because there was no backing in the market for them, no support in the market for them." This was the time for Minpeco to start hedging, Ferro advised.

"And what was said on that subject?"

"We talked a lot about this, because one of the goals of his trip was to try and get Minpeco to get started [hedging] with some strength," meaning a large short futures position.

"What was said when you and Mr. Ferro spoke with Mr. Munar [Minpeco's President] and Mr. Alvarez Calderon [General Manager] on the question whether Minpeco should start hedging at that point in Lima?"

"We spoke about the price levels of silver, which were really extremely high. At the same time, we also said that we at Minpeco were now in condition to start operating—the infrastructure had been put in place, the people had been trained, and the financial resources were available to cover original and variation margins as they might come up. The market was presenting this opportunity, Minpeco was ready, and E.F. Hutton was ready to give us all the support needed to turn this into a success."

At the time, Jim Ferro was also a broker for Naji Nahas. Among the unsolved mysteries in a case of many mysteries was whether Jim Ferro had been tasked by Nahas to lure Minpeco into the futures market, whether Ferro had sufficient visibility on Nahas's whole position to understand what he was up to, or whether his sales pressure on Minpeco was just one more coincidence. Hutton and Merrill Lynch had both been defendants, but they had settled for many millions well before trial.

Two days after Ferro departed, Merrill Lynch brokers showed up in Lima and stayed until October 5. At Merrill Lynch, the connection between the Hunt team and Minpeco teams was not as close as within E.F. Hutton. They had come with much the same message as E.F. Hutton. Fonseca summarized the conversation for the jury. "The only thing I could add to that was a feeling that we were being put under pressure to get started."

"Why was the decision made in late September to begin entering short silver futures trades for Minpeco's own account?" I asked.

"Due to the fact that the market situation and the price situation showed an advantageous situation, we considered that we were sufficiently trained, we had already hired the brokers who would place our operations, and market events were affecting prices on the exchanges for mining products. Summarizing this, we thought we were safe, we had efficiency, and we would, thus, achieve the goals of hedging."

The Board of Directors authorized Fonseca to start placing futures trades and the company made arrangements with its principal bank, Banco de la Nacion, to pay the original and variation margins. Fonseca was now speaking daily on the phone with the E.F. Hutton and Merrill Lynch brokers who were providing information about political and economic events and prices but made no mention of a possible squeeze or the Hunts' or Conti Group's interest in silver, even when they appeared in the major financial press.

"Did you consider the information you were receiving from the brokers valuable?"

"Yes, very much so at that time."

"So who were you relying upon for the most up-to-date market information?"

"Exclusively on the brokers, Merrill Lynch and Hutton."

"In entering the short silver futures trades that Minpeco entered in September, October, and November 1979, were you relying upon the information you received from the brokers?"

"Totally."

Both E.F. Hutton and Merrill Lynch continued to express the opinion that silver prices would decline once they reached $18.10 per ounce on October 2, 1979. And they seemed right, prices softened back to $16.74 over the next ten days. Several weeks after Minpeco started trading, from October 17 to 20, 1979, another Merrill Lynch broker, Frank Granados, came to Lima with the same message about silver prices. My exchange with Fonseca gave the jury another insight into what traders who seemingly were not plugged into the Hunt conspiracy were thinking about the unusual price movements.

"What was said in those discussions?"

"The topics were very similar, but I want to illustrate it with a comment by [Frank] Granados which he gave us in the course of a dinner with the president and me. As far as Granados was concerned, what was happening in the market was inconceivable, because a huge interest in silver had been awakened at the national level here in the United States, and he said the market ought to be only for producers and buyers, eliminating all those who wanted to make money through speculation. I found this rather remarkable because it was my feeling that brokers were trying to increase the number of people participating in these markets as much as possible. I think what Granados was saying is in a market like that, supply and demand could be considered the only factors that should set prices. From this conversation one can deduce that Granados also shared the thought that the market at that point was distorted and might fall at any time."

"Did Mr. Granados give any opinion as to why the prices were at the levels that they were, the high levels they were at that time?"

"Well, actually, no one could clarify the situation and the comment was always the same, too many people running after money and that was what was pushing the price of silver up."

At Granados' request, Fonseca introduced him to some of the major mining companies in Peru, including Centromin, the largest with 40 percent of Peru's silver production. Some of the mines, including Centromin, began hedging their production through Minpeco.

I went over with Fonseca the risks inherent in futures trading, a subject I expected to be the focus of cross-examination. I wanted to touch that subject first, and at the same time, make the point that traders—both hedgers and speculators—should only be exposed to those risks in an honest market. The account opening documents had a Risk Disclosure Form, which described the risk of futures trading, but it also described protections in the US legal system against price manipulations. I went over both provisions with Fonseca.

"When you signed this risk disclosure statement did you understand that these risks were supposed to be risks taken in an honest market?"

"That was so. I thought we were dealing in a honest and trustworthy environment, which not only assigned responsibilities but had its own, too."

I also wanted to anticipate the defendants' attack on Minpeco's trading strategy. I had Fonseca make the point that the Minpeco's trading strategy had come from the experienced US brokers and not from a rogue employee thinking he could be a hero by speculating in volatile silver markets.

Both Paul Curran and Peter Fleming had focused the jury on Minpeco's trading strategy during their opening statements, arguing that Minpeco should blame itself for its own losses, not find rich men as scapegoats. Fleming had framed the argument elegantly, pacing before the jury and talking in a smooth, philosophical voice: "We live in a world where it may seem to each of you there is a lowering of standards. We live in a world where it appears to be increasingly impossible for individuals or corporations to say I am to blame. We live in a world where increasingly our mistakes or our misconduct are never our fault but the fault of someone else. We don't believe we have jurors who live by those lesser standards. We believe we have jurors who live by higher standards." The defense also accused Minpeco of misrepresenting itself to the brokers as a hedger while it was really speculating on silver price movements. That started a battle with the defense over the complex definition of hedging.

Fleming had described a pure hedge, which means that a silver dealer with one long silver contract will have 5,000 ounces of certificated bullion to deliver to the exchange at the maturity of a short futures contract. Thus, when the dealer loses money on its short futures side of the hedge, it will make money on its inventory of physical silver and can deliver certificated silver to the exchange, if necessary, to settle its futures contracts without a loss. The two transactions offset: losses on futures are offset by profits on physical silver or vice versa. In that way the dealer locks in the price at the time the future contract is acquired. The purpose of the transaction is to provide predictability and reduce risk. Speculating on price movements is for others.

However, many legitimate hedgers do not sell silver in the form of certificated bullion; like Minpeco, they are middlemen, hedging future commitments, so they do not have silver bullion in a form that they can readily deliver to the market to offset their futures positions. Kodak, for instance, used hedging to establish its cost of manufacturing because silver was an important element in photographic film in those days, and it ran into trouble during this period containing its costs.

In Minpeco's case, many of its sales were on behalf of others (state or private mines), and thus it would not make a profit on the physical silver sales when it lost money on hedges. Minpeco was responsible for selling approximately 45 million ounces of silver annually. The brokers recommended that Minpeco lock in the current high prices of future physical silver sales by selling short futures for one-third of that volume.

Starting in late September 1979, Minpeco began selling futures (thus, a short position) at $16 to $18 per ounce for delivery in March 1980. If, as anticipated, silver prices declined, Minpeco would close its short futures contracts at or prior to March 1980 and reap the profit on their futures contracts as prices dropped, as all the brokers were predicting. The physical sales would be at the lower prices, but the profits on the futures contracts effectively locked in the September 1979 price for silver sold in March 1980. The fallacy was that Minpeco had to pay the daily variation margins as prices increased (and the value of its physical silver sales increased). Minpeco's margins would have been manageable in a relatively stable market but started mounting into the tens of millions and more with the unanticipated and extraordinary price spiked in December 1979. Minpeco was losing big on the hedge but not making the equally big profit on the physical silver owned by others (which in any case would not be available until March 1980); Fonseca became swamped by the financing requirements.

The strategy devised by the US brokers had the same fallacy that tripped up other major metals dealers—like Mocatta and Engelhard Metals, major silver dealers—during the unprecedented price surges of September and December 1979. In advance of a renewed Fleming attack on cross-examination, I asked Fonseca to explain the situation to the jury.

"During the time you were trading with Merrill Lynch or E.F. Hutton in the period September 1979 into December 1979, did you believe that all the trades you placed were hedge trades?"

"Fully."

"It says here," I read from the Risk Disclosure Form, "that you should have legitimate hedges against our spot position or *commitments in accordance with accepted definitions of hedge transactions.* With respect to the short silver futures positions that you placed for Minpeco, what were the spot positions or commitments that you were hedging?"

"We were hedging firm purchase operations and those back-to-back contracts. Both are ways of trading at Minpeco."

Fonseca explained that Minpeco bought silver from small miners and then resold it, in which case it had an inventory of silver to hedge. Minpeco also sold silver for the large miners through back-to-back contracts: Minpeco would buy the silver from the miner but have an immediate contract to sell it abroad. Minpeco only made a commission on those transactions and never owned the silver. In those cases, Minpeco was hedging its legal obligation for future sales of Peru's annual silver production.

"Was it your understanding that Minpeco had the responsibility for setting the price on the back-to-back contracts?"

"That was so, and there was a [board] resolution of 65-1-76 that says that Minpeco had to hedge necessarily not only its own production, but also the back-to-back production."

"When you were selling short silver futures contracts, were you using those as a means of hedging Minpeco's obligation to get the best price on these back-to-back contracts?"

"That's right. We were paralleling that responsibility."

With the entry of Minpeco, the hunters and the prey were now arrayed in the silver markets. One of the September prey turned out to be Mocatta Metals, whose venerable chairman, Henry Jarecki, was an influential member of the COMEX Board of Governors. Bunker had to save Mocatta or risk a strong reaction from regulators that could halt his scheme.

Part Five

Bunker Staves off the Regulators

Chapter Twenty-Five

The historic upsurge in silver price in September 1979 had dramatic consequences: the exchanges were in disarray—at lock limit much of the time—speculators were losing millions beyond historic experience and the financial plans of commercial users became frenzied and ineffective. Nobody understood the cause. Paul Curran directed Bunker Hunt to a very public consequences, the threatened bankruptcy of Mocatta Metals, one of the world's oldest and largest metals dealers. Mocatta's dire finances graphically displayed the extreme condition of the silver markets, making it a subject Paul Curran could not avoid.

The Hunts' negotiation with Henry Jarecki, the powerful Mocatta chairman, opened the next phase of the drama—the Hunts maneuvering to neutralize industry regulators.

The futures markets are self-regulated by industry representatives on the boards of governors of the COMEX and Chicago Board of Trade (CBOT), among others, with oversight from the CFTC, a government regulator. With silver prices surging in September 1979 beyond any relationship to supply and demand, the CFTC and the exchanges were investigating.

Some board members, like Henry Jarecki of Mocatta, were losing millions on short positions that hedged their physical silver inventories, and they had the power to influence the exchange boards to impose regulations that could stop Bunker's plan. To stay their hand, the Hunts bailed out Mocatta and later other major silver dealers, which, some said, left the exchange boards content to sit back and watch a well-anticipated debacle in December 1979 that cost Minpeco and many others millions. Henry Jarecki was the first to receive Hunt assistance.

Mocatta had been a centerpiece of the metals markets for more than 300 years. In 1671, a Jewish diamond dealer, after emigrating from Amsterdam to London, formed Mocatta and became the bullion dealer for the Bank of England. The Mocatta family became a storied family in England as architects, scholars, and founders of the Jewish Reform Congregation. They eventually expanded their bullion operations into six countries. The family remained involved in the company for almost 300 years until 1957.

By 1979, Dr. Henry Jarecki, another colorful character in our story, owned Mocatta. Jarecki fled Nazi Germany as a child, obtained his medical degree from the University of Heidelberg in 1957, and became a Diplomaté of the American Board of Psychiatry and Neurology and an Assistant Clinical Professor of Psychiatry at the Yale University School of Medicine. After a decade, he took a detour into the business world to build an empire that included Mocatta Group, an investment bank, a brokerage firm, and MovieFone. But for all his business acumen, Jarecki's oversight of 300 years of history was teetering at the end of September 1979.

A silver dealer usually holds short silver futures contracts (commitments to sell silver) as a hedge against its physical silver or commitments (a long position). That arrangement usually takes the price risk out of their dealings: When prices go up, the short positions lose value while the physical silver gains value in approximately the same amount and vice versa as prices go down. In normal times, the daily margin requirements for the short positions are manageable. But in the extraordinary times of September 1979 with silver prices surging, the margin calls on Mocatta's short positions—like Minpeco and many dealers—became astronomical and unmanageable.

In response to Curran's questions, Bunker explained what happened. He and Herbert had borrowed from Mocatta "maybe $50 million," secured by silver bullion. "And so rumors got around that Mocatta might be in financial trouble . . ." Concerned by the rumors, Bunker and Herbert went to visit Jarecki, who admitted he was having financial difficulties. That should not have been a problem for the Hunts; they normally could have repaid their loan and recovered their silver, which was now worth substantially more than it was mortgaged for. But Jarecki's surprising admission was that Mocatta had re-pledged their silver for its own loan. In other words, Mocatta no longer had control over the Hunt silver, threatening the loss of 10.7 million ounces of very valuable silver if Mocatta were forced into bankruptcy. Mocatta reportedly had a market capital of $40 million and $400 million in bank loans; it was effectively broke.

After much handwringing and perhaps Hunt anger, Jarecki hatched an idea, a transaction that would save Mocatta and the Hunt silver—an exchange of futures contracts for physical silver, known in the trade as an EFP. After some negotiating, they reached an agreement. The Hunts would repay their $50 million loan to Mocatta, which would allow Mocatta to repay its loan and recover the 10.7 million ounces of Hunt silver held by Mocatta's lender. IMIC would exchange 4,583 long silver futures contracts for an additional 22,995,000 ounces of Mocatta's physical silver. Mocatta would use IMIC's long contracts to offset its short positions, thus closing those contracts and ending its incessant margin calls. And Mocatta, with Jarecki who was viewed as one of the major figures on the COMEX board, would no longer have an incentive to stop the surge in silver prices.

There also was a kicker that gave Jarecki a secret incentive to support upward prices. In one clause in the EFP contract, Mocatta could buy 800 March 1980 long silver futures contracts and IMIC would guarantee any losses in excess of $2 per ounce. Jarecki's future actions on the COMEX board now had to be viewed through the lens of the IMIC guarantee and his new 800 long positions, which were not known to his colleagues at COMEX or to the CFTC until much later.

The sheer size of the deal had made a big splash in the financial press. Paul Perito, pushing Curran's broad day-light conspiracy theme, had laid down another challenge to us during his opening statement: "You now ask yourself, if these alleged conspirators want to put a squeeze on the market would they do [a transaction] with 23 million dollars for God and the world to see, a press release issued by Mocatta . . . Some conspiracy!"

We took up the challenge. Although the Hunts told the exchanges that the EFP silver was all nondeliverable in form, the reality was that IMIC took control over additional silver bullion in the COMEX and CBOT warehouses, as well as London Metals Exchange (LME) deliverable silver bullion in Zurich. The transaction also included non-deliverable silver coins and options on additional bags of silver coins, which was what the Hunts told the press and the regulators. Our main point, however, was that the Hunts had omitted the key fact that the EFP gave IMIC additional control over warehouse silver bullion. In his testimony, Bunker tried to contort a potential disaster brought about by IMIC's silver hording into an effort to help the futures markets.

However, before he testified, the COMEX lawyer, Mark Buckstein, helped us show the jury that the regulators were told only part of the Mocatta EFP story. He testified that

COMEX considered the EFP helpful "as long as at the same time it did not reduce the available deliverable supply that was then in COMEX licensed depositories." Buckstein did not know that Henry Jarecki—a COMEX board member—had arranged for delivery to IMIC of millions of ounces of certificated silver. Thus, the EFP did exactly what Buckstein said was unhelpful to the markets. And Buckstein also did not know that the EFP agreement gave Mocatta an option over 800 long March 1980 silver contracts where the Hunts had a concentrated position, two unhelpful facts withheld by a COMEX board member.

Undeterred, Paul Curran asked Bunker: "Did you have any understanding as to whether this EFP was helpful to the silver market?"

"Yes. We had advisers on the deal . . . they both thought that was a very good thing and I think somebody representing our organization talked to some other officers of the COMEX."

"Did you understand that the COMEX, having learned of the transaction, approved it?"

"That was my understanding, yes."

Bunker's testimony that the Mocatta EFP was to help the market was a target for cross-examination. The silver futures markets were supposedly helped by the reduction of IMIC's December 1979 long futures position that reduced the potential nearby demand for silver bullion. I began by asking:

"And you actually completed those negotiations and offered that transaction to IMIC as a way of getting back control of your 10 million ounces of silver; is that correct?"

"Yea, in effect."

"And so this transaction was never undertaken to help the market, was it? It was undertaken to get your silver back; isn't that true?"

"Well, that was my main—my main interest was to get my silver back . . ."

When I pointed out that the Hunts and IMIC had hired the very law firm advising the COMEX, the stench had both Paul Curran and Paul Perito on their feet objecting. But Judge Lasker allowed the question. Bunker blamed the lawyer, as if the lawyer's relationship to the COMEX board was of no consequence to him, saying, ". . . later I did hear that his firm or himself had some connection with the exchange. Perfectly legitimate on our part. If there's a conflict, you're a lawyer, if you have a conflict, you don't get in the case. So, I just assumed that it was all right." As the fall went on, Bunker's transactions with COMEX board members multiplied many times.

For the Hunts, the Mocatta EFP represented a coup. They saved one of the major shorts from a bankruptcy that may have effectively ended their scheme if it prompted regulators to act more decisively. They recovered their silver bullion and took control over more. And they secretly brought an important short on the COMEX board to the long side of the market with a guarantee of 800 March 1980 long contracts. They could argue, when challenged, that they had helped the market because IMIC gave up its December 1979 silver position, thus relieving pressure on the demand for silver bullion in December.

But Bunker did not stand pat. The Mocatta 800 long contracts immediately replaced some demand for bullion, and his coordination with the Conti Group showed just how organized he was in reacting to changing conditions.

At the same time, Mocatta, a victim of the sudden September upsurge, was exiting the short side of the silver futures markets and moving to the long side, Minpeco was suckered in to take its place as a short futures trader. Two victims passing. Henry Jarecki, however, was a COMEX insider. He did not stay a victim for long. He later boasted he made a killing on silver.

Chapter Twenty-Six

On October 3, 1979, Bunker Hunt left his brother Herbert with Henry Jarecki to finish the Mocatta EFP negotiations while he flew to Paris (presumably in coach) to attend the biggest thoroughbred horse race of the year, Prix de l'Arc de Triomphé. Thoroughbred horse enthusiasts from around the world—kings, sheikhs, and billionaires—gather each fall at Longschamps Racecourse. The pomp and circumstance rivaled the Kentucky Derby and Royal Ascot. But L'Arc de Triomphé is not just a horse race. With the Eiffel Tower in the background, this is Paris; it is a fashion event, of course. Chanel, Louis Vuitton, and Yves St. Laurent are on regular display. And one fashion accessory is obligatory, the outrageous hat. Of the twenty-three horses in the L'Arc de Triomphé in 1979, Bunker's horse, Trillion, "ran a very good second but she was a mare," Bunker said, "She was beaten by about a half a length." Not bad for a girl, I suppose he meant.

Bunker, Naji Nahas, Norton Waltuch, and Jean-Jacques Bally all converged on the Bristol Hotel. They had much to discuss. The Mocatta EFP was about to reduce IMIC's positions in the December 1979 silver futures contract, and the Conti Group commitment to the COMEX to reduce its December 1979 long positions put its plans to take delivery of large quantities of silver bullion under regulatory attack.

And while in Paris, the schemers were confronted with other complications. On October 3, 1979, the COMEX board created a Special Silver Committee headed by a former Federal Reserve Board member, Dr. Andrew Brimmer, and made up of four members with no silver positions. The committee's mission was to conduct a more in-depth investigation of the goings-on in its silver market—to identify the members of the Conti Group, to determine whether they were trading together, and to monitor whether they would comply with the newly negotiated commitments to reduce their positions in the December 1979 silver contract. And on October 6, 1979, newly appointed Federal Reserve Board Chairman Paul Volcker put up another roadblock. He announced a historic series of economic measures designed to attack the raging 12 percent inflation rate. Among those changes was a directive discouraging US banks from lending for commodities speculation, including silver. The Federal Reserve prohibition meant the two groups had to come up with cash or find foreign sources of financing for their bullion deliveries.

Bunker and Nahas had another meal at the Bristol Hotel dining room, another luxurious, public locale to add to Paul Curran's broad daylight conspiracy theme. But this was no casual encounter: Bunker and Nahas were together not just at a meal, but also staying in the same hotel, and after their meetings, important trades were made that advanced their silver scheme.

When Bunker refused to admit that he stayed at the Bristol, I pulled out another hotel receipt and began walking across the well of the courtroom. After three months of travel records, Judge Lasker was losing patience: "We don't need to take time to show these records to the witness, do we, Mr. Curran? Can't you and Mr. Cymrot agree as to what the records show?"

I detoured from Bunker toward Curran's chair. He took the receipts without looking at me, briefly thumbing through them, and begrudgingly agreed. But then Bunker did not remember whether Nahas was at the Bristol Hotel, I started reminding him but the judge was having a testy day, interjecting again:

"We all know that he usually stayed at the Bristol Hotel, right?"

"I think so, yes, your Honor," Bunker obliged him.

Bunker did not remember that Waltuch and Bally were there also or whether they discussed silver futures. He had escaped into not recalling to almost every question, which left unchallenged our version of events. He did not remember whether he saw Fustok on this occasion, but acknowledged that Fustok spent most of the year in Paris.

From this early October 1979 meeting came a series of coordinated actions reacting to the consequences of the

Mocatta EFP and regulatory pressures. Bunker decided not to wait until December to grab more silver bullion. Between October 5 and 8, 1979, Bunker bought 245 October 1979 silver futures contracts and almost immediately took delivery of 1,225,000 ounces of silver bullion. It seems Bunker now shared with the IMIC Sheikhs an interest in bullion. Bunker also increased his position in December 1979 silver futures contracts from 225 to 1,200 long contracts, replacing the contracts IMIC gave up in the Mocatta EFP.

Bunker did not have a good explanation for buying 245 October 1979 contracts and taking delivery; he just said he was bullish on silver in October. I laid out for the jury Bunker's trading that coincided with the Conti Group's, asking:

"Now within a couple of days of the time when you placed orders for 245 October contracts on the COMEX, Mr. Nahas, through the BPS account, placed orders and took delivery of 300 October contracts (1.5 million ounces) on the COMEX. Did you know that?"

"No, I did not know."

"Did you know that Mr. Fustok took delivery of 492 silver futures contracts (2.46 million ounces) on the COMEX in October?"

"No. I didn't know what anyone else was doing other than myself and IMIC."

"In your view, it's just a *coincidence* that the three of you placed orders for spot contracts in October and took deliver?"

That brought a chorus of objections from the three defense counsel that the judge sustained. When I rephrased the question, Bunker still had no explanation: "I was bullish on silver and I didn't mind telling people I was bullish on silver . . . In any event I don't know why they took it." And Bunker also had to concede there was no tax reason for placing spot orders for silver and taking delivery: "There might be. But I don't know of any," he said, sounding frustrated.

When Banque Populaire Suisse bought another 792 October 1979 contracts (3.96 million ounces) about the same time, the conspirators had suddenly taken control over almost 8 million additional ounces of silver bullion in COMEX warehouses, worth more than $120 million. I doubted taking control over millions of ounces of silver bullion in its warehouse was what the COMEX had in mind for reducing December 1979 congestion.

But Norton Waltuch's reaction when I asked him about Conti's commitment to the COMEX was sarcastic: "I was very appreciative of the commission business." I sucked in my breath and grasped for a question. But he continued to show no concern for Conti's regulatory commitments.

In response to Paul Volcker's new rule, the two groups began ramping up their financing for another assault on the warehouse bullion. Bache, apparently not feeling constrained by the Volcker directive, increase their trading limits from 5,000 to 7,500 contracts and extended their credit lines from $35 to $50 million. Bache's loans were to grow to $176 million by the end of February 1980. For all their talk of independent trading decisions, Bunker and Herbert Hunt had a joint stock account at Bache, and in October 1979, they jointly began buying stock in Bache, starting with a 3 percent interest, which grew to 6.5 percent in March 1980.

On October 10, 1979, Merrill Lynch, feeling similarly unconstrained by the Fed rule, increased the IMIC and Hunt combined credit limit by $50 million to $175 million. On October 11, 1979, Nahas introduced Bunker to Banque Arabe et Internationale d'Investissement (BAII) in Paris, which advanced a $50 million loan to IMIC, the beginning of their combined efforts to find foreign financing. Bank Leu A.G. in Zurich offered another $50 million.

Even though they were together in Paris only shortly before, Bunker denied he knew Nahas was heavily concentrated in December 1979 futures contracts. And he denied he was trying to put pressure on the futures markets by replacing the 985 long December 1979 contracts IMIC had surrendered as part of the Mocatta EFP. I attacked his assertion that with the Mocatta EFP he was being helpful to the silver markets, caustically asking Bunker:

"You weren't trying to be helpful to the market when you put on those 1,200 December 79 contracts, were you?"

Curran did not like my tone; he jumped up, insulted: "Objection, your Honor." I kept my gaze on Bunker, not looking to Curran or the judge.

The judge did not oblige him: "Overruled."

"I was buying silver," Bunker straightening up responded brusquely. "There were serious problems with the markets, there were rumors the market might close and I thought it was the time to buy some silver."

"Well, you didn't really care one way or the other whether your buying silver was helpful to the market or not, isn't that true?" I asked with a rising voice.

"I was—let's put it this way," Bunker started, apparently taken aback by the change in my usual calm demeanor. "I wasn't trying to cause any problems with the market, I was buying silver and if—I don't think there was anything negative or sinister about buying silver."

However, Bunker had choices other than December 1979 contracts. "Well," I said, leaning forward to press the point, "you had a lot of other choices other than buying December positions, isn't that true, Mr. Hunt?"

"Oh, I guess you could buy something else if you wanted to," he said, trying to sound casual.

"That's right. And so there was some special reason you wanted to buy December contracts, isn't that true?"

"I liked the way the market looked; I thought December was a very good month." That must have seemed lame to Bunker because when I pushed him, he came up with an alternative explanation.

"And what was it about December that you liked as opposed to buying another one?"

"Well, I think, I think there was not much liquidity in the market, as I recall, and it was hard to buy futures at that time. You could buy the spot, but you couldn't buy futures very easily. I think that affected my judgment."

Bunker's refuge in "liquidity" opened another line of attack based on his brother's trading, a point we had prepared but were not sure how we would use. I did not need my notes to remind me of the trades. "And the reason that you say that is because, as far as you are concerned, there was no liquidity in any other months is that true?"

"That liquidity by that time had gotten very, very difficult in the market. There was very little liquidity because of, because of the margin, the exchange margins had gotten so high."

"Well, on November 14 of 1979, your brother Herbert bought 150 March 1980 contracts, so he didn't have any trouble buying March contracts apparently, so liquidity doesn't seem to be the reason, does it, Mr. Hunt?"

"You will have to ask Herbert," Bunker grumped but had no other explanation.

After that rapid exchange, our timeline had been repeated through Bunker's mouth, the key events were being connected for the jury, and wherever possible, his excuse for buying spot October 1979 contracts and taking a 1,200 contract position in December 1979 silver futures was being undermined, at least I hoped that was the way the jury was seeing it, as the story turns back to the Conti Group.

Chapter Twenty-Seven

About this time, Norton Waltuch and Naji Nahas took a ride out to Mahmoud Fustok's farm in Chantilly for a chat about silver. Waltuch described the scene: "Well, we drove in. It was a very impressive looking place, huge walls around it and electronic fences that swung open when we pulled in. He has a beautiful facility. Mr. Nahas pointed out the various buildings and the stables in back." Fustok's mother had a house in one section and Fustok had his own house and a separate building for his office, which was where they went.

Nahas introduced Waltuch as the "silver man." Although they had met briefly in Lexington the prior spring, it was Fustok's first extended encounter with Waltuch. Waltuch and Fustok told different versions of the meeting. According to Waltuch, the talk was about silver; he told Fustok the silver markets still had upside potential. "I continued to be very, very friendly to the silver market," Waltuch testified. "I thought the situation in the world continued to deteriorate even worse that I had thought sometime ago and the world political situation was on the verge of chaos, inflation was rampant. I thought all these things would have a major effect on the price of silver, gold, and all commodities in general."

Waltuch tried to pick Fustok's brain about the Middle East. But Fustok was distracted and disinterested as he described the scene: "I kept on interrupting him because I wanted to talk about horses. He wanted to talk about silver." However, Fustok absorbed Waltuch's message despite his annoyance: "Norton told me at Chantilly [silver prices] would go very high. He told me the Arabs are doing a very good thing."

Fustok saw Nahas at the racetrack every two days during this period. Nahas would come to the paddock, annoying him more by constantly talking about silver—what Waltuch was saying, what Bunker was doing. Bunker had $150 to $200 million invested in silver, Nahas told Fustok, which impeached Bunker's testimony that he never told Nahas how large a silver position he had.

"What did [Nahas] tell you about Bunker Hunt's investment in silver?" I asked.

"He said he is the big man," responded Fustok. "The king of silver."

"When was this said?"

"All the time."

Nahas also told Fustok that he was talking to Advicorp, thus tying tighter those coordinating trading. When Nahas said silver was going to $100 per ounce, Fustok "loved it," but he was planning to hold onto his silver at any price, he insisted.

Although supposedly irritated by all the talk about silver, Fustok joined the others in stockpiling financing: He signed two letters of credit totaling $65 million from Banque Populaire Suisse to ContiCommodity to pay margins on silver futures contracts and obtained another $50 million line of credit from Swiss Bank Corporation. Jean-Jacques Bally, one of the Advicorp partners, testified the letters of credit were "precisely in order to respond to Mr. Fustok's desire to increase [silver] purchases . . . Fustok understood it was to meet margin calls on his silver futures contracts." This $115 million in financing impeached Fustok's defense that he had limited his silver investments to $30 to $40 million and everything else was fraud by his advisors. Fustok insisted he was not paying attention; he had not read the documents. And Waltuch did not walk away empty handed; Fustok opened a personal commodity account with him.

We were now in the midst of competing stories: Ours was about silver trading, while Bunker and Fustok wanted to talk about their beloved horses.

Chapter Twenty-Eight

While Bunker Hunt was in Paris on October 3, 1979, Herbert Hunt got word that the CBOT was concerned about the "illiquidity and disorderliness" in its silver market. In an unusual move, the Business Conduct Committee asked the CBOT's President Robert Wilmouth to call the Hunts directly; the exchanges usually talk to their members, the brokerage houses. Robert E. Goldberg, the Business Conduct Committee (BCC) chairman, explained: "In a general sense we wanted Mr. Wilmouth to convey that we were concerned about the silver situation . . . We wanted to get Mr. Wilmouth to get the Hunt brothers to pledge their cooperation."

"What type of cooperation was the BCC looking for from the Hunts?" I asked.

"Well, in a broad sense we felt that they had an obligation to maintain an orderly market and, secondly, we would be looking for some good-faith efforts to starting to reduce the size of their positions."

The CBOT was already considering aggressive action. Goldberg explained to the jury. "We should have some sort of a game plan to impose some emergency rules and regulations." Those options included shutting down the market at a particular price or liquidation-only trading, which means allowing the purchase or sale of no new contracts, only contracts to close positions. The conditions that prompt consideration of such extraordinary actions, Goldberg explained: "That the [Hunt] positions were so large, and that they would not be liquidated in an orderly manner [so] that we would have to force the liquidation of the contracts rather than just let them sit there and *possibly attempt to influence or dictate the prices.*"

"And if they took delivery over the next four or five months," I asked, "what was the concern of the BCC?"

"*The possibility that the deliverable supplies could be exhausted.*"

This was important evidence that the Hunts and Conti Group bullion demands were a threat to a fair market. I pressed further:

"What would be the result of running out of silver?"

"*It would lead to a sharp increase in price.*" Goldberg responded.

That was the very point we were trying to make to the jury. By taking delivery and taking control over silver supplies, the conspirators were intentionally increasing prices, conduct which was illegal—as the judge had instructed the jury at the beginning of the case.

In response to the Business Conduct Committee request, Wilmouth dialed Herbert Hunt. At that point, the Hunts' struggle with the exchanges became more direct and personal; the call began a series of conversations between Herbert and Bunker Hunt and the governing bodies of the two exchanges and the CFTC. Wilmouth told Herbert Hunt about a lengthy meeting the prior day of the Business Conduct Committee, which was considering "drastic measures" should the disorderliness in the silver market continue. Herbert tried to calm Wilmouth, saying he was in New York working on an EFP that would "dramatically change" his positions in Chicago. The exchange should have no concern about his positions or those of "his international company"; he would work with them to keep the market functioning.

Wilmouth "reported back with basically the thought process that the Hunts had said that they have always been in the silver market, have always adhered to the idea of maintaining an orderly market and would see no reason that this situation would be any different." The problem, in Herbert Hunt's view, was high margins, referring to a margin increase on September 18 to $20,000 per contract.

Over the next week, Herbert's conversations with Wilmouth continued. Herbert claimed he "had the same number of long contracts as he has had for the past several years," a statement that was untrue. More important to the exchange, he committed that, "He would not take any personal deliveries except when necessary for capital gains."

That statement certainly was untrue as to Bunker's positions that Wilmouth undoubtedly thought was part of the conversation. According to Wilmouth, Herbert repeated on several occasions, "I recognize my responsibilities if the shorts cannot come up with it," meaning bullion close to fulfill their contracts. He continued: "Regarding my February positions at the Board of Trade, I intend to move them forward after the first of the year," another statement that proved untrue. He could not move them any earlier because of "serious tax consequences." When the CBOT continued to worry about the bullion supply to satisfy demand in December 1979, Herbert repeatedly referred to his "horrendous tax consequences" if he made silver available to the market.

As Wilmouth continued to press through one of the Hunt brokers and directly with Herbert, the Hunt tax people came up with a solution for the bullion supply issue: Herbert could swap Chicago bullion receipts for bullion in London and Zurich without incurring a taxable event. That would maintain the silver bullion supply in Chicago warehouses. Herbert called Wilmouth, promising to make bullion available from his inventory if the exchange needed it. For his part, Herbert urged Wilmouth to maintain "a viable market," and he questioned Wilmouth's concern that "the game could be all over in December." That certainly proved true for Minpeco.

While Herbert was talking in soothing tones to Wilmouth, Bunker was taking delivery of 1,225,000 ounces of bullion deliveries at the COMEX and replacing IMIC's December 1979 long positions with his own 1,200 contracts (6 million ounces), thus, maintaining the same pressure on the December 1979 contracts that the exchange was trying to relieve. The COMEX did not react.

But the trade that provoked the CBOT into action came on October 16 to 17, 1979, when Houston Hunt, Bunker's son, added 1,700 straddles contracts on the Chicago exchange with long legs in June 1980, a position that paralleled his father's, only a month later. It appeared to be a direct challenge to the exchange, and the Business Conduct Committee responded angrily by recommending to the CBOT Board of Directors to impose "liquidation-only" trading. That means traders could only close positions, not open new ones, effectively closing the Chicago silver futures market.

Robert Goldberg testified to the committee's frustration: "Well, again, you can't exactly apply science to all these things. But the basic reasons were we felt that our jawboning efforts had been exhausted . . . We were concerned that the positions in the marketplace were attempting—*were starting to influence the price*." The CBOT Board of Directors did not accept the recommendation, concerned that it was too drastic. They sent the committee back to review other options, including meeting with the Hunts.

On October 22, 1979, Herbert Hunt, and this time Bunker, flew to Chicago to meet with the Business Conduct Committee, which expressed directly to them their concern with congestion in the silver market. In his testimony, Robert Goldberg described the committee's concerns: "Well, we . . . wanted them to declare their intentions to the committee and to the exchanges and we wanted to tell them that we were concerned *about an undue influence on prices.*"

"The undue influence on prices would have been the result of what?"

"Of their positions."

Thus, the committee put Bunker and Herbert directly on notice that their silver positions could be affecting silver prices, which they knew would be unlawful. When the committee questioned Houston Hunt's 1,700 straddles, Bunker's response was "I can't control the actions of my son." That certainly did not comfort the committee. Several times during the meeting, Bunker and Herbert insisted they were trading independently.

"Did the committee accept the response?" I asked.

"Not necessarily, no," Goldberg responded. "For our analysis we basically considered them to be one position."

According to Goldberg, both Hunt brothers pledged their cooperation. The Hunts spun the Mocatta EFP as helpful to the markets, saying it involved noncertificated (silver bullion not qualified to deliver), yet another untrue statement. To assuage the committee's concern about the bullion supply, the brothers promised to make 10 million ounces of bullion available to the market to ensure an orderly liquidation of the December 1979 contract, and to roll forward their large February 1980 positions after January 1. "They would be willing to help liquidate the [December] contract and not just stand there and do nothing," Herbert told them. Herbert acknowledged making these commitments in his testimony, although sticking to the Hunts' separate trading theme, he would make available 5 million ounces and Bunker would make available 5 million ounces and with the caveat "provided it was economically viable to do so."

Also on October 22, 1979, the CFTC sent Bunker and Herbert telexes asking for more details about their silver positions: the names of all their domestic and foreign brokers and the list of any persons or entities with silver futures positions they controlled or had a financial interest in. After the Business Conduct Committee meeting, Wilmouth and the two Hunt brothers apparently walked back to Wilmouth's office to call CFTC Vice Chairman Read Dunn. The trio found Dunn in the midst of a meeting with his staff about the imposition of "speculative position limits" on precious metals, which would be a limit to the number of contracts any trader or group of traders could hold. Wilmouth explained the substance of their conversations and put Herbert on the phone, who gave Dunn more details about IMIC's recent EFP transactions. Bunker got on and asked for a meeting.

The next day, Bunker flew to Washington for a meeting with Dunn and three staff members in a small, spare government office building in the business district. He pleaded for a "neutral market." According to the cold tones of a CFTC memo, Bunker told Dunn that he and his brother trade independently, convincing nobody I am sure. He gave his usual lecture about silver demand outstripping supply and assured Dunn that all his positions are reported to the CFTC. He said, "He did not want to do anything that would be detrimental to the futures market," which "has been good to him over the years. Therefore, he and his brother will try to avoid causing any problems." He planned to roll forward his positions as he had done in the past, but he would wait until after the first of the year. They would not sell bullion due to the "tax consequences" but would swap deliverable silver stock for silver that did not qualify for delivery. He preferred to have his bullion in Europe; "he was afraid the U.S. government might expropriate silver from individuals as it did in the 1930s when individuals were no longer permitted to own gold."

When Dunn asked about Arabs in the silver markets, Bunker claimed the IMIC Sheikhs Mussalem and Al-Amoudi were "the only two Arabs that he knows are investing in the silver market," one more untrue statement. The CFTC memo continued: "However, he has reason to believe that there are a number of other wealthy individuals who are acquiring silver. He based that statement on conversations with Arab individuals that he has met on his various trips to Europe." He made no mention of his "friend" Naji Nahas or his buffet dinner host, Mahmoud Fustok. Bunker assured Dunn he planned to roll his futures positions forward after the first of the year, one more sop to Dunn's concerns that proved untrue.

Dunn thanked Bunker for coming to Washington. He expressed the CFTC's concern with the "volatile and rapid price run-up." He gave Bunker a not-too-subtle warning: the CFTC questions "whether silver prices are reflecting a legitimate demand for silver or whether someone is *forcing the price up artificially.*" When he warned that the CFTC was considering the imposition of speculative position limits, Bunker expressed the hope that they would wait until after the first of the year or he would "incur a substantial tax on his position if he had to liquidate." One CFTC staffer described how the government participants felt: "we all had an amount of skepticism."

For good reason. When I asked Bunker about his omission of Nahas and Fustok in response to Dunn's questions about Arabs in the silver markets, he barked: "Nahas is Brazilian," obviously a prepared but limp response. When I pointed to his earlier testimony that Nahas was Lebanese, Bunker shot back, "He carries a Brazilian passport." As for Fustok, Bunker said, "I had only read that in the *Wall Street Journal* and trade publications." He failed to mention the August 1979 conversation at the end of which Fustok ordered his bankers to buy $30 to $40 million of silver.

An aging trial lawyer should not read old transcripts. In writing this narrative, I kept turning the pages of Bunker's cross-examination looking for the portion where I pummeled him with his repeated reference to Nahas as his "good friend." It wasn't there.

Their meeting with Bunker and Herbert did not appease the Business Conduct Committee, which remained skeptical and concerned about the silver supply. "Plus," said Robert Goldberg, "we weren't satisfied with the statement of Bunker Hunt that he couldn't control the action of his son." On October 25, 1979, the BCC again recommended a liquidation-only trading rule to the CBOT governing board. The Chicago board again balked and opted for a lesser but nonetheless severe remedy, imposing position limits of 600 contracts per trader effective by February 1, 1980. The Hunts would have to shed the excess before they could take bullion deliveries on their huge February 1980 futures positions, which were the positions most concerning to the Chicago exchange. The Chicago board's position-limits rule effectively closed the Hunts out of that market.

The game would have to be played at the COMEX in New York, which at that moment was focused on the Conti Group.

Chapter Twenty-Nine

Meanwhile, senior ContiCommodity officials were trying to calm anxious COMEX officials. Silver prices had remained flat around $16 to $17 during October but they were not sure how long that would last with large positions overhanging their December 1979 contract. At an October 25, 1979, Special Silver Committee meeting, the COMEX lawyer, Mark Buckstein, reported that the Conti Group had made "no material change" in its December 1979 positions despite the group's commitments of September 27 to roll forward those positions. He apparently did not report the October 1979 bullion deliveries by Bunker or the Conti Group. In an era before the electronic transfer of information, the regulators may not have known about them yet. Nonetheless, Lee Berendt, the COMEX president, reflected the exchange's concern by calling Conti officials, warning that: "If the clients did not voluntarily reduce their positions, COMEX would take measures to force liquidation."

In response, a senior Conti official scurried over to the Special Silver Committee meeting offering a "foolproof plan" to avoid a squeeze. After some modifications, the COMEX and Conti agreed to a plan under which the Conti Group would take no more than 2,000 December 1979 deliveries and would move their other futures positions to contracts beyond May 1980. That limit would not overwhelm the bullion supplies available to short traders who have to make delivery. The COMEX seemed less concerned than the CBOT about the impact of such large bullion demands on silver prices, as long as no short defaulted.

At the same meeting, Buckstein reported more comforting words from a Hunt lawyer. The committee minutes of October 25, 1979, reported that the Hunts had a net long position of 12,281 contracts, which the Hunts said were "the residue of positions held for a number of years," a representation that was untrue. As for their intentions, the Hunts said that: "Their basic practice has always been and continues to be, to move their positions forward; *they have no present intention of increasing their position; and they have no present intention of standing for delivery.*" Herbert Hunt later testified he authorized his lawyer to make these representations.

The Hunt and Conti Group assurances either calmed jittery nerves or simply provided the regulators with an excuse for ducking their responsibility to impose more harsh restrictions. Generally, the insiders were doing fine at that point; like Mahmoud Fustok, they loved the high prices. Despite the imposition of position limits in Chicago, the COMEX postponed any action on position limits, but the next day the COMEX Special Silver Committee imposed a $50,000 per contract margin rule. The margin increase required speculative traders to put up five times the margin to hold their contracts, although hedge positions were exempt, thus exempting most board members. Along with the Federal Reserve's directive on bank lending, the regulators hoped the new super margins would put financial pressure on the Hunts and Conti Group to reduce their positions.

The COMEX Board of Governors held another special meeting on the afternoon of October 29, 1979. Andrew Brimmer, the Special Silver Committee chairman, initiated a discussion of the so-called "super margins." The Hunt and Conti Group's misleading assurances were of crucial importance to the discussion, according to the minutes. "No significant risk of a squeeze, manipulation, or congestion exists at the present time," Mark Buckstein reported. He later explained: "If there were no understandings with the clearing members involved, there would be a concern about the possibility of a corner or manipulation. In light of the existing understandings, however, and the indications that all parties involved were acting in good faith." Relying on these representations, Buckstein gave his recommendation: "The appropriate course of action for the exchange, under those conditions, was to monitor the progress of the parties involved in reaching the goals set forth in the understanding."

Henry Jarecki quickly jumped in to express his opinion. Unbeknownst to the COMEX board, Mocatta had bought the 800 March 1980 silver contracts (4 million ounces) guaranteed by IMIC between October 16 and 25, 1979, in the range of $17. (When Mocatta reported its positions to COMEX on November 19, 1979, the 800 March 1980 long contracts were not included, which would explain why the COMEX lawyer, Mark Buckstein, testified that he did not know about those contracts even eight years later at trial.) Jarecki sought to undermine the call for super margins, arguing that market conditions did not show evidence of a squeeze or manipulation and the Board Trade Group, which he chaired, was concerned about the lack of liquidity caused by the $50,000 margin requirement; they recommended reducing the margins. A robust discussion ensued. During a recess, the Special Silver Committee reduced the super margins to $30,000 per contract and $400 per month per straddle. The silver committee's minutes parroted Jarecki's reasoning for the change: "in order to improve the liquidity of the marketplace." When the board meeting reconvened, Jarecki made one more effort to sidetrack the Special Silver Committee, proposing a Special Margin Committee to consider margin issues. That suggestion was tabled.

When Paul Curran asked about the regulatory pressure, Bunker developed another theme of the defense—almost a battle of good against evil—by ascribing these regulatory changes to the "shorts" on the Boards of Governors manipulating silver prices lower. By shorts he was referring to traders who sell futures contracts, while longs like the Hunts buy futures contracts. Major metals producers—like Mocatta before the EFP transaction, Engelhard Metals, Sharps Pixley—held the largest short positions to hedge the value of their inventories or commitments. As prices went up, their short futures positions lost value (while their less liquid metals inventories increased in value), but their futures positions prompted large margin calls. Bunker's allegation was that the emergency regulations were a manipulation by insiders who were hurting from large margin calls as prices shot upward. To stop the pain, the shorts influenced the exchange boards to impose the new rules, according to Bunker's version of events.

Bunker explained his theory of corruption at the exchanges: "I didn't realize it at the time, but I know it now, that the shorts are made up of seven or eight or ten major firms, and they take the overwhelming position of the short side of the market, and the general public, such as people like myself, are on the long side of the market, and so that's what I am referring to."

"Were there representatives of the shorts on the boards of the two commodities exchanges, Mr. Hunt?" Curran asked.

"Yes, unfortunately, the shorts ran the futures market pretty well. I didn't realize that until later on. But the longs were not represented on the board and the silver committee. They were all manned by the shorts, members of those major firms."

"So the boards of the two exchanges had shorts representatives on them, but no long representatives, is that your
understanding?"

"That's my understanding, yes."

Bunker's apparent failure to anticipate regulatory action
was a fundamental fallacy in his planning. He seemed surprised and offended that the exchanges and the US government would not allow him and his Arab cohorts to buy the
entire visible supply of silver bullion in order to set up an
OPEC-style silver cartel. From time to time, I would muse
about his reaction, which seemed one of his more genuine
emotional reactions. His father was wildly successful in the
relatively lawless and unregulated days of the Texas oil
boom. H.L. Hunt was not beholden to government restraints
or even personal ones. Bunker seems to have missed the
transition to a smaller world with bigger governments. He
was the victim of arbitrary government action in Libya, and
again, in his view, in the boardrooms of New York and
Chicago.

By portraying regulation as a private battle between
wealthy shorts and the general public longs, Bunker was
advancing his defense that he was merely a big investor in
silver, not a manipulator. After all, what is a billionaire to
do, buy small?

The Hunts responded to the margin increases by jawboning. They urged the COMEX to maintain a viable,
liquid market. He told the CBOT: "They needed a viable

market and that the recent margin increase from 10 percent to 50 percent reduced the liquidity of the market in
effect; just stopped the buyers and so they were causing an
illiquid market situation." The margins, Bunker went on,
"just pretty well stopped any potential buyers from buying
silver, because no one is going to pay 50 percent margin for
the right to buy a futures contract. I shouldn't say no one. I
would say 99 percent of the people won't do that."

Bunker continued: "Well, I said, the law requires that you
all be market neutral, that you not do anything to affect the
market, either pro or con and that's what the people that
buy contracts are depending on and that I hoped that they
would do that."

"What response, if any, did you get to that?" Curran asked.

"Well, it was sort of a no comment kind of response. They
wouldn't really say what they were doing except they were
just doing things that they thought would improve the
market."

Curran went back to the one-sided nature of the new
"super margins" that favored the insiders; they did not apply
to legitimate hedge positions, which included the major
shorts on the exchange boards, Bunker testified: "They
would be the beneficiary; it did not cause them problems."

When my turn came to cross-examine Bunker on his
skirmishes with regulatory officials, I started with Bunker's assertion that the short representatives dominated
the COMEX board and was imposing regulation to protect

their firms. Bunker admitted that Charles Mattey, the Hunt broker at Bache and a former COMEX president, was still a member of the board in fall 1979. The Hunts provided Mattey with 90 percent of his income.

"So when you're talking about the shorts on the Board of Governors of the COMEX you're not referring to Mr. Mattey; is that right?"

"No."

"Mr. Mattey, in fact, represented your interests on the Board of Governors of the COMEX, didn't he?"

"Well, I hope he did. I think he would have—I think he tried to help us. Yes. I asked him to and I think he did try to."

So the Hunts were not just any members of the public with long positions; they had their own representative on the COMEX board. I took the opportunity to bring out that Bunker and Naji Nahas must have talked about specifics in the silver markets, rather than the generalizations Bunker had been spewing.

"And you and Mr. Nahas both believed that the COMEX Board of Governors was dominated by the shorts; is that true?"

"It was dominated by the shorts, yes."

"I'm asking you whether you know whether Mr. Nahas had that same belief?"

"I think he did. I think he expressed that to me, certainly, at some point in time. It was obvious that the board was dominated by the shorts."

With the blizzard of information we had to absorb, we had not yet put together the significance of the 800 March 1980 long contracts that IMIC guaranteed for Mocatta, whose president, Henry Jarecki, was actively undermining the super margin rule as an influential COMEX board member. And for all the talk with the CFTC and COMEX, Bunker and the Conti Group were retaining their hold over massive long positions in the December 1979 contract. Talk is cheap—but only for some. Others like Minpeco were hurtling toward disaster.

Chapter Thirty

From his meeting in Washington with CFTC Vice Chairman Reed Dunn, Bunker Hunt flew to Zurich where he entered into one of the most significant secret transactions of the run-up to December 1979. This was the first of four transactions at Swiss Bank Corporation that put the lie to everything he and Herbert were telling the CFTC and the exchanges. Bunker must have believed that these transactions would forever stay hidden behind the wall of Swiss secrecy. Bank secrecy was an industry in Switzerland at the time. Conducting forbidden transactions behind that impenetrable wall must have seemed safe to Bunker.

Unraveling Bunker's story began, once again, with a hotel receipt showing Bunker and Nahas stayed at the Dolder Grand Hotel from October 31 to November 2, 1979, "the perfect environment for people who are looking for pleasure, exclusivity, and relaxation." Norton Waltuch, Jean Jacque Bally, Bob Guinn and Jim Parker were also in town. They were staying at other luxury hotels around town, the

Savoy and Baur a Lac. The hotel receipts, led to questions, which eventually led to this breakthrough.

Waltuch was the first to put Bunker and Nahas together at Swiss Bank Corporation. While waiting for Nahas in the lobby of Swiss Bank Corporation, Bunker walked out and said a quick hello, according to Waltuch. When Nahas came out shortly later, he told Waltuch he had just "bumped into" Bunker. As it turned out, Waltuch also identified the purpose of their visit to the bank—to ensure that Nahas would pay his margins to ContiCommodity. Bullion deliveries on his December 1979 contracts were about to cost Nahas millions.

According to Advicorp's Jean-Jacques Bally, Bunker and Nahas's presence were a lot more than a casual "bump"; they met at the Dolder Grand Hotel and rode, along with him, in the same car to Swiss Bank Corporation.

This meeting required an explanation from Bunker. More vague talk but no scheming was his version in response to Paul Curran's questions. He borrowed some money and bought some silver forwards contract. "Swiss Bank Corporation was a very big factor in the silver business," Bunker explained. The bank was "hustling business," so he opened an account and they also discussed a loan using silver as collateral.

"Why did you have to go all the way over there to get money?" Curran asked Bunker.

"Well, the American banks had virtually stopped," Bunker said, then paused and restarted, "I guess they had stopped lending on precious metals at that time, gold and silver. I think there was some kind of instruction from the Federal Reserve not to, not to loan gold or silver. Maybe I think it was more specifically silver." He needed the extra money because the exchanges had imposed super margins on his large positions. Bunker was not planning to trade silver on that trip, he claimed, but with the increased margins at US exchanges and rumors more regulation was coming, "so I was looking for alternate places to do business in the event I wanted to do business to financing, trading, whatnot."

Although Bally's testimony had put Bunker and Nahas in the same car, Bunker had another story: "I was walking through the lobby of Swiss Bank Corporation and here walking right at me was Norton Waltuch," Bunker said. "And I said 'Hello, Norton. What are you doing here?'" According to Bunker, Naji Nahas was with Waltuch, implying a casual encounter with Nahas at the bank, which conflicted with Waltuch's story that Bunker walked out first and then Nahas. With so many actors, they could not keep their stories straight. They were vague about their business, according to Bunker: "I was friendly with Nahas and, you know, I talked to him freely and I'd say, 'Well, what are you doing here in town?' And he would say, 'Oh I'm here doing something.' I think he said he was checking, doing some banking."

This supposedly chance meeting in the lobby of Swiss Bank Corporation was anything but a coincidence I wanted to show when it was my turn. I started with their accommodations.

"And how did it happen that the two of you ended up at the same hotel?"

"I don't recall. We were friends and if I were going there I would tell him where I was going to stay. There was no secret about that," Bunker said, trying to sound casual. The fortuitous meeting in the lobby of the bank was thus a planned get-together, which was not as Bunker had portrayed it.

I moved to the key transaction that Curran had sidestepped, some of the most direct evidence of conspiracy. I supposed there was no good explanation.

During the pretrial stage of the case, Judge Lasker had ordered the Hunts to sign waivers of their rights under Swiss bank secrecy laws. The Hunts resisted until Judge Lasker threatened to grant our motion for sanctions including potentially a default judgment. Bunker and Herbert signed the waivers but immediately went to Swiss court to block Swiss Bank Corporation from providing any information, arguing the waivers were not voluntary and, thus, a violation of Swiss law.

We did not know about the Swiss lawsuit until after it was concluded. But the Swiss court refused to block the disclosures, finding that the threat of a civil money judgment was not sufficient compulsion to make the waivers involuntary. It seemed to me it was a case in which the highly visible mess Bunker had made by crashing the silver markets overwhelmed any other concerns the Swiss might have had about their secrecy laws.

When we finally received the Swiss Bank Corporation documents, our team was shocked into silent disbelief. The cache of documents disclosed a series of joint transactions involving Bunker and Herbert Hunt, Nahas and IMIC. The hard-fought battle over the Swiss secrecy waivers was about to pay dividends as I pressed Bunker about these trades.

The first of those transactions occurred between October 29 and November 1, 1979, when Nahas purchased 3.5 million ounces of forward contracts (similar to futures contracts) from Swiss Bank Corporation for deliveries on the LME in February, April, and May 1980. The contracts were worth almost $56 million. Between November 8 and 11, 1979, half of those positions were transferred to Bunker and Herbert Hunt at their original price. I asked Bunker:

"Did Mr. Nahas transfer half of his Swiss forward account to you and your brother Herbert at about that time?"

"I don't believe so. I bought some forward contracts from Swiss Bank Corporation. I don't know what Nahas did."

"Mr. Hunt, let me show you a telex from Naji Robert Nahas to Mr. Bruderer at Swiss Bank Corp. It says, 'Please transfer 50 percent of all silver futures purchases made on my account as following: 25 percent to the account of Mr. Nelson B. Hunt and 25 percent to the account of

Mr. Herbert Hunt.' Now, Mr. Hunt, is it your testimony you had no idea that Mr. Nahas had done that?"

"No, I, I—that's correct," Bunker stumbled but he seemed to have a prepared story. "I didn't have any idea . . . I bought some forwards and how the paperwork was handled I don't know."

There was the paperwork excuse again. The paperwork, however, which I went over with Bunker in detail, showed that he, Herbert Hunt, and IMIC had opened commodity accounts at Swiss Bank Corporation on October 25, 1979, the same day his lawyer was lulling the COMEX with promises of cooperation. Two weeks later, Nahas's forward positions were transferred into Bunker and Herbert's accounts, but at the same price at which Nahas bought them even though the market price had moved in the interim. Bunker had no explanation for these transactions. It appeared the Hunts was guaranteeing Nahas's silver trading and providing him with $28 million that Nahas would need to take bullion deliveries just a few weeks away in December. The joint nature of the transactions put the lie to Bunker's repeated assertion that his business with his friend Nahas was principally about horses, and, at the same time, showed yet another joint transaction between Bunker and Herbert.

I was surprised by Curran's omission of these trades during the direct examination and even more surprised by Bunker's lack of some facile explanation other than paperwork, which did not seem too convincing. These trades were dramatic evidence of the coordination between Bunker and Nahas. And Bunker could not explain how he and his brother, who supposedly was trading independently, ended up with identical transactions.

"How did it happen that you and your brother Herbert bought silver forward contracts for the exact same amount and exact same prices at the same time in November of 1979?"

"I guess we bought them together," Bunker said, before remembering that was not the practiced line. "I mean, he bought—I bought some and he bought some and it was the same time, time, amount. I don't, I don't know," he concluded in frustration.

I did not want to let this subject pass. "Well," I said, "he wasn't in Zurich in late October, early November 1979 with you, was he?"

"Not to my knowledge, no."

"Well then, how did it happen that he bought the same amount of silver forward contracts at the same price at the same time as you?"

"I don't have a recollection, but I'll speculate that maybe he asked me to buy some for him also."

Bunker also admitted knowing that IMIC had opened an account at Swiss Bank, but he denied knowing Mahmoud Fustok had done the same thing a few days later. When I asked how all these accounts were opened at the same time, Bunker said only, "I suggest you ask Swiss Bank Corporation," again sounding exasperated but providing no innocent explanation.

The day ended with a dinner at the Dolder Grand Hotel. Before the dinner, Bunker, Nahas, and Jim Parker, Hunt Energy's CFO met in Nahas's room to discuss silver. When they went down to the dining room, Waltuch and Bob Guinn from IMIC joined them. Much to Bunker's surprise, he said, Guinn was in Zurich to set up more storage facilities for silver, even though IMIC had given up its December 1979 long positions in the Mocatta EFP. Curran again made a point of the "broad daylight conspiracy" in a hotel dining room with 300 to 400 seats. "I don't have any recollection of any discussion [about silver], Mr. Curran," said Bunker, "but let me say this, I'll speculate that since virtually everybody at the table was involved in silver, I would have said something about it, but I don't recall what I said."

The picture of the two Hunt brothers, IMIC, Nahas, and Fustok opening accounts in Switzerland at the same time and Bunker and Herbert assuming Nahas's positions at their original price could not be explained by a chance meeting in the lobby of a Swiss bank. The $28 million that Bunker and Herbert paid for Nahas's forwards contracts would come to good use in several weeks when the December 1979 COMEX silver futures contracts matured, breaching the so called "foolproof plan" to avoid a silver squeeze. Bunker had not given a series of coordinated transactions an innocent explanation for another damning coincidence. I moved on satisfied.

Chapter Thirty-One

Naji Nahas and Jean-Jacques Bally went from Zurich to Geneva on November 1 to 2, 1979, where they met with E.F. Hutton broker Jim Ferro, who was talking to Minpeco's Ismael Fonseca regularly. Ferro was soliciting an account from Banque Populaire Suisse. He also told Nahas that there "was discussion within the commodity community about the possibility of a squeeze or corner in the silver market." I imagine that was no surprise to Nahas; he probably looked innocent and shrugged. But it would have been a surprise to Minpeco if Ferro had done his duty and warned Fonseca, which he did not.

On November 7, 1979, Fonseca began a trip to London to set up Minpeco's trading account at the LME. When Fonseca flew through Chicago, one of the E.F. Hutton brokers told him that his firm had agreed to send him to London to help Fonseca. When the two stopped in New York, Merrill Lynch saw what was happening and quickly had one of its brokers join the trip. Fonseca had become a celebrity, representing one of the world's largest metals

dealers that had just started to trade futures. He represented the potential of huge bonuses for the brokers. As to
why he took them along, Fonseca said, "As I trusted them,
I thought their advice to me would be very valuable in
London."

His trust was misplaced, it seems. Before leaving New
York, Fonseca had breakfast with Jim Ferro at the St. Regis
Hotel, back from his Geneva meeting with Nahas. Just off
Fifth Avenue, the St. Regis is described with words like
glamour, *elegance*, and *chic*, while Lima at the time had one
rundown Sheraton and a few small business hotels, modest restaurants, and a dreary aspect. I am not sure Fonseca
would have seen anything as elegant as the St. Regis in his
life.

"What discussion took place at the breakfast?" I asked
Fonseca.

"I got a feeling that Ferro's impressions were not optimistic concerning the future of silver prices."

"You had a feeling or did he tell you that? What did he
tell you?"

"I say I have that impression because I don't remember
his exact words, but his words left in me the feeling that
prices could not go up any more."

Ferro was obviously being cagey. By leaving the impression that silver prices could go down, he was encouraging
Fonseca to hedge more of Minpeco's silver commitments,
which would mean more commissions for E.F. Hutton.
Even worse, there was no evidence that he warned Fonseca

about the talk of a squeeze on silver futures that would send prices skyrocketing and Minpeco's margin requirements with them. As a hedge trader, Minpeco was not subject to the super margins, but even the lower margins levels would soon become unbearable. Instead, Ferro offered to introduce Fonseca to big Arab silver buyers in Zurich.

When the Merrill Lynch broker heard about Ferro's invitation to introduce Fonseca to an Arab group in Zurich, "he told me that Merrill Lynch worked with a very powerful family, Messrs. Hunt, who were also buyers of physical silver and very important people in this area of marketing in general. One of them would tell me I have A and the other one would tell me I have B and the competition between them—"

Judge Lasker leaned forward, interrupting: "You mean they were what we call in America name dropping?"

"I think so, yes," Fonseca responded, but with a quizzical look on his face. Then he continued to describe the conversation with Jim Ferro at breakfast. He "told me that taking advantage of this trip to London we could visit— and he gave me the name of something like four Arabs— that I could deal with since I would be in Europe, concerning the sale of physical silver." The only name Fonseca could remember was Nahas. "Jim Ferro thought that in this way Minpeco would have other customers for its physical silver production." Despite our many pretrial conversations, Fonseca had never told me this story, which provided further fuel for the idea that Nahas had focused on locking up

Minpeco's silver supply. And Nahas undoubtedly would pay Ferro handsomely if the introduction accomplished his goal.

Bunker's plan was thus be moving from controlling the silver bullion in exchange warehouses to monopolizing the sources of silver around the world. Peru was the third largest producer of silver in the world and Minpeco was its exclusive sales agent, making it a prime target for monopolists. Ferro seemed to be suggesting that Nahas and his unnamed partners might buy Minpeco's annual silver inventory, taking it off the world market and restricting world supplies. We also found evidence that the Hunts were approaching Mexico, another major silver supplier, with an offer to lock up its annual silver sales. Removing Peru's and Mexico's annual production from the market would have sent silver prices skyrocketing more effectively than futures trading and for a longer period of time.

Ferro explained to Fonseca that he had arranged a helicopter to pick him up, along with Ferro's E.F. Hutton colleague in London, and fly them to Switzerland.

"How did you respond to this invitation from Mr. Ferro?" I asked, feeling uncomfortable that I was moving into an area in which I did not know what Fonseca would say.

"Well, no doubt about it, very human," Fonseca responded. "First I liked the idea, but then on the way to London I thought that I was meddling with the functions of other areas so I turned the invitation down when we arrived in London."

Fonseca's answer did not entirely capture the new world he was being offered. Peru was in the midst of a decade-long recession. The agricultural economy was breaking down under the weight of a land expropriation program by the military government. Large farms had been split up into small lots and given to the peasants. But the resulting small farms were uneconomical. Poor families were giving up their land in the face of a failed socialist experiment and a growing terrorist movement, flocking to a huge shanty-town that was growing on the hills around Lima. Minpeco's offices in a Lima suburb were in a converted mansion that must have been luxurious once, but now was bare. One peculiarity struck me when I first visited several years later. There was no toilet paper. The workers would bring their own and keep it in their desks, which they would quickly offer to their American visitors as we headed toward the public restrooms. Breakfast at a five-star hotel and a heli-copter ride were unthinkable for Fonseca and his cowork-ers in Lima; public toilet paper, now that was a real luxury.

At trial, I asked Fonseca about his trip to London. He, with the E.F. Hutton and Merrill Lynch brokers in tow, vis-ited their London offices and opened accounts for trading on the LME. Both brokers continued to express the opin-ion that silver prices would go down and encouraged Fon-seca to add to Minpeco's short futures position, which he did after tracking down on the phone Minpeco's President, Juan Munar. As Fonseca told it: "With their advice we placed another four or five million ounces hedged in London with maturities from December 1979 on, we also closed some of the operations we had opened. We carried out a full hedging operation as a team that were together morning, afternoon, and evening carrying out this activity."

With those trades, Minpeco's short position reached 13 million ounces. Fonseca was riding high, probably too high. He was opening a new chapter for his company, traveling internationally, and being wined, dined, and entertained as brokers often do with hot new clients. And then it all fell apart very quickly within a few weeks: his new project, his company, and his career. And the brokers did what they often do; they shrugged and walked away, or in the case of Ferro, he vanished at least from the view of his soon-to-be desperate Peruvian client.

Chapter Thirty-Two

While Bunker Hunt was in Zurich, Herbert Hunt began a letter-writing campaign against the Chicago position limits rule. Herbert's November 1, 1979, letter expressed his anger to CFTC Chairman Stone and Vice Chairman Dunn. "I deplore the adoption of retroactive position limits in silver future contracts by the Chicago Board of Trade," Herbert wrote. He continued with the Hunt theme that the exchanges were forcing silver prices down "benefiting the holders of short positions who traditionally are exchange members." He asked for public rule-making hearings and an investigation of the silver positions of the CBOT board. After asserting that he was one of the principle targets of the exchange action, he wrapped himself in the public interest: "You must recognize that the major victims of that action will be the trading public and the major beneficiaries will be the [exchange] members."

Herbert's letter the same day expressed "dismay" to Chicago President Wilmouth based on the two commitments he and Bunker had made to the exchange: "We did not intend to take delivery in fulfillment of February silver contacts unless the spreads widen unreasonably. Rather, we intend to follow our *long-standing and established practice of rolling these positions forward*. In response to the committee's request, we expressed our willingness to make 10 million ounces of silver available to the Board of Trade market." He accused the exchange of benefiting the shorts.

The next day, Norton Waltuch returned from Zurich—on the supersonic Concorde, he insisted on telling us—and called Herbert Hunt. Waltuch's description of the call may have supported Paul Curran's broad daylight conspiracy argument, but also highlighted what Minpeco was not being told: "Well," said Waltuch, "*The New York Times* and *Wall Street Journal* each had an article about squeezing the silver market and my name was mentioned, the Hunts' names were mentioned, and I was kind of upset about it and I called him up and wanted to know if he had read the article." The *Times* and *Journal* were not generally available in Lima in those days and Fonseca did not speak or read English, but neither sets of brokers said anything to Minpeco about these alarming reports.

"What was disturbing about it?" I asked Waltuch.

"Well, I mean the article mentioned my name and mentioned the Hunt name as if we were operating together, which was completely erroneous. Also I was very upset with the margin credits that the COMEX had put in. I guess it was a day or two before and I had just wanted to discuss the situation because these articles were terrible."

Herbert acknowledged he was upset too, but when Waltuch suggested the Hunts file a lawsuit against the exchanges, Herbert deferred. "He said he would look into it." Waltuch added dryly, "He is not a man of many words." On that point, I had to agree with Waltuch; I do not think that Herbert ever said a word to me despite many days together in court.

Nahas, however, wanted to pursue a lawsuit. "How did you go about pursuing it?" I asked Waltuch.

"Well, Nahas had mentioned to me that he had read Louis Nizer's book, I guess it was *My Life in Court*"—which had inspired me as a young lawyer—"and he says why can't you go to his law firm and see if you can get him, he's an influential attorney. See if you can get him to represent you and to bring some action against COMEX, which I did. I never got to see Louis Nizer, but I saw some other attorney there. I believe they sent a letter to COMEX."

Waltuch introduced Nahas to another lawyer, Howard Schneider, former CFTC chief counsel. Nahas never filed the lawsuit, but Schneider made a comment to Nahas and Bunker Hunt in an elevator in New York that would force Paul Curran into a difficult spot later in his direct examination.

While Nahas was talking lawsuits, the Hunts were engaged in another strategy—to put off exchange action with charming but meaningless talk. Both exchanges invited them to meetings. Herbert Hunt met with the CBOT Business Conduct Committee first on November 5, 1979. He reiterated his earlier commitments, and, according to Robert Goldberg, "he said that if he didn't live up specifically to the commitment for February silver that he would not take delivery, we could publicly go ahead and say that he was not telling the truth."

On November 6, 1979, Herbert Hunt and his lawyer met with the COMEX Special Silver Committee. Herbert's described the Hunt efforts to alleviate congestion made no mention of the new December 1979 positions Bunker had recently added, or their financing of Nahas' upcoming delivery demands, which put pressure on the rest of the market participants. Herbert continued that, "he never met or spoke to Mr. Waltuch prior to November 2, 1979," again not mentioning Bunker's meetings with Waltuch. Herbert again claimed his positions during the past five or six years have been larger than his present ones, another misrepresentation. And he repeated promises to roll forward his large positions in March and May 1980 contracts and not take bullion deliveries, which were promises that went unfulfilled. Herbert criticized the super margins but said he would comply with them.

Before he entered the room, Lee Berendt had expressed concern that the deal with the Conti Group was falling apart. He told the committee that the Conti Group "may not be cooperating in a desirable manner." The day before, Nahas bought another 131 December 1979 contracts through Norton Waltuch, but, apparently in an effort to hide them, cleared the trades to his account at E.F Hutton.

If that were not enough reason for COMEX officials to doubt the Conti Group's intentions, they should have been resolved the next day when Advicorp—on behalf of Mahmoud Fustok—moved 800 December 1979 contracts into November and took delivery of another 4 million ounces of silver bullion, paralleling the moves of Nahas and Hunt. The bank shipped the bullion out of COMEX warehouses to Zurich. Despite these signs of bad faith and the increased risk of a squeeze in December, the COMEX took no action.

Fustok's order resulted from a telex to Advicorp sent from his London office at 98 Baker Street, just down the street from the Sherlock Holmes Museum at the famous 221B Baker Street. I often say I learned to litigate from Sir Arthur Conan Doyle, author of the Sherlock Holmes mysteries, which I studied more than my law books. Fustok testified that he simply could not recall sending the telex to Banque Populaire Suisse giving it instructions for the 4 million ounces. But Fustok's passport put him in London on that day, and Fustok testified no one else in his London office had authority to send the telex. So there was no one else who could have placed the order but him.

Four million ounces cost about $60 million, which further undermined Fustok's defense that he had only authorized his advisors to invest $30 to $40 million in silver. Fustok continued with his absentminded performance when he was asked how $102 million was transferred from Swiss Bank Corporation to Banque Populaire Suisse to pay for the silver. He did not know, he testified, and I reacted with incredulity:

"And you didn't notice that the money was gone?"

"How would I notice? I'm not sitting at the door of the bank."

"And you never asked for a bank statement?"

"I did in March after things went wrong; I asked everybody for statements."

"And while the price of silver was going up you didn't?"

"*I was enjoying it.*"

Obviously, he was not paying his bills paycheck to paycheck like many of the jurors. And I am quite sure the great Sherlock would not have bought Fustok's self-portrayal as the distracted millionaire obsessed by his thoroughbred horses, not silver. I hoped the jury felt the same way.

But despite this open breach of the Conti "foolproof plan," the COMEX took no action on position limits and postponed the effective date of the super margin requirement until February 4, 1980. As far as the Special Silver Committee was concerned, there was enough silver bullion to deliver when the December 1979 contract expired, so the market was working fine. Unlike the Chicago exchange, the Silver Committee was not sure whether distorted prices fell within the COMEX's definition of a disorderly market. So they asked their lawyer to draft a legal memorandum: Was it supposed to worry about artificial prices that had already inflicted grievous injury on many other innocent traders? While the lawyers pondered, they sat watching and hoping for the best.

Chapter Thirty-Three

This time it was Herbert Hunt who flew to Washington, DC, where he met with CFTC Vice Chairman Reed Dunn. "The exchanges should be fair to both sides and not loaded on one side," Herbert reportedly complained almost before settling into a chair opposite Dunn. The new emergency regulations—position limits in Chicago and super margins in New York—are not "market-neutral," he continued. The exchange board members held large short positions, which "would benefit those members to the detriment of non-members" like himself. Herbert asked Dunn to hold public hearings before allowing the exchanges to impose new regulations.

Herbert also "claims to have played no part in the rise in silver prices in the last few months. His holdings today are no larger than they were in August," a sleight of hand because he put on his large long straddles in June 1979. And he knew the exchange viewed him as a representative of his brother Bunker, who had taken deliveries in October and added to his December 1979 contracts. His statement was disingenuous even for Herbert's own long contracts that were positioned to take delivery in early 1980, thus creating the congestion that was driving prices upward.

For his part, Dunn responded judiciously, "expressing concerns about the market concentrations, the large positions and the price movements, relating the two, but not drawing any conclusions or pointing any fingers, and perhaps in somewhat a rhetorical style saying this is an issue that is of grave concern to the commission." Herbert repeated the Hunt commitments to reduce their positions and limited their delivery demands.

The Hunt lobbying onslaught had an impact on the CFTC and the exchanges. The CBOT delayed the effective date of its position limit rule from February 1 to April 1, 1980, and the COMEX delayed the imposition of retroactive margin requirements until February 1980. The regulators' discussions were not recorded, but they are not hard to imagine: the billionaire Hunts had large wallets to pay for lawsuits, in which they could argue that they had made promises that should have resolved the regulators' concerns.

Also, the Hunts seemed to have gotten an unintended message from the regulator meetings: they had to relieve the pressure on influential firms, particularly those with representatives on the exchange governing boards. Within weeks, IMIC and Banque Populaire Suisse had negotiated EFPs and swaps with Sharps Pixley, J. Aron and Engelhard, each a major metals dealer with a representative on the COMEX board. In all, they exchanged 10 million ounces of silver bullion and future positions in New York and Chicago for 10 million ounces of London and Zurich silver bullion, which was a pathway to resupply the US warehouses when bullion supplies became low. Minpeco, an outsider in the hinterlands, was not on the Hunt list of bailees.

Herbert Hunt laid down another challenge to the regulators. On November 15, 1979, he purchased an additional 150 March 1980 long contracts. The Conti Group was not reducing its silver futures in December 1979 silver. Both the Hunts and Conti Group appeared to be ignoring their promises, but the exchanges did not react. For all the Hunt talk about the shorts controlling the exchange boards, they never mention shorts on the COMEX board who helped them garner more control over deliverable silver bullion.

The Hunts' successful strategy of intimidation and appeasement left their plan intact: they and the Conti Group could take delivery of bullion in December 1979. Silver bullion in exchange warehouses had grown from 111 million ounces in July 1979 to 127 million ounces by mid-November. But the two groups already owned almost half of that bullion and their combined positions far outstripped supplies; growing from 321 million to 365 million ounces in six weeks, then worth in excess of $6.5 billion, three times the visible bullion supplies. The two groups were primed to monopolize the silver bullion that backed futures contracts.

The US regulators—guardians of supply and demand prices—were adrift, like a small dingy bobbing in the ocean as the Titanic sped toward an iceberg: they did not wave, honk a horn, or set off a flare. They watched, hoped, but took no action to protect the markets as the December 1979 contract expired.

Part Six

Debacle in December 1979

Chapter Thirty-Four

Lima was a long way from all the regulatory maneuvering in New York and Washington. But Minpeco was about to feel the volcanic effects from the out-of-control silver markets. Silver prices opened on November 27, 1979, at $16.28, after weakening for two months from $18.10. Prices jumped $1.69 the next two days. Minpeco began getting crushing margin calls, $13 million for each dollar silver prices rose. In two days, it was required to come up with more than $22 million in daily margin payments, an unfathomable amount to Minpeco. And silver prices kept marching upward, sowing panic throughout Minpeco's management.

Ismael Fonseca had no idea what was happening; he had no access to the financial press in New York, and despite Paul Curran's talk about a "broad daylight conspiracy," Minpeco's brokers were giving him no explanation for the sudden upward surge. The private battle between the Hunts and Conti Group and US regulators was invisible to most traders, and E.F Hutton's Jim Ferro and his counterpart at Merrill Lynch were not inclined to tell Fonseca a squeeze might be in progress, even when the New York financial press reported publicly on Bunker Hunt's large appetite for silver.

Minpeco executives were experienced metals traders, but none had seen silver prices move so violently. By November 30, 1979, Minpeco created a hedge commission to figure out what to do about the profound financial drain. Fonseca was a member. "Now, the effort within the company was huge to comply with these requirements day by day," Fonseca explained, then added defensively: "By the way, I want to make it very clear that Minpeco met every one of its margin obligations." By December 3, 1979, silver prices were up $3.60 in a week to $19.88 and kept climbing. On December 4 or 5, 1979, Fonseca was relieved of his duties as hedge manager.

On December 11, 1979, the Minpeco Board of Directors was told that Minpeco had paid almost $50 million in variation margins—money that went directly to the billionaires in Dallas, Riyadh, and Sao Paulo. Silver prices were still rising. In response to my question, Fonseca described the tense scene:

"I'll sum this up in three ideas: extreme nervousness, total ignorance, resulting in a tremendous unease when it came to taking up a position, because we really did not understand what was happening."

"What do you mean by total ignorance?"

"We did not know the reasons that prices had shot up in this way starting on November 27, 1979."

As we approached the events that brought the downfall of his career, Fonseca became agitated, his answers became longer, and Judge Lasker began interrupting him to keep him on topic. Concerning the interactions at the December 11 board meeting, I asked him what the general manager had said about the situation. Fonseca went into a long, rambling explanation, which Judge Lasker tolerated: "I remember that in his report there was this figure of speech of spreading responsibility without assigning it specifically, without making any mention of what was really happening in the United States where prices were shooting up, something never before seen in any other metal or any other product that's quoted on an exchange. Very little was said about this, about the true reason for Minpeco's problem, which was not our responsibility, whoever 'we' might have been."

Finally, Judge Lasker interrupted: "You have answered the question."

Fonseca nodded, lowered his head, and stopped talking.

The board decided to invite the brokers to come immediately to Lima to consult. Only the Merrill Lynch brokers came for a packed board meeting on December 14, 1979. E.F. Hutton's Jim Ferro failed to come, abandoning Minpeco to its fate.

Fonseca continued describing the meeting: "I remember that first we spoke about the situation the company was facing. The guests [from Merrill Lynch] were asked to give their opinion as to what was happening, to give the background of what was taking place ... Well, they apparently—well, not apparently, I am totally convinced that their job at that point in time—"

Judge Lasker interrupted again: "Excuse me. We just want to know what they said, not what your conviction was."

"I see," Fonseca stopped with a grimace and restarted, still excited. "They talked about what was happening on the silver market at that moment ... They considered that this had been something surprising. They mentioned several factors that might have influenced prices, the hostages in Iran. In general they were trying to relay the political economic situation with the rise at that moment."

The hostage crisis had started on November 4, 1979, but silver prices had not significantly moved at that time. In late November and early December 1979, the *Associated Press* and *Wall Street Journal* (which were not available in Lima in those days) had reported extraordinary demand from the Hunts and Conti Group, but the Merrill Lynch brokers made no mention of the "broad daylight conspiracy" to the Minpeco board. They were no longer name-dropping their big clients, the Hunts. The board members were left groping for an explanation and how to react to it.

As the meeting continued, Fonseca, up at a chalkboard, laid out a proposal for moving Minpeco's positions to London where he had been told during his November trip that margins were not required, but a letter of credit would suffice. The brokers sat quietly, but after Fonseca left the room they rejected that option; Merrill Lynch would insist upon cash margin payments in the midst of this crisis, they said. From Fonseca's perspective, the meeting was inconclusive. He did not know his fate had been sealed the day before in a conversation between Minpeco and its chief banker, which left Minpeco no choice but to close its positions.

When the margin demands started, Minpeco turned for funds to its line of credit at Banco de la Nacion, Peru's largest state bank. By mid-December 1979, Minpeco had blown through its $80 million line of credit, which was supposed to fund its entire operations. The line reached $120 million when the bank started to run out of money, a graphic reminder of Peru's poverty. On December 13, 1979, the bank called a halt to additional advances, insisting that Minpeco close its short futures positions. Silver prices had reached $20.52. Minpeco was hoping to ride out the steep price upturn and recover its money as prices returned to normal levels. In retrospect, it would have taken another $396 million (a total of approximately $451 million) to ride the market to the top of $51 per ounce, funds Minpeco, Banco de la Nacion, and Peru did not have.

Minpeco officials hoped for a magic solution from the brokers at the December 14 board meeting. When the brokers had nothing to offer—close the positions if you think prices will rise but leave them open if you think they will drop—Minpeco had to close its short positions, which took days to accomplish. Minpeco suffered a $120 million

loss; $40 million was later attributed to losses on the min-
ers' hedge positions, which the miners had to assume. That
left Minpeco with a still-whopping $80 million loss.

Fonseca was fired a few days later. His career was over.
The stress on the company's top executives and board must
have been intense. In Peru, like in many countries, public
employees have personal liability for their decisions, including potential criminal liability. In December 1979, the
Minpeco board members and executives all faced political
disgrace, financial ruin, and even possible jail time; they
needed someone to blame.

The December 14 board minutes, like those of December
11, blistered Fonseca, blaming him for speculating in silver
futures, exactly as the defense was arguing. An internal
Minpeco report and a later ministry report laid blame on
him and Juan Munar, Minpeco's president. Munar spent
three years in pretrial detention and Fonseca fled into hiding. They were never convicted of wrongdoing; the courts
eventually rejected the ministry's conclusions. The indignity was nonetheless hard to imagine. In the run-up to trial,
I asked Fonseca what he was doing, but he was vague,
which I took to mean not much. His life was shattered.

And now, eight years later, Fonseca was sitting waiting
to be cross-examined. And he must have been thinking
that he could be blamed once again if the trial went badly.

Chapter Thirty-Five

"A broad daylight conspiracy," Paul Curran had repeatedly called it, and he was not far from wrong for those with access to the New York press in pre-Internet days. What was happening as the December 1979 silver futures contract matured was no secret to those in New York paying attention, including Minpeco's brokers. On November 26, Norton Waltuch went on the COMEX trading floor and, in his usual flourish, bought 500 more December 1979 contracts for Banque Populaire Suisse, an open and provocative breach of Conti's "foolproof plan" to avoid a squeeze. Bunker bought another 250 December 1979 contracts. This coordinated effort to create a frenzy was reflected in an *Associated Press* article on November 28, 1979: "The price of silver continued to soar Wednesday, propelled by renewed investor interest and fear of a near-term shortage of supplies on major world markets." The *Associated Press* left no doubt who might be behind the shortage: "The markets became more nervous on widespread talk that Texas oil heir Nelson Bunker Hunt, a top silver speculator, and

Norton Waltuch, a New York broker affiliated with Conti-Commodity Services Inc. who is believed to be representing prosperous overseas interests, have been buying even more silver in recent days."

As Bunker and the Conti Group followed these trades with massive silver bullion demands, the *Wall Street Journal* reported concerns about inadequate silver bullion supplies in exchange warehouses and the possibility of a squeeze of short traders. A silver bullion shortage is the key element of a squeeze of shorts. Silver prices reacted to the turmoil by jumping $3.60 in a week and spiking from $16.28 to $32.20 by the end of December, more than five times the price at the beginning of 1979.

Once more, our years of painstaking analysis of credit card records and hotel receipts paid off when we put Bunker Hunt and Naji Nahas together on November 29 to 30, 1979, this time at the Regency Hotel in New York just as the December 1979 contract was maturing. Our chart of telephone calls showed a microcosm of the conspiracy. Bunker called Waltuch's home at 5:34 p.m. on November 29. The next morning, two lengthy calls were made from Nahas's room to a telephone number Fustok testified was that of the nephew of Saudi Crown Prince Abdullah, and calls were made to Advicorp, Hunt Energy, and Waltuch's home again.

And what all the talk was about seemed apparent: a coordinated demand for more bullion deliveries. Despite Herbert

Hunt's representation to the exchanges and CFTC that he and his brother had *"no present intention to take delivery,"* Bunker took delivery of silver bullion on 985 of his 1,200 long December 1979 silver futures contracts he had purchased only six weeks earlier, and the Conti Group—Banque Populaire Suisse, Nahas, Fustok, and Norton Waltuch—took deliveries on a total of 3,589 contracts, far exceeding the 2,000 contract limit of the Conti "foolproof plan" to COMEX.

In total, the two groups took delivery of 22,490,000 ounces of bullion in COMEX exchange warehouses, alone about one-third of the total. Even as additional silver bullion flowed in, COMEX warehouses had only 69.4 million ounces of silver bullion, of which the Hunts and Conti Group already owned a substantial percentage. Combined, the two groups held long March 1980 silver contracts for 91 million ounces, almost three times the available supply. Bunker's position in the COMEX's March 1980 contract alone represented commitments for 63 million ounces. The Hunt domination over the Chicago warehouses was similarly overwhelming with their massive February 1980 contracts still outstanding.

And those figures did not include the silver bullion the two groups removed from the United States in swaps and bullion shipments that would normally have served to resupply the US warehouses. On December 7, 1979, Mahmoud Fustok instructed Banque Populaire Suisse to make arrangements to accept 315 tons, 10,080,000 ounces of silver bullion, which he flew from New York to Geneva, another graphic threat to the markets. Nahas told him, Fustok testified, that he and Bunker Hunt were moving their bullion out of the United States for fear the US Government would seize it.

When confronted with the amount of bullion he owned, Fustok continued to maintain that he was innocent because he was oblivious; he never realized his silver was in futures contracts converted to bullion. When confronted with the storage agreements he had signed, he claimed again that he had no idea how much he owned.

"Is it your testimony that you never knew you owned $500 million worth of silver?" I asked skeptically.

"I did not," Fustok shot back.

Fustok also supposedly did not know that from within the Banque Populaire Suisse account, he bought silver from his brother-in-law, Crown Prince Abdullah.

When their worst fears were realized, the CFTC commissioners and the COMEX board did not seem to be reading the newspapers. The regulators did nothing. I doubt any member of the exchange governing boards thought that silver prices in excess of $20 per ounce was a true reflection of supply and demand. When they took no action, Minpeco lost $80 million and thousands of traders lost much more. But the COMEX board members were safe from the carnage thanks to the EFPs and swaps with the Hunts and Banque Populaire Suisse.

On December 12 when the COMEX Special Silver Committee delivered an interim report to the COMEX board, it made no mention of the surging prices or the Hunt and Conti Group's misrepresentations and broken promises. The problems were in the future; according to the committee, "There is a likelihood of congestion continuing to plague the market during 1980." That means no one had yet defaulted on short contracts. However, the extraordinary nature of the deliveries is reflected in the report's list of deliveries: an average of 5,000 per year in the three prior years and 44,958 in 1979. Even though price manipulation is illegal, the COMEX still did not seem to think it was responsible for obviously distorted prices caused by these deliveries.

However, the many false statements by the Hunts and Conti Group were reflected in the committee's conclusion: "To date no evidence has been discovered which would prove or suggest that the [Hunt Group] and [Conti Group] were or are acting in concert."

Although the committee's report listed board member silver positions, it still did not reflect Mocatta's 800 March 1980 silver contracts guaranteed by IMIC, even though Henry Jarecki was sitting in the meeting.

In response to the report, the COMEX board barely blinked. It thanked the staff for its assistance, filed the report, and let the debacle continue without any response.

Toward the end of the month, the CBOT increased silver margins while confirming position limits would be imposed by April 1, 1980, well after its warehouses would be empty of silver bullion if the Hunts took delivery in February.

We did not necessarily disagree with Bunker's complaint that self-interest at the exchanges was affecting their decision making. We just did not agree that the regulators' decisions were an excuse for Bunker's brash and illegal price manipulation. Minpeco had also sued the COMEX and CBOT for not maintaining an orderly market, but Judge Lasker had dismissed those claims before trial because regulators have qualified immunity. That means we had a high burden to prove that "self-interest or other ulterior motive unrelated to proper regulatory concerns was the 'sole or dominant' reason for Comex's actions and inactions." After detailing in his opinion the many conflicts on the COMEX board, Judge Lasker concluded: "In sum, while it is undisputed that a number of the COMEX governors were associated with businesses which either held net long silver positions, had net long customer accounts, or did business with the Hunt defendants, there is insufficient evidence of record that any of these business affiliations actually influenced the actions of any COMEX governor . . . Bad faith cannot be inferred from these theoretical conflicts," the judge continued. "Moreover, there is no evidence of record that any alleged conflict of interest, even if proven to exist, tainted the actions of the Board as a whole." The regulators got a pass.

When silver prices surged to $32.20, nightly variation margin calls transferred billions to the Hunts and Conti Group from thousands of losing traders. This small group held a silver stash that grew in value to $13 billion, more than the gross domestic product (GDP) of Peru.

Chapter Thirty-Six

Paul Curran had to confront the dramatic events of December 1979. In response to Curran's questions, Bunker was vague about his meeting with Naji Nahas at the Regency Hotel. He kept to his thoroughbred horse theme: "I had plans to come to New York in connection with various business things, as well as silver and my horses." He and Nahas talked beforehand and agreed to stay at the same Park Avenue hotel, the Regency, and they had dinner together with Maurice Zilber, their horse trainer. Bunker's story remained the same on the topic of silver: "I have no recollection of any specific discussion, but I would say that I would have discussed it, yes. I would have asked him what he thought, what was going on as far as he thought about the market and so forth." He might have had breakfast with Nahas, again at another public dining room. Curran did not ask Bunker about his December silver bullion deliveries or his breach of faith with the two exchanges.

Curran turned to a strange topic, I thought. Nahas had a lawyer with him, Howard Schneider, who was introduced to him by Norton Waltuch when Nahas was considering a lawsuit against the exchanges. Earlier, I had slipped into Norton Waltuch's direct examination a warning that Schneider had reportedly given to Nahas and Hunt at the time of this breakfast:

"Did Mr. Nahas tell you that Mr. Schneider, after working on this matter for a month, told Nahas and Mr. Hunt that it was inadvisable for them to be seen in public together?"

To which Waltuch had simply responded: "No."

My question was objectionable as it called for hearsay—what Nahas, a party not in court, had said—but it had gotten by without objection and Waltuch's response had not given it any credence, in my view. But Paul Curran apparently felt he had to address it, or perhaps that Bunker's response would advance his defense.

"Do you recall," Curran asked, "any conversation that you had with Mr. Schneider or that he had with you before breakfast or at breakfast?"

Bunker puffed up and ignited with emotion: "Yes, Mr. Schneider and Mr. Nahas and I were in the elevator and Mr. Schneider says: 'I don't think you and Nahas should be seen together, it doesn't look right.' And I said, 'My God, what is this, are you talking about Nazi Germany or something? This is a free country. Why would I have any concern about being seen with Nahas or anybody else?' And I remember the guy from that thing, because it was such an outlandish statement, that it sort of insulted me."

Bunker's emotional outburst could not wipe away the sting of Schneider's observation, as far as I was concerned. He confirmed that a prominent New York lawyer had seen a conspiracy in progress. If anything, Bunker's show of emotion made the exchange more memorable.

Curran skipped quickly back to Bunker's alternative reality, horses. Bunker went to Aqueduct Racetrack. When asked for the horse names, he could recall only Goldclad— "Not a very good horse," we learned. Curran took the time to pull out the program of November 29, 1979, to refresh Bunker's memory that his filly Honorary ran in the eighth race at the Meadowlands. Curran then moved on without relating the meetings to any of the explosive events in the silver market. It was all just about thoroughbred horses.

When he returned to the subject of silver, Curran had Bunker recount the price surge in December 1979 without mentioning the many silver bullion deliveries he took, along with the Conti Group. Bunker had to explain his own demand for bullion. He could not blame it on the IMIC Sheikhs' religion. Once again out of chronological order, Curran asked Bunker to explain.

"Why did you take delivery in December 1979?"

"Well, there were very strong rumors circulating, and it wasn't rumors it was actually being articles in the paper would allude to the possibility of the exchanges closing and not making deliveries as guaranteed. That was one of the reasons. And tax reasons was a very big factor, because if I rolled forward from a very profitable December contract and rolled it forward, I created a tax event or a great deal of tax that had to be paid at the rate of 70 percent, whereas if I took delivery and waited until after the first of the year, then thereby I would have no tax due in 1979."

"Did you understand that it was somehow illicit or improper to take delivery on a silver futures contract?"

"Not at all. That's what a futures market is, that's why they call them futures market, because they provide for the ability for you to take delivery, and I'm told there is not a successful futures contract in the world that doesn't provide for the right to take delivery. That just goes with the market."

Curran later went back to the subject so Bunker could blame the exchanges for his deliveries. He asked Bunker about exchange action, and Bunker obliged by referring to the margin increases. "There was proposition that you had to pay so much margin that you virtually might as well take silver and not worry about paying the margin and things in general. There were strong rumors that the market might close and you might not be able to get silver for what contracts you had."

And even later in the testimony, he gave yet another explanation. As silver prices rose, he was receiving huge margin payments from the losers in the markets. The deliveries, which had to be paid in full, were another way to plough gains back into the same investment.

Bunker also acknowledged that he bought 750,000 ounces of bullion in Switzerland and one hundred contracts

(1 million ounces) in London because: "They were both sizeable, large silver markets and so I was just curious about how they functioned and wanted to see what the market was like." According to Bunker there was nothing illegal or improper about buying silver in Europe, and his purchases had nothing to do with the new exchange regulations.

Chapter Thirty-Seven

With my turn, I continued to associate Bunker's silver trading with his encounters with Naji Nahas. Bunker denied discussing the December 1979 deliveries with Nahas at their November 1979 stay in New York: "Not, not on my part. Somebody else might have been discussing something with someone, but I have no recollection of discussing it."

"But you and Mr. Nahas did discuss the silver market on that occasion, isn't that right?"

"Oh, we were friends, we would talk about I knew he was a long, he knew I was a long. He knew we were both involved in the same side of the market, so, sure, I talked to him about it, but I would talk to anybody about it."

"Didn't you and he talk about the fact that you were both having trouble with the exchanges at that point in time?"

"Well, the newspapers were full of problems with the exchanges and increasing the margins, rumors of rule changes and so forth . . . The whole world was. All, all of the longs. There were thousands of longs having trouble with the exchanges."

The judge did not like his evasion, interjecting: "The question is whether you and Mr. Nahas talked about it."

Bunker finally admitted: "I don't have a recollection of it, but I'll speculate that we talked about it."

I reminded the jury that the COMEX had not wanted Nahas to take delivery on his December 1979 silver contracts, but Bunker denied knowing about that commitment. "I never talked to him about that," he said.

"Is it just a *coincidence* that you and members of the Conti group took delivery in December of 1979?" I shot back, knowing I would get an objection.

This time both Paul Perito and Paul Curran shouted at the same time: "Objection, your Honor!"

I did not wait for the judge to sustain their objection; I asked my next question. The jury had just heard that Bunker and Nahas were at the same hotel, with large positions in the same December 1979 futures contract, taking delivery of bullion at the same time, and watching prices take off to their great pleasure—but they did not talk about it except in a general way, according to Bunker. The jury might think otherwise.

I moved on to the Hunts' misrepresentation to the COMEX Special Silver Committee that they had *no present intention of taking delivery* in December.

"Is that a representation that you authorized one of your representatives to make to the Special Silver Committee?" I asked.

"No, I didn't," he responded emphatically.

"Would [your lawyer] or your brother make representations to the COMEX without you authorizing them to
do it?"

"Well, he might have, he might have made, made it on
behalf of Herbert Hunt."

"Do you believe that either Mr. Herbert Hunt or your
lawyer made a representation that you had *'no present
intention of taking delivery* on silver futures contracts'
without being authorized to do that? Is that the kind of
thing that they would do?"

Bunker must have thought his answer did not sound too
credible; he shifted his ground in a way that largely confirmed the representation and walked himself into dangerous territory: "Well, I don't know. You know, you might
make a representation or a statement at one time and a
month or two later the economic conditions may have
changed greatly, the actions of the market may change
greatly and that changes what you can do as based on what
you said you might be able to do . . . What your intentions
are today doesn't necessarily control what you will do 45
or 60 days from now."

"You don't contest that the representation was made on
your behalf, you just don't recall it occurring right now, is
that your testimony?"

"I don't recall, but I think what I said, though, any representation that was made has to be relevant to what happens

in the future and what happens to the market. What your intentions are today doesn't necessarily control what you will do 45 or 60 days from now."

"So as far as you are concerned, a representation made on October 25 that you had no present intention of taking delivery was simply irrelevant at the end of November, is that true?"

"No, I said—I didn't say that. I said conditions could change, and you got vast economic investments here and you don't set in stone that you are going to do something forever."

But Bunker did not wait for conditions to change; he was building his December 1979 long contracts as his brother was making the commitment to the Special Silver Committee. And his brother added 150 contracts to his March 1980 positions about a week later. The source of Bunker's December 1979 bullion deliveries were 985 new contracts he had purchased in October 1979 after his meeting with Nahas in Paris.

I had earlier attacked Bunker's so-called good intentions to relieve congestion in the December 1979 silver contract with the Mocatta EFP. Now, I attacked his tax excuse for those deliveries. Bunker and I had a tense exchange:

"So, what you had in mind when you bought those December contracts was to take delivery on them?"

"Well, not necessarily. I don't recall that that specifically was in my mind. It could have been."

"At the time you put on those December contracts you knew that you could not get long-term capital gains except by taking delivery; isn't that true?"

"Well, that would have followed, that you have to hold more than six months to get long-term capital gains."

He would have to take a short-term gain if he closed his positions without taking delivery and pay a considerably higher tax rate on his gains, which was contrary to his investment philosophy and Jim Parker's tax advice, Bunker was forced to admit: "Yes. I preferred naturally—I preferred long-term capital gain at the much lower rate."

Thus, Bunker's purchase of 985 long contracts added in October 1979 was contrary to his explanation that the Mocatta EFP helped relieve congestion, was contrary to his commitment to the COMEX that he had "no present intention of taking delivery," and was contrary to his tax excuse for the deliveries.

Bunker's tax excuse for putting on 28,000 straddles in June 1979 also fell apart at year-end. "That was considered good tax planning," Bunker proclaimed. In those days, straddles were often used to reduce income taxes without significant risk. As prices moved, one leg would become more valuable, while the other would lose money. By closing the losing leg at year-end, the taxpayer could report the loss to reduce net income.

Bunker testified that Jim Parker, Hunt Energy's chief financial officer and "a top-notch" taxman, had advised him to buy straddles because silver prices had risen so much in the first six months of 1979.

When I asked Bunker about the straddles, he came up with another new story: "I was advised by our tax people, Mr. Parker, and recommended to me by Les Ming that it might be a good idea to place some straddles at that time."

Les Ming was a name that was new at trial. Ming was a broker and a very good friend from Oklahoma City, Bunker testified. The reason for this new story quickly became apparent. Ming had passed away. Ming joined Naji Nahas and the IMIC Sheikhs as another empty chair in the courtroom; we could not cross-examine Ming about his tax expertise or his purported conversation with Bunker about tax straddles. I pulled out Bunker's deposition in which he made no mention of Ming:

"When you talk about your tax people, who are your referring to by your tax people?"

"Well, Jim Parker and Shank Irwin [his Dallas law firm]?"

Why, I asked, had he made no mention of Ming?

"Well, my memory is not perfect," was Bunker's explanation. The reason for introducing Ming's name became apparent with the next exchange. Parker denied advising the Hunts to purchase tax straddles. I read Parker's testimony:

"Q. Now, did you ever recommend straddles to Bunker or Herbert or Lamar Hunt?"

"A. I don't recall that I ever did."

When I asked whether he was wrong about Parker's advice, Bunker adjusted his testimony. Ming gave straddle advice and he did not need straddle advice anyway, he already knew about straddles. Parker "recommended that I do something trying to get long-term capital gains instead of short-term capital gains and one way to do it was by rolling out beyond six months. Another way was to use tax straddles." Bunker was now caught in a maze among his direct testimony, his deposition testimony, and his trading records. It was complex stuff that I could have left alone at that point. But I tried to spell out the distinctions for the jury because I had additional points to impeach Bunker's explanation.

"There are really two pieces of tax advice that you referred to, aren't there? First of all there is simply moving a position out beyond six months, which would give you a long-term capital gain versus a short-term capital gain; is that correct?"

"That's correct."

"And the other piece of advice is to put on a tax straddle; is that correct?"

"That's right."

The first impeaching testimony came from Bunker's deposition. I went back to the theme of a newly created story; in his deposition, Bunker had no explanation for the short positions, "I just don't have any recollection of them," he testified.

At trial, I pressed: "So at the time of your deposition two years ago you couldn't recall whether these were tax straddles or not, isn't that true, Mr. Hunt?"

"Well, Mr. Cymrot, if you remember, after 14 days of trying to answer your questions, it's lucky I could recall my own name."

The judge interjected: "You seem to have recovered." My head swiveled toward the judge; I had not expected his tone. It seems I had scored a point.

"Well, not all the way, your Honor," Bunker shot back. "I don't believe I'll ever be the same." That was probably an honest emotion given the way his life had changed in the eight years since he crashed the silver markets.

After additional fencing, I went to the next point: Bunker did not take Jim Parker's advice to use the short positions to reduce his income taxes. With rapidly rising silver prices in December 1979, his short positions were losing money while his long positions were making tons. By closing his short positions before year-end, he would have incurred losses that could have offset other income and thereby reduced his income tax bill. When I directed Bunker to the income section on his 1979 tax return, Bunker had no explanation for his failure to close his short positions and take losses to offset his income; he said the return was too complicated for him to offer an explanation.

But we had an explanation; if silver traders had seen Bunker closing short positions in December 1979, it would have dampened the huge price surge or even precipitated a crash. In order to take advantage of the straddle tax strategy, Bunker should have closed the losing position before year-end to offset other profits. In December 1979, the short positions were clearly the losers because they lose value as market prices shot upward from around $8.50 in June to past $30 per ounce. But neither Bunker nor Herbert closed their losing short legs. If they had it would have dampened the surging prices, which is exactly what they did not want. They were up to something else—an effort to manipulate silver prices was our explanation.

At times, all this technical talk about longs and shorts, tax straddles, and spreads masked the very personal impact that the Hunt's activities had on some lives. As silver prices unexpectedly shot higher, those on the short side of the market lost many millions. And some lost their jobs; others went bankrupt. The panic among Minpeco executives was palpable from Ismael Fonseca's testimony. But we still had to prove hoarding exchange silver bullion caused silver prices to spike.

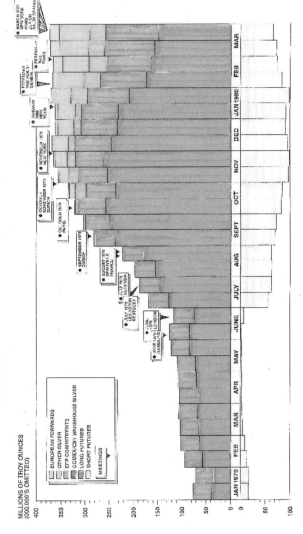

Mountain of Silver: Conspirators' Meetings and Silver Accumulation

Steve Groo, FTI Consulting

Chapter Thirty-Eight

Our 10 x 20-foot historic silver price chart hanging on the north wall of the courtroom showed an unprecedented spike in December 1979, coinciding with the Hunts and Conti Group accumulation of silver futures and bullion. That convinced me that silver prices had been manipulated. But the law demands more.

Establishing that "more" was the job of our economics expert, Hendrik S. Houthakker. The intellectual debate between Houthakker and defense economist, Stephen A. Ross, was one of the mini-dramas in the trial. Houthakker, distinguished and near retirement, was a former chairman of the President's Council of Economic Advisors for both Presidents Lyndon Johnson and Richard Nixon. He was head of the Economics Department at Harvard University and held a string of awards and honors. He was credited with unifying several economic theories on consumer demand and was considered an expert on pricing in the commodities and energy futures markets.

Stephen Ross was up and coming. A PhD from Harvard and an economics professor at Yale, he already had several pricing theories named after him on arbitrage and options pricing and interest rate movements—all arguably relevant to understanding the surge in silver prices in 1979 to 1980. Houthakker was gray-haired, bespectacled, thin, and slightly slouched. Ross was young, good looking, and energetic on the stand. The past and the future were in battle on a very public stage.

After covering his impressive credentials and the mass of information he had reviewed, Houthakker expressed his opinion that silver prices on the COMEX, CBOT, and London Metals Exchange (LME) had been manipulated from August 1, 1979, through April 1, 1980. Futures and forwards prices did not reflect the underlying fundamentals of supply and demand, he said, a key element of manipulation. And he opined that the competitive prices for silver should have been between $8 and $10 per ounce.

For more than a day of direct examination, he described the many factors supporting his opinion, which included the unprecedented price, silver prices compared to gold prices, supply and demand statistics, econometric analyses, and many others. He divided his opinion into three sections: price distortions, the specific activities of defendants that were of a manipulative nature, and defendants' effect on price. About Bunker's main defense—political and economic events—Houthakker was unforgiving. ". . . [I]t turns out that the impact of these political and economic events on the price of silver were quite small . . . between one and two dollars."

We kept the seventy-year-old Houthakker sharp during another long day of cross-examination by putting chocolate milk, instead of water, in a thermos he took to the witness stand. The defense lawyer pressed him on almost every front, but the changes in his reasoning since his pretrial deposition seemed to hit home. Houthakker had not been sufficiently prepared for his deposition, the product of his well-earned hubris. *Who is not going to believe me*, I imagine he was thinking before the defense lawyers bore into him. Fear of appearing foolish has always motivated me, and it appeared to have motivated him as well; he did considerably more work before trial.

On the stand Houthakker doggedly defended his opinion, but one quip displayed his frustration at some of the points the Hunt examiner was making. Houthakker was using a laser pointer to illustrate his points on our large price chart on the wall. In response to a particularly difficult question, Houthakker let out an exasperated breath, pointed the laser at the lawyer, and cracked, "If you ask me another question like that one, young man, I'll zap you with this laser." The lawyer hesitated and blinked, the jury and gallery roared with laughter, and Paul Curran sat stone-faced, staring straight ahead. Houthakker was not laughing, either.

Although Houthakker focused on the silver futures and forwards markets, Stephen Ross saw the market as consisting of 6 billion ounces of silver worldwide that had been mined since the beginning of eternity. Ross went over many of the same factors as Houthakker had but reached exactly the opposite conclusion—that silver prices were not manipulated in 1979 to 1980 but were affected by world political and economic events. Ross attacked Houthakker with econometric models.

We worried that it was all dry fare for the jury, but we learned later that several jurors had extrapolated the economic arguments into additional explanations for the silver price movements. After listening for six months, they had developed quite a sophisticated understanding of the silver markets. During jury selection, Judge Lasker had subtly ensured we had a jury that could understand the case by releasing jurors who did not seem up to the task. It was difficult to argue with Houthakker's impressive credentials, simple logic, and authoritative style. Ross might have had an easier task if he had acknowledged that the defendants' accumulation of silver had some effect on prices but was not the only influence. That argument might have lowered the damage award, but admitting that the Hunts and Conti Group trading had any impact on silver prices would have been too much of a concession to our conspiracy theory.

At the final argument, one of the Hunt lawyers attacked Houthakker by arguing that: "he made it up," meaning his analysis did not fit Ross's econometric numbers. I responded with rage: "Can you believe that a man who gave advice to three Presidents, is the head of the economics department at Harvard University, is at the pinnacle of his career, would come here—for what reason would he come here and make it up? You know that it demonstrates, when they don't have an answer and need to fill in a hole in their argument, they say Dr. Houthakker made it up. I just think that's wrong!" He did not make it up, I declared; his analysis was impeccable.

Ross also was undermined by the cross-examination of the young, but highly credentialed, economist whom he had relied upon to build his econometric models. For most of a day, my colleague, Tom Gorman, engaged in a highly technical cross-examination, filled with hotly contested interactions about regressions, correlations, and statistical associations. Gorman, who had the jargon and the theories down pat, used his droll, sarcastic style to undermine the economist. How much of their debate the jury understood was questionable. Once Gorman had the economist fully committed, he pulled out the guy's unpublished doctoral thesis, a discovery that was an unexpected research coup in pre-Internet times. Gorman quoted the key passage discussing the December 1979 price rise:

"Thus, a *manipulation* of the market tests the wisdom of nearly every rule of the exchange. The recent machinations in the silver market . . . show that *manipulations* can still place great strain on many of the rules."

Each repetition of "manipulation" Gorman read slowly with emphasis and then asked, "Isn't that your thesis that you wrote for your doctorate?"

The first sound was the economist's wife letting out an involuntary screech from the packed visitors rows, reflecting the common surprise. In the hushed courtroom, the sound reverberated off the walls. No one reacted, acting like nothing had just happened. The economist blanched, paused, and asked for a moment to read the complete passage. The time provided him no relief. He stammered, ". . . the margin rules worked to aggravate some of the price moves I believe . . . I never published this, Mr. Gorman." That answer walked directly into Gorman's next point. He had the economist confirm he had written his thesis in June 1980 shortly after the silver market crash, but in 1986, when he had published a book derived from his thesis, he omitted the damning passage. Then Gorman drove home the point:

"And that passage was deleted from your book which came out after you went to work for the Hunt defendants; is that right?"

"Objection," howled the Hunt lawyer. He must have been as surprised as the witness's wife and now had recovered his voice.

"Sustained," barked Judge Lasker.

I could not see anything wrong with the question; it seemed only to violate the judge's politeness principle: Nobody gets ravaged in his courtroom. But the question made the point. "No further questions," Gorman announced, and sat down. I exhaled. I had known what was coming but not how it would work out.

The Hunt lawyer made an effort at redirect but could not take the sting out of the dramatic exchange. The woeful witness rose, rushing, eyes down, shoulders fallen past me. As I turned to watch his exit, his wife rose, shuffled hurriedly past several spectators, stumbling on feet until she reached the aisle. I caught a glimpse of her stricken face as she turned and pursued her husband out of the courtroom.

When I think of that exchange, I often put myself in the economist's place. I imagine the conversation between husband and wife the night before, anticipating the glory from being invited onto the big stage, and the silent dinner the night after his thumping. It could have been me if the case had turned out differently. The economist survived, continuing to teach at his stellar university, though perhaps he could not exorcise the demons of that day. Seven years later he published a book supporting the economic arguments the Hunts had presented to the jury.

And Tom Gorman wrote the forward.

Chapter Thirty-Nine

The dramatic events at Minpeco in December 1979 were about to be replayed through Ismael Fonseca's cross-examination. After I had completed Fonseca's direct examination, the judge announced a mid-morning break. When we returned, one of Paul Curran's colleagues rose first. Peter Fleming was back observing with his long arms and legs dangling out of a too-small chair. He was prepared to question Fonseca next with his well-earned, lofty reputation for scorching cross-examination. He looked on impassively.

The Hunt lawyer focused on Minpeco's trading strategy that had gone so wrong in December 1979. Was Minpeco hedging or, in reality, speculating—as the defendants defined those terms—questions designed to advance the Hunt theme that Minpeco had only itself to blame for its losses. It was not a point that I particularly feared; both hedgers and speculators are entitled to an honest, unmanipulated market; Fonseca had made a convincing case that Minpeco had been following the advice of two

internationally respected brokerage firms; and he was
convinced that he was hedging—no one was going to shake
him from that belief. When the lawyer got bogged down in
a long, complex hypothetical about Minpeco's operations,
Judge Lasker lost patience.

"Can I ask you a question?" he said. "Thank you for a complete discussion of why Minpeco conducts its affairs as it
does. We, in this trial, are facing a slightly different question. That question is what the economic consequences of
Minpeco's acts have been. Are we correct in now understanding that in the back-to-back contracts if Minpeco
hedges and prices go up Minpeco takes the loss?"

"Yes," said Fonseca, turning toward the judge.

"And if prices go down, in such circumstances, Minpeco
reaps the profit?"

"Yes."

With these questions, the judge encapsulated the issue,
shrugged and called a lunch break. The Hunts would argue
that Minpeco was speculating, misleading its brokers to
get the lower hedge margins, and responsible for its own
losses. We would argue Minpeco was involved in typical
middleman hedging. A hedger does not want to be at risk
for price movements, so it establishes a balanced position
between physical silver or silver commitments and short
futures positions. But a middleman, like Minpeco, must pay
nightly margin on its short futures contracts while its physical position does not produce immediate cash as prices
move. Usually those payments are usually manageable, but as

Mocatta, Engelhardt and Minpeco learned, in a volatile market they can become overwhelming. That does not turn those companies into speculators when they keep a balance position.

We took Fonseca to have lunch with us, sandwiches brought into a conference room. We stayed clear of any subject that the judge might consider preparation for his cross-examination. He ate quietly, looking nervous, and then headed back to the courtroom. We were all anticipating a difficult afternoon.

The Hunt lawyer restarted by quoting Minpeco's board minutes from December 11 and 14, 1979 that pummeled Fonseca for violating the board's dictates on hedging by placing short futures positions that were not backed by physical silver, which was speculating by the Hunt definition. Fonseca repeatedly denied the minutes were accurate until he unleashed a rather charitable speech given what he had been through: "Mr. Munar and Mr. Alvarez Calderon and all of us that were taking part in this meeting were extremely nervous. *Plows fell upon us we knew not whence.* We didn't know the market was being upset by something we had never thought of." Fonseca explained he first learned about the Hunt manipulation allegations from a *Newsweek* article in April 1980, and continued, "So, things were said and unsaid in a state of total nervous tension because in Peru we were answerable not only to the company but also politically. Image is very important for people that play in that area. If we had known exactly the facts affecting our operations, many things that I later could explain to myself as human attitudes of self-defense would not have been registered in this document, which I rejected."

I was surprised. I had not heard Fonseca express that benevolent emotion before; in our pretrial meetings he had sounded bitter and angry. The Hunt lawyer did not flinch; he continued quoting from the minutes for an extended period until the judge lost patience again, suggesting he move on. "Thank you, your Honor," the lawyer responded but did not mean it.

He continued on a related topic: "You believe the Board was wrong to close the positions it closed as of the last two weeks in December of 1979, don't you?"

"Yes, I believe so, and that's why I voted against it," Fonseca responded and continued. "According to my calculations, Minpeco would not have lost anything, it would have obtained a profit."

That testimony might have concerned me, but we had a ready answer. It would have cost Minpeco more than $451 million in daily margin payments to keep its positions open, money even Peru's largest national bank did not have. But before the jury would hear that testimony from another Minpeco executive, Fonseca would have to survive the remainder of the afternoon with Peter Fleming's cross-examination.

Chapter Forty

Peter Fleming took his time unwinding from a small wood-framed chair, projecting calm and confidence. I watched him tensely, well aware of his reputation. He had many notches on his belt. One of his most memorable was defense of John Mitchell, Richard Nixon's Attorney General during the Watergate scandal. Fleming had destroyed the credibility of former White House counsel John Dean, the key prosecution witness. While interrogating Dean, Fleming was asked by the judge how much longer he planned to continue. "Till he cracks," Fleming reportedly snapped. When Mitchell, along with Nixon's commerce secretary, Maurice H. Stans, was acquitted of obstruction of justice and perjury, Fleming strode down the courthouse steps to a barrage of reporters and reportedly bragged, "We pitched a no hitter!" *The New York Times* concluded, "He did not mind the limelight." I doubted I could do so well, either the cross-examination or the walk down the courthouse steps.

As Fleming organized himself, I thought back to our first confrontation, which came when Fleming challenged one of Judge Lasker's more important pretrial rulings. In a lengthy opinion, Judge Lasker had barred the defense from making the argument that Minpeco's losses should be off-set by gains the Peruvian government had made in its state mines and elsewhere when silver prices soared. Minpeco, a corporation owned by the Peruvian government, was enti-tled to recover its own losses, the judge had ruled, even if other parts of the Peruvian government had benefited from the price rise.

Both sides had undertaken jury research before trial. The defense's pretrial jury research must have shown that their "single entity" argument would resonate with jurors. In his opening statement, Paul Curran had skirted the issue while criticizing Minpeco's trading decisions, but Fleming turned explicitly to it in his opening. He began calculating Peru's purported profits for the jury: "Let's assume," Flem-ing continued, "[Minpeco] only had three million ounces instead of the 13 million ounces . . . So that a silver pro-ducer in Peru, who has authorized Minpeco to sell its sil-ver, as a part of this transaction, is holding silver and the price of that silver is going up . . ."

I saw where he was going. Objections during opening statements are disfavored, but before Fleming could com-plete the calculation for the jury, I shot up and objected: "Excuse me, your Honor," I said in voice loud enough to interrupt Fleming, "I'm sorry to interrupt. I believe you have ruled in this area and Mr. Fleming is stepping over into this area that you have ruled on."

Fleming stopped, turned toward me, looking surprised.

Judge Lasker nodded and agreed: "I'll have a special instruction for the jury."

Fleming flinched and reacted: "I'm aware of it."

"I'm sure you are aware of it," the judge scoffed. "It may require some clarification." My insolence had paid off; the jury must have seen the judge unhappy with Fleming's argument.

"That's fine," Fleming responded, quickly turning back to the jury and moving on to complete his other arguments.

After the judge dismissed the jury for the day, we marched straight to the judge's robing room where the judge, even before sitting down, started after Fleming: "I am not quite sure, Mr. Fleming, what your point was when you referred to the fact that people of Peru might be making money on silver while Minpeco was losing it, but whatever it was I think it muddied—"

Fleming interrupted: "I would like to make my point." The judge and Fleming went into a lengthy, increasingly heated exchange. The judge was sitting at his small, metal desk with Fleming towering over him, leaning forward with his hands on the metal desk arguing that either Minpeco was grossly negligent or intentionally withholding its silver from the market. And the judge kept reminding him that he could not offset Minpeco's losses with gains made by others in Peru, including the government.

Finally exasperated, the judge said, "Let me be blunt about it." I held my breath; I thought he was going to unload on one of New York's most prominent lawyers. "I came away with the very distinct impression that it was *confusing*, and I'm not out to state anything which I think is adverse to your position, in fact, I haven't thought about the state of mind proposition before . . . but I want the jury to know what the rule is."

The judge had blinked, at least, a little. I did not think it was confusing at all; it was a direct attack on the judge's ruling. But I held my tongue; I did not want an angry judge turning his attention away from Fleming. Paul Curran saw the same dynamic; he jumped in to change the subject and save Fleming from further debate with the judge. The battle lines were drawn.

As the court session opened the next morning, Judge Lasker turned to the jurors just as they sat down and gave them an additional instruction in response to Fleming's argument. "The question of damages is way down the road . . . But I want you to understand what the rules are . . ." he began, "if you ultimately decide Minpeco is entitled to damages then you must consider only whether Minpeco has suffered any damages after offsetting its own benefits, if any, as the result of the rise on the market price. It is irrelevant and you must not consider whether the government of Peru or the people of Peru or any other person or corporation suffered any losses or experienced any gains as a result of those alleged activities." That made our point rather directly. Coming from the judge, jurors will usually follow the instruction. But I was not sure whether I had diffused the issue or only helped to emphasize it.

Now, months later, Fleming walked to the well of the courtroom as Fonseca sat waiting for him. I wondered whether he would repeat his challenge to the judge. He began questioning Fonseca with the technique for witness control for which he was so well known: short questions that required yes or no answers. That is easy to describe but it requires a strong personality to pull off.

"Mr. Fonseca, my name is Fleming. I am one of the attorneys representing Mr. Fustok. I would like to ask a series of questions. I would like to ask you to respond yes or no unless you cannot respond yes or no. You are from Peru?"

"Yes."

"Peru's major export is silver, physical silver?"

"No, it's one of the most important products, but it's not the major one."

"With regard to the silver in Peru, am I correct that Peru, the nation, owns the silver?"

But sometimes the give and take of sparing with a hostile witness can take unexpected turns even for the best cross-examiners. When Fleming asked this question, Fonseca seemed to freeze; there was a silent pause. Fleming turned to the bench. "That can be answered yes or no, your Honor."

Perplexed, the judge said, "I don't know."

The interpreter chimed in, "Translate?"

"Yes, go ahead," Judge Lasker said, as everyone looked at Fonseca, who seemed puzzled. Finally he began to explain: "The Peruvian state owns the mines. That is in the ground and in mines—" Then Fleming jumped in to interrupt, first turning toward the judge—"Your Honor, I'm sorry—" but changing his mind and turning back to the interpreter: "Please, Mr. Interpreter, will you tell Mr. Fonseca that I will get to all of that. Would you explain to him that I am simply trying to ask questions so that I can fully understand his testimony and I appreciate him coming here from Peru."

"Yes, sir," Fonseca interposed.

"And explain to him," Fleming continued, "if he believes that he is being tricked in some way, please tell me." While the question was laboriously translated, Fleming turned and took several long strides toward the jury box, scanning the jurors for theatrical effect. And then came Fonseca's delayed but all too honest answer, in a barely audible voice:

"Well, since I'm under oath, I must say that I do think that part of what you are going to do is to *trick* me!"

I was watching Fleming closely; he stopped, his eyes burst wide open, looking shocked, and he broke into a genuine belly laugh. The courtroom erupted in laughter. Fonseca sat blankly. Fleming turned back toward Fonseca and retorted in triumph: "Now we understand each other!"

The exchange worked for Fleming. As Fleming began to bore into him, Fonseca responded with a series of one-word answers. It quickly became obvious that Fleming was pursuing the theme that had gotten him into trouble with Judge Lasker during opening statements, the "single entity" theory, trying to offset Minpeco's losses with Peruvian government gains. Fleming and I were heading for another confrontation. That was now clear.

But I had to pick my spot. Some of Fleming' questions were justified by Fonseca's answers to my questions. If I jumped up too soon, the judge might deny my objection, which would leave Fleming free rein to make his point. I had to let him expose his point, which was a direct challenge to Judge Lasker's earlier ruling.

"Am I correct that Peru, the nation, owns the physical silver in the ground?"

"Yes."

"Am I correct that the producers in Peru are licensed to take that physical silver ore out of the ground?"

"Yes." . . .

"Yes. So I won't trick you," Fleming chuckled, "I am talking about the period up through 1979. Correct?"

"Yes."

Fleming continued with a series of questions confirming the Peruvian government owns the silver in the ground and licenses it to producers, and Minpeco was Peru's exclusive seller of the silver with the obligation to realize hard currency, usually US dollars, for the silver. The dollars were paid to Peru's central bank in exchange for local currency, Soles, which were transferred to the silver miners. The dollars were counted on by the Peruvian government to fulfill its budget every year. So far, the exchange was only an explanation of Minpeco's operations, but then Fleming moved deeper into the threatening area.

"And it is a part of Minpeco's obligation to satisfy and realize the hard currency revenues which the government of Peru has budgeted for the year in question?"

"Insofar as it can do so."

Fleming had set up his point but seemed to understand that I was getting ready to object; he did not want to risk that the judge would sustain an objection. He skipped away for some time, directing Fonseca's focus to the hedging process and Minpeco's efforts to lock in the current high prices for future sales of silver bullion. He moved back to the issue of Peruvian government involvement, and began attacking the Peruvian government involvement from another angle, asking whether Minpeco's hedging policy came from the government. Fonseca agreed that the general policy came from the Ministry of Energy and Mines. Once again, Fleming mixed the discussion of hedging with his point on government profits:

"And by hedging those 13 million ounces at $18 an ounce, you locked in $234 million hard currency to be paid to the central bank upon the sale of that 13 million ounces?"

"Yes."

"And you did that to eliminate price risk for those 13 million ounces?"

"Yes."

"And that was price risk for the nation of Peru?" Fleming must have realized he had gone too far; as I started to rise, he quickly stopped, "I will withdraw it," he said before I could object. He and I knew we were in a pitched battle that was being fought largely in our heads at that moment.

Fleming swayed away and then back toward his main point. He asked whether silver prices three times higher than the prices ordinarily realized on the sale of Peruvian silver would realize foreign currency revenues into Peru's national bank far in excess of any expectation at the beginning of 1979. It seemed to me Fleming was about to put directly to Fonseca a question tying the Peruvian government's profits from the sale of physical silver to Minpeco's losses. I was about to object when Fonseca threw him a curve. "It seems to me that you may have the wrong idea about what it means to turn over a foreign currency to the Banco Central Reserva," Fonseca said. "It's not a payment, it's just an exchange." He was referring to the exchange of dollars for Soles of equal market value.

"And the hard currency, the dollars, are kept for the government of Peru?"

"For the state of Peru." Fonseca responded.

At this point, Fleming's direction was clear enough. I objected: "Your Honor, may we approach?"

"I am puzzled," said Judge Lasker shaking his head, "but you may approach."

Since it had been months since Fleming had challenged his ruling, the judge did not seem to realize where Fleming was going. I was ready for another donnybrook to begin. The lawyers huddled around Judge Lasker out of earshot of the jurors. I pointed out that the judge had already ruled that the Peruvian government's gains were not relevant. Fleming said he was making another point. When I argued he should not tie Peru's gains to Minpeco's loss, the judge agreed.

When we stepped back from the brief exchange Fleming asked: "Just one last question in this area. The $18 per ounce, which you locked in for the physical silver you have described, was three times the ordinary price that Peru had realized for silver?"

The judge was now onto Fleming's point: "That has been asked and answered."

"So in the last situation it was hedging for the nation?" Fleming decided to challenge the judge.

"Objection," I shouted.

"I will sustain an objection," Judge Lasker said, and continued his reproach of Fleming: "It isn't important whether it is for the nation or not."

"Your Honor," Fleming said, "I—"

The judge shot back, now displaying a flash of anger: "I ruled on that as a matter of law in this case."

"I think I am within your Honor's ruling," Fleming responded defensively, "but it's time for a recess." Fleming did not want the fight in front of the jury because the judge had already made one unhelpful remark and was likely to make more.

Judge Lasker quickly agreed: "Let's take a recess."

We all rose and watched the jurors file out, and then marched into the judge's robing room adjacent to the courtroom. Fleming started in almost before we were all gathered: "Judge, I think I'm entitled to ask to that question. . . ." A heated exchange ensued first with the judge and then I interjected: "We had a sidebar where I specifically asked that that question not be asked and that my understanding is you instructed Mr. Fleming not to ask that very kind of question."

Judge Lasker tried to calm the situation: "The way to handle this out in the open is I'm going to tell the jury it doesn't make a difference what the effect on the country was. It was the effect on Minpeco. . . ." Fleming objected, arguing he was entitled to his theory that Minpeco's losses as agent for Peruvian miners should be excluded, which was a diversion since those losses had already been removed from Minpeco's damage calculation. Fleming changed directions again, interjecting: "We are entitled to understand whether he is speculating or hedging."

"He said he's hedging," the judge retorted.

And I jumped in: "It's another issue."

"It's not another issue!" Fleming snapped.

"You've asked that question and you've gotten an answer," the judge rejoined. We were all talking over each other at this point. Fleming continued, "If they were not hedging for something, then they were speculating."

Fleming was challenging a judge who knew the answer: ". . . [T]he definition of hedging under COMEX as I understand doesn't simply mean are you taking a risk or not taking a risk. It means are you in the business of dealing in silver or not."

Fleming's colleague jumped in. "It's only if they got an authorization—from the CFTC and they didn't. There's no evidence to support that proposition."

Judge Lasker tried to call a halt to the bickering: "It isn't such a clear-cut question as sheer speculating or sheer hedging. I will allow you to ask that last question."

Now I was alarmed: "Which question?"

"Mr. Fleming, I'll allow you to ask the question of whether what was done was as a result of policy set at a higher level." Then he cut off debate, saying, "Let's take five minutes longer for everybody to cool off."

When the jury filed back into the courtroom, nobody had cooled off—at least I had not. Fleming took one last stab at making his point.

"And did that authority of Minpeco to hedge a producer's silver without a request from the producer, did that authority come from levels higher than Minpeco?"

"No, it seems to me not."

"From where did that authority come?"

"From the highest body of Minpeco, the Board of Directors."

Fleming decided to make his point whether the judge liked it or not.

"So, you were locking in a price for the production of Peru?" Fleming asked.

"Yes."

"And by doing that you were acting in the interests of the State of Peru?"

I woke up and stood. "Objection," I announced, in what I hoped was a calm voice so as not to bring too much attention to the point for the jury.

To which the judge responded, "This is a matter of argument."

"All right," Fleming said; it seemed he had enough of arguing with the judge.

"Assuming it's relevant," the judge said, getting in the final word.

With that, Fleming moved on. When he stopped, he offered Fonseca an olive branch. "I mean it, Mr. Fonseca, when I say I'm very grateful that you came up here to answer these questions."

After I asked a few clarifying question, the judge turned to Fonseca. "Very good. Mr. Fonseca, we all thank you very much and wish you a fine trip home."

"Thank you," Fonseca responded.

"You see, nobody tricked you," Judge Lasker said, smiling, as Fonseca rose to leave. He looked and nodded, but seemed too uncertain to smile back. I imagine after all he had been through, he was wondering whether he would be blamed again if the trial turned out badly for Minpeco. Despite the roadblocks put up by the judge's rulings, Fleming's persistence probably put Peru's gains as an issue before the jury. What the impact would be I could not guess.

I thought Fonseca had come across as an honest, intelligent guy, philosophical about the ugly turn in his life, ruined by forces he could not see or foresee. He had not displayed the obnoxious, angry behavior that we had seen in our interactions with him earlier. I watched him walk quickly out of the courtroom. I never saw him again.

Minpeco was now out of the market and out of the story. The trial turned to other topics. We still had to tell the story of the open warfare that had broken out in January 1980 between the regulators and the Hunts.

Part Seven

The Unrelenting Ascent
Continues

Chapter Forty-One

After the 1980 New Year's festivities subsided, Robert Wilmouth, Chicago Board of Trade (CBOT) President, began walking the trading floor, anxiously looking for Hunt orders to roll forward their enormous February 1980 silver futures positions, as Herbert Hunt had personally promised. The year-end had passed; tax strategy was no longer a viable Hunt excuse. Silver prices had doubled again during December 1979 from $16.28 to $32.20 and jumped more than $7 on January 2, 1980, to $39.95, driven by Hunt and Conti Group demands for more bullion deliveries. Neither the Hunts nor the Conti Group had kept their commitments to the COMEX and CFTC: the ContiCommodity "foolproof plan" to avert a squeeze had been a worthless promise, and Bunker Hunt had taken large bullion deliveries in December 1979, which made the brothers' puffing about the benefits of the Mocatta EFP and representation that they had "no present intention to take delivery" more empty words. Although disaster, as defined by the regulators, had been averted—no shorts had defaulted—silver prices were up more than 650% in one year, undeniably at artificial levels. Yet, the regulators seemed hypnotized; they sat and watched the December debacle without taking any action.

Now the CBOT faced its biggest challenge. The trap that the Hunts had laid in June 1979 was about to snap shut. After the unknown traders—IMIC and the Conti Group—had absorbed a large percentage of the certificated bullion supplies, Bunker and Herbert were poised to take control over the remainder. The Hunt long futures in the February 1980 contract represented more than 27 million ounces, and the Hunt and Conti Group positions in COMEX March 1980 silver contract represented another 96 million ounces, far exceeding the remaining silver bullion in exchange warehouses and beyond. The Hunts and Conti Group also owned a substantial portion of the secondary sources of bullion in London and Zurich. Bunker and his cohorts were about to monopolize world bullion supplies.

On the trading floor, Wilmouth found no Hunt sell orders. After two days of pacing, Wilmouth picked up the phone to call Herbert Hunt. Just back from vacation, Herbert tried to defer a substantive conversation. Wilmouth pressed, reminding him of his promise to liquidate his February 1980 positions after January 1. Herbert corrected him, saying he promised not to take delivery, which Wilmouth conceded was correct. Wilmouth told Herbert "that he would like to see him start moving his positions today

[Friday] or Monday—an indication that he was starting to move his position would be helpful at the meeting on Tuesday," a meeting in Washington at the CFTC among the silver regulators. Herbert was noncommittal. They agreed to talk on Monday.

While lulling Robert Wilmouth, Herbert took bullion deliveries of 1,250,000 ounces of bullion on Thursday and Friday, January 3 to 4, 1980. Herbert later claimed he was stuck in "an illiquid market"; there supposedly were no orders in the pit and he "caught deliveries." A trader's usual reaction to unwanted deliveries is to redeliver the silver back into the market. Herbert kept the silver and bought more.

The skyrocketing prices were no longer just a trader's game, according to a *Wall Street Journal* headline: "Silver-Price Surge Taking Toll on Consumers, Manufacturers." The article detailed the carnage: "GAF Corp. has stopped taking new orders for silver-using x-ray and graphic-art film until the company can figure out how to set prices for those products. Shillito's Department Store, a division of Federated Department Stores, has seen a decided drop its bridal registrations for sterling silverware as suggested gifts. Star Dental, a division of Syntex Corp., says the average price of silver alloys commonly used in dental filling has increased about five times since early last year." And Eastman Kodak announced that it would raise x-ray prices by 48% as a result of spiraling silver prices. Analysts were still skeptical of Kodak's prospects. Bache estimated that each $4 increase in silver prices cost Kodak 1% in earnings.

The regulatory battle was about to enter a new intense stage. Quiet jawboning had failed miserably; the regulators were finally moved to action. On Monday, January 7, 1980, the COMEX joined the CBOT by imposing position limits of 500 silver contracts a month and a total position of 2,000 contracts per trader. The Hunts and Conti Group had thousands of contracts beyond the 2,000 contract position limits. If position limits and increased margins forced them to sell their long positions, the price bubble could burst, driving prices quickly downward. Bunker and Naji Nahas scrambled to organize a multifaceted counteroffensive. The unspoken, seesaw battle continued.

Bunker, Herbert, Nahas, and others in the Conti Group immediately reacted by buying new January 1980 contracts and demanding delivery on another 7,515,000 ounces of certificated warehouse silver. The COMEX board struggled to keep up. On January 9, 1980, it amended its position limit rule to fifty spot contracts—cutting off the January purchases—and the next day it increased margins to $75,000 per spot contract.

But Bunker and his allies were still staying ahead of the regulators. To evade the new position limit rule, Nahas opened new bogus accounts at ContiCommodity, ACLI International, and E.F. Hutton in the name of shell companies where he could park some of his positions. The Hunts joined that strategy with a new account at Merrill Lynch for a company called Eighth Crescent Investment, and IMIC opened new accounts at other brokers. The war of wills continued.

The COMEX quickly caught on and countered again by aggregating the accounts of the Conti Group, Banque Populaire Suisse, Nahas (Litardex, Gilion), Waltuch, and others, for position limit purposes. All the Hunt family accounts, including the Hunt children and IMIC, were given the same treatment. That meant the each group was required to have no more than 500 contracts in each contract month and a total position of no more than 2,000 contracts. Even with the January deliveries, they were still many thousands above those limits. It was like two heavy-weight prizefighters throwing punches, absorbing blows, grunting, not talking.

Except in the press. In a *Wall Street Journal* interview, Bunker threw another haymaker at the regulators. If the new regulations block him from the US futures exchanges, Bunker said: "He would look elsewhere for his bullion . . . and he suspects that other cash-rich traders, such as Arabs, will do the same." CFTC's Reed Dunn, who had asked Bunker about Arabs in the silver markets, must have read that quote and wondered.

As the Hunts and Conti Group continued to accumu-late bullion, silver prices marched relentlessly upward beyond $44 per ounce in mid-January 1980, a price that nobody had anticipated even at the beginning of Decem-ber 1979—up from $6 just twelve months earlier. Bunker was absorbing everything the regulators could throw at him while continuing to press his strategy and collecting millions in margin money each evening. Using his father's scoring system—money is just for keeping score—Bunker was winning big.

Norton Waltuch gave an insight into the intense pressure felt by one major short as the silver price surge persisted. COMEX board member Ray Nessim of Engelhard Minerals, one of the nation's largest silver refiners, came into Waltuch's office appearing "white—under severe pressure," according to Waltuch, and unloaded his anguish: "I have been informed by my management that we can no longer keep our short position in futures. I have to do something to relieve the pressure." Engelhard's banks would not extend it any more credit for its daily silver margin calls, Nessim explained, a precursor to default and bankruptcy.

According to Waltuch, Engelhard was making "untold millions" buying scrap silver and refining it into bullion. Although they had a hedged short futures position, "the only thing they didn't figure on was that if the market went up, they had to come up with a lot of margin on their futures and they couldn't convert the silver bullion into cash." In other words, one of the world's most sophisticated silver dealers had fallen into the same trap as Mocatta in September 1979 and the unsophisticated Ismael Fonseca at Minpeco in December 1979. Another major metals dealer was being driven to the precipice of bankruptcy by the unusual price surge.

But unlike Minpeco, and like other metals dealers with representatives on the COMEX board—Mocatta, Sharps Pixley, and J. Aron—Engelhard knew the key long players to approach. "He said that he was under pressure from his management to do something about it," Waltuch continued, "and if he couldn't do anything with Conti's client then he would make sure that the COMEX board would do something. There was an implied threat there."

To which Judge Lasker immediately leaned forward and reacted: "Sounds like a *direct* threat."

Waltuch turned to the judge and agreed: "I guess you're right. I wanted to be nice to him."

Waltuch called Nahas and Jean-Jacque Bally who came to his office to huddle with Ray Nessim. After an hour, they came out with a deal to do an EFP—exchange their futures contracts for Engelhard's silver. To Waltuch, it appeared that Nessim "was making a very, very good deal for himself. He was going to lock in a $10 profit by giving them the scrap at what the market price was and not reflecting the discounts you could buy scrap at that time."

But the deal did not close. Nahas and Bally figured out they were being taken. Waltuch continued the story: "They were rather naïve about that kind of transaction and I think when they made some inquiries round with other people in the market they realized they had been taken advantage of."

Our lifeless travel receipts and telephone records suggested Nahas's consultations were not random. The same day the COMEX adjusted its position limit rule, January 9,

1980, Bunker Hunt and Nahas made a reservation for the plush Regency Hotel in New York for January 14 to 15, 1980, booked by ContiCommodity. It appeared to be another strategy huddle to counteract the regulators. After the meeting with Nessim, Nahas and Bally probably walked back to the Regency Hotel to consult with Bunker, who must have explained that they had negotiated a bad deal. Nahas and Bally withdrew and the Hunts stepped into the void.

Engelhard's troubles and Nessim's threat fueled the Hunt storyline about manipulative shorts on the COMEX board, but what came next showed the COMEX insiders at work. Bunker saw an opportunity. Instead of liquidating futures positions as seemingly required by the new position limits rules, the Hunts wanted Engelhard's silver bullion and Engelhard wanted the Hunt long futures contracts to offset and close its short contracts. They quickly negotiated the deal that, just two months later, would rock the financial markets and cause Paul Volcker to intervene.

The Hunts agreed to pay $1 billion for 10.8 million ounces of bullion, and swapped 2,172 futures contracts. The deal allowed Engelhard to exit the futures market and put an end to the threatening daily margin calls, and the Hunts reduced their long futures positions that were beyond the position limit rule, but they also took control over an additional silver bullion, which tightened their grip on bullion supplies. The Hunts paid $400 million down with the remaining $600 million due in sixty or ninety days, which led to one of the Hunts' biggest problems when silver prices crashed.

Thousands of short silver futures traders were collectively losing millions of dollars that were being transferred to the Hunts and Conti Group accounts nightly as margin payments. However, the shorts on the COMEX board had a way out. Like the Mocatta EFP in September 1979 and Sharps Pixley and J. Aron in November and December 1979, Hunts EFP with Engelhard neutralized another major short with a member on the COMEX board, the very people the Hunts were accusing of manipulating silver prices downward. Ray Nessim no longer had a conflict of interest; his firm was out of the silver markets in a way that advanced the Hunt aim to take control over all certificated silver bullion.

But that is not how Bunker explained it in response to Paul Curran's questions. When Curran wanted to know why Bunker had not started reducing his futures positions after January 1, as his brother had promised the exchanges, Bunker leaned forward and huffed that the new regulations "made it almost an inactive market as far as the volume of trading."

"When you told those people in October of 1979, sort of trying to forecast ahead two or three or four months, did you intend to do what you said?" Curran asked.

"Yes, we did," insisted Bunker. "It was subject to them maintaining the viable market and not changing the rules and making it impossible."

Bunker argued that he could not roll his silver futures positions forward as was his practice for many years; his only options were to offset them (buy short positions that would close his long positions), take bullion deliveries, or conduct EFPs.

"I think you said that as a result of the rules changes you among other things took deliveries of some physical silver?" Curran asked.

"Yes, sir."

"You could do that, right, under the rule?"

"Yes, that's right," came Bunker's clipped response.

"I think you said you did additional EFP's; is that right?"

"Yes, I did some exchange for physicals."

"That was all right under the rules?"

"Yes. I think we inquired of the commissions and actually I guess we got a letter saying that that was fine," responded Bunker, more contemplative now.

"Did those actions allow you to keep your investment in silver to some extent?"

"Yes."

And Bunker was right; his actions were legal—that is, until he was intentionally increasing prices, like by taking extraordinary bullion deliveries and coordinating his trading with the Conti Group.

So when the topic turned to his coordination with the Conti Group, Bunker reverted to another rambling, witty story. Since we had put Bunker and Naji Nahas together again in New York on January 14 to 15, 1980, Curran had to ask Bunker about that meeting. From stiff and polite, Bunker sat up taller and became animated: "Well, as I recall, Mr. Curran, the silver market had gotten a tremendous amount of publicity in all the press and the media at that time and I received a call from Barbara Walters, the television commentator, the lady, the woman that does interviews on television. I had met her once before, and so she wanted to get me to come on her program."

Bunker did not want to do it. But Barbara Walters had not become a television icon without persuasion skills. Bunker continued, "She called a mutual friend and he urged me to, and she got my wife on the telephone—she is a very persuasive woman—convinced her that it was a good idea, so I came up at that time to be on her program."

Curran urged him to continue: "Was that then shown on television?"

"I believe it was. I never did see it," Bunker said thoughtfully. "But that was the first time I had been interviewed like that, and I was sitting on a couch next to Barbara Walters and the program was getting ready to go on. Barbara Walters pulled out a powder puff and she put a little powder on her face, and then she handed the powder puff to me, and I was stunned. I never had anybody offer a powder puff to me; that's why I remember it so well. And I said, 'Good Lord, Barbara, as ugly as I am; that powder puff won't do me any good.'"

I was too focused and tense to notice whether the line got the laugh it deserved.

Bunker repeated for Walters his speech about silver as a long-term investment. When Walters asked whether ordinary people should buy silver futures, he said no, it was too risky. "And I heard later, it sort of surprised me, but some of the brokers at the COMEX sort of held that against me, said I was bad for business because I was telling people that they shouldn't buy futures contracts."

After the interview, Barbara Walters invited Bunker to Tavern on the Green, a famed restaurant that once housed the sheep that grazed on Central Park's Sheep Meadow. The restaurant "invites patrons into a warm, celebratory gathering space that captures the spirit of Central Park and the energy of New York City," it says of itself. "We had a nice lunch, and as I recall I pretty much left town and went back home," Bunker drawled nonchalantly.

But when Curran got to the heart of the issue, Bunker could not remember much:

"Do you recall where you stayed on that visit to New York for the Barbara Walters interview?"

Bunker paused, as though trying to recollect: "I think maybe I stayed at the Regency again, but I'm not entirely sure about that, sir."

"Did you meet with Mr. Nahas on that visit to New York?"

"I don't, I don't recall whether he was there. He could have been there, but I was just there it seemed like one day."

Curran was content to move on. Barbara Walters must have found Bunker's speech convincing. She ignored his warning and invested in ten silver futures contracts (50,000 ounces) in January 1980, presumably long positions. Based on what silver prices did next, it may have been a very expensive interview for her.

Chapter Forty-Two

When I got up, I wanted to draw a different picture for the jury. Bunker Hunt had implied he had come to New York in mid-January 1980 solely for the Barbara Walters interview. However, the ContiCommodity reservation for Bunker and Naji Nahas at the Regency Hotel for January 14 to 15, 1980, suggested otherwise. I pulled out another hotel receipt, walked it over to Bunker, and asked:

"According to the Regency Hotel, that indicates that on January 9 of 1980, ContiCommodity made a reservation for you at the Regency Hotel, and it says at top, 'See Naji Nahas.' Does that refresh your recollection that Mr. Nahas made arrangements at the Regency Hotel on this occasion?"

"Well, apparently he did. I didn't recall that, but apparently he did."

And the hotel's phone records were even more telling: twenty telephone calls from Nahas's room from January 13 to 16, 1980, went to Hunt Energy, Waltuch's home, Crown Prince Abdullah, Advicorp, Jean-Jacque Bally, and Bunker's Lexington farm, suggesting intense discussion and planning. After Bunker flew to Lexington, his phone records recorded a call back to the Regency Hotel. We had earlier played Bunker's pretrial deposition, during which I had asked him whether he had called Nahas from his farm and his attorney had interrupted:

"Hunt attorney: Regency Hotel has about 400 hotel rooms."

"Mr. Cymrot: I see."

"Hunt attorney: Plus a restaurant."

"Q: Did you call the restaurant for 13 minutes?" I shot at Bunker.

"A: I don't recall," Bunker responded, seemingly puzzled by the exchange.

This time, when I asked Bunker if he had called Nahas from his farm, he conceded, "I could have." Hotel receipts and telephone records are not nearly as amusing as the Barbara Walters story, but they were telling our story in crystal clear terms. They gave me the opportunity to tell the jury our alternative explanation for Bunker's trip New York trip, asking:

"Did you and Mr. Nahas decide to get together as a result of the COMEX rule changes?"

From not recalling the meeting, Bunker's memory recovered: "No. I came to New York to be on Barbara Walters' program and I think in talking with [Nahas] on the telephone I told him I was going to be here, so he said, 'Why don't you come stay up at the hotel, I'll make a reservation,' so I did."

That alone did not explain why they had gotten together. Bunker, however, continued to insist he and Nahas were not plotting: "We are good friends," he responded, "if I heard he was in town, I would get together now all that has gone over."

But again it was the colorless trading records that rebutted Bunker's story. The new position limit regulations created a problem, according to Norton Waltuch; silver bullion was flooding into the warehouses. Waltuch provided a colorful picture: "Silver was coming out of the woodwork. Every grandmother with a pair of silver candle sticks or sterling silver flatware was bringing it down to these little stores all over the country and selling it at $12 under the value of silver." The refineries could hardly keep up with the demand. COMEX records showed the certificated bullion in its warehouses had grown from 57 million to 76 million ounces. Bunker had to find a way to absorb additional bullion in order to keep his plan going.

I walked Bunker through what he did rather than what he was willing to say. He was absorbing the extra silver bullion like spilt milk on a kitchen counter: he took delivery on 453 January 1980 contracts and Herbert Hunt took 250 January 1980 deliveries. Bunker was not prepared to acknowledge that he had coordinated bullion deliveries with the Conti Group, but the records showed their parallel actions. We went slowly through those deliveries: Nahas 172 January deliveries, Fustok 50 January deliveries, and Banque Populaire Suisse took delivery on 474 January contracts.

Bunker denied knowing about the Conti Group bullion deliveries: "That's news to me. I didn't know." But the jury, I hoped, was getting the picture of meetings and coordinated trading.

The Hunts also repeated the EFP strategy—exchanging futures for bullion—on an even more massive scale. Bunker and Herbert exchanged their February, March, and May 1980 futures contracts for more than 30.8 million ounces of certificated silver bullion in New York, Chicago, and London warehouses. The transactions were largely with the major metals dealers who Bunker portrayed as the devils, shorts on the COMEX board: Bunker Hill, Sharps Pixley, Johnson Mathey, and an EFP with Bunker's old acquaintance Asharf Amin. To a lesser extent, Banque Populaire Suisse mirrored the Hunt strategy with EFPs. Although COMEX board members escaped the carnage through EFPs, prices continued their relentless march upward from $32 toward $51 inflicting pain among those the COMEX was supposed to protect.

Bunker did not have to take control over silver bullion in order to close his enormous long February 1980 positions; he could have rolled forward those positions as he had been doing for years, which was exactly what Robert Wilmouth was asking Herbert to do. But Bunker—like Herbert—claimed he had faced an illiquid market; there supposedly were no shorts willing to sell. The Chicago exchange's yearbook, however, showed 88,000 contracts traded in January 1980, more than enough to cover Bunker's positions. And

I had anticipated Bunker's excuse by asking Andrew Brimmer, former Federal Reserve Board governor and chairman of the COMEX Silver Committee, his opinion:

"Was there any period of time during the period of September 1979 through March 1980 when in your opinion, the silver market was so illiquid that a trader for a long position who wanted to roll forward could not roll forward his position."

I got a simple answer from Brimmer: "No."

We were continuing to put the events in sequence and drawing connections for the jury. Bunker could buy large amounts of silver, but the law did not allow him to conspire with others to increase silver prices intentionally by buying the entire stock of warehouse bullion. Bunker's memory failures or affable stories were not providing an alternative innocent theory that was well grounded in the facts.

Between the January 1980 spot deliveries and the EFPs, Bunker and his cohorts had taken control over another 40 million ounces of certificated bullion in a breathtaking series of transactions. And the two groups still held a combined long position of 123 million ounces in the Chicago February 1980 and the COMEX March 1980 futures contracts, which would mature in a matter of weeks. Silver prices continued to surge upward despite the rules changes designed to dampen them, resulting in millions of dollars of daily margin payments gushing into their brokerage accounts every night. The regulators had delivered a blow with the new regulations, but Bunker had responded with a vengeance. In mid-January 1980, Bunker was at the height of his powers.

A surging bank account, a TV interview, and lunching in a famous restaurant with an iconic luminary must have felt very different from the bland description Bunker was offering eight years later in a packed Federal courtroom. *The New Yorker* described the glass-walled Crystal Room of the Tavern on the Green as decorated with "seven-foot-tall Baccarat chandeliers from Indian palaces, a molded-plaster ceiling in 'light mint green, birthday-candle pink, and telegraph-blank yellow,' and a 'fantasy mural' with flowers, birds, and butterflies." Bunker must have been beaming as brightly as the room, although he would not have admitted that then and surely no longer felt as buoyant as he sat on the hard, wooden seat on the witness stand.

The Hunts and Conti Group silver stash (futures and bullion) hit its height in January 1980 of 371 million ounces worth $16.4 billion ($50.6 billion in 2016), which was pretty good if you used H.L. Hunt's scoring system. That was before it all changed.

Chapter Forty-Three

As for us, we were just trying to survive a six-month trial. Friday nights were the time we got to relax and blow off some steam. We were at Christos on East 54th Street. We often went out as groups to a restaurant or some other entertainment. Amazing in retrospect, I rarely, if ever, went to a movie and never went to a Broadway show or the ballet—which I enjoyed frequently during law school in New York.

At Christos, we were six or eight chatting it up when I drift off. One of our dinner companions, Brenda Nelson, our chief secretary, noticed me staring at the next table. The daughter, about nine or ten in a pretty dress, was talking intently. The two younger boys were listening, neatly outfitted in matching gray sweaters. The young parents, also well dressed, were leading a family conversation. They looked like a Midwest family, perhaps from Kansas, on vacation.

"It's time for you to make a visit home," Brenda interrupted my thoughts.

"I've decided they must be drugged," I sighed, "no squirming, no getting off their seats, good manners—even the little one. I can't get over him. He can't be more than four. It never happened that way in my house at their ages."

"That's true," Brenda nodded. "We gave up restaurants for years until my boys were older. But you obviously need a visit home. You've been away too long."

I was thinking about our efforts to teach discipline at the dinner table. The first time I ordered Isaac to his room from the dinner table he was about three. I don't remember the offense, but I do remember being flabbergasted that he actually got up and went. I told the story for weeks. But by the time I stopped telling the story, he had stopped going.

However, Erin always knew better how to deal with Dad. I ordered her to her room when she was about two. She made it as far as the third step, stopped and made enough noise to be sure I knew she was going no further. I started after her, stomping mad and roaring:

"I said go to your room."

"You don't talk to me that way," she responded in a small voice.

"I said go to your room!"

"You don't talk to me that way. You go back and finish your dinner!"

Her first retort was given somewhat timidly. But this second speech was delivered sitting straight up, her little finger wagging directly at my nose, and her voice imitating my best authoritative growl. At that moment, I knew I had lost to a two-year old. My scowl was gone, and my face was contorted, fighting hard not to smile, or, more accurately, laugh. Fortunately, memories are merciful. I do not remember exactly how I surrendered. If the usual pattern held true, my wife rescued me. But I do know I made little progress thereafter with dinner discipline, and I am sure I never ordered either one of them to their rooms again.

Brenda was right; I needed a visit home. But the weekends were only slightly less intense than the weeks, as we prepared for the upcoming witnesses. Early in the trial, I had gone home when I did not have a witness to examine on Monday and the team seemed organized to their tasks. But I would show up home late on Friday, strung tight and leave early on Sunday. It was too disruptive to the family that was missing my presence all week. I was distracted and only made them tense. We had moved to a new neighborhood shortly before the trial; my wife told me the neighbors thought she was lying when she said she was married. We decided I should stay away for the sake of calm and the family routine, but we did not anticipate the trial would last six months. With the exception of one week in June when the judge gave everyone a vacation, I did not go home for most of four months.

We spend most of the weekends in office space we had rented from a large law firm. We had mostly internal offices except the conference room overlooked New York Bay. The Statute of Liberty was far off to the right, looking smaller than I remembered it. Verrazano Narrows Bridge was straight in the distance with Queens and Brooklyn close to our left. I would take breaks by staring out the window at the harbor traffic; the large ocean-going cargo ships would slide under bridge and move slowly to the wharfs in New Jersey for unloading, as other boats would zigzag to avoid them. As spring morphed into summer, hundreds of sail-boats would be gliding across the bay during the weekends. At times, it was hard to pull myself away from watching the families enjoy the sun and the water. My sarcastic exchange with Norton Waltuch was quite apt:

"There is more than silver in the world, Mr. Cymrot."

"I hope to get back to it some day," I responded. That was more than a mere retort to his wisecrack.

Part Eight

The Hourglass Empties

Chapter Forty-Four

The day silver prices hit an intraday high of $51 per ounce, COMEX finally called a halt to the mayhem. On January 21, 1980, COMEX effectively closed its silver market by imposing "liquidation-only" trading, which meant traders could close their silver futures contracts but could not open new ones in order to lay claim to additional bullion. Even *The New York Times* seemed overwrought with a headline that did not entirely make sense: *"Comex Curbs Trade in Silver Futures; How Futures Protect Merchants Trade in Silver Is Curbed Near Chaos in Markets Actions to Curb Trade."*

Silver prices immediately dropped almost $10, closing at $41.55. Long speculators who had been riding the Hunt coattails began fleeing silver markets worldwide, including many traders from the Middle East where Bunker Hunt had spent five years virtually advertising his scheme. With subsiding demand and the upward price psychology shattered, silver prices began to spiral downward.

The next day the Chicago Board of Trade (CBOT) followed suit, imposing liquidation-only trading in its market, prompting prices to drop further to an intraday low of $33.50, $18 in two days. *The New York Times* reported: *"Chicago Board Limits Silver Futures Trading; Sharp Response in Market Averting Squeeze on Shorts."* The *Chicago Tribune* quoted an analyst saying: "'People were stampeding over each other to sell.' He said traders reasoned that the demand that had propelled prices was cooled by the order." The article was next to one about a roof collapse, an unintended observation of what was happening.

Now the gushing money reversed course; the Hunt and Conti Groups were forced to pay huge daily margin calls. However, even with the price splash, they were still well into the black, at least on paper. In June 1979, Bunker and Herbert had put on their huge straddle positions at prices in the range of $8.50 per ounces; those positions were still very profitable. When Bunker took delivery of bullion in the period of October 1979 to January 1980, the prices were still below $33. Even this expensive bullion was still no worse than breakeven.

The COMEX Board of Governors finally acted after the Special Silver Committee concluded that the Hunt and Conti Groups controlled most of the 76.4 million ounces of deliverable silver bullion in the exchange's warehouses, and the inventory was not going to increase significantly over the next six months. The Silver Committee felt it was not appropriate for a group of four to take drastic action; they turned the issue back to the COMEX board, which imposed the liquidation-only rule. Charles Mattey, the

Bache official and Hunt broker, did not attend the meeting. Mocatta's Henry Jarecki and Engelhard's Ray Nessim voted for the rule.

Two exchange officials explained to the jury the reason for the new, liquidation-only rule. Mark Buckstein testified that the COMEX observed "a number of new positions being opened in the marketplace that seemed to be affiliated to at least one of the existing groups . . . The concern, therefore, was that while the exchange was trying to cool down what seemed to becoming a volatile situation, the size of the positions was increasing and increasing in a circuitous way which was troublesome for the exchange." That was a reference to Nahas's new accounts in the name of shell companies at ContiCommodity, ACLI International, and E.F. Hutton and the Hunt new Eighth Crescent account.

Robert Goldberg of the CBOT was more direct: "We felt that we could no longer live up to the representation that the Hunts would not take delivery in February." The Hunt positions in the February and March 1980 futures contracts—put on the prior June—appeared to dwarf the available supply of bullion.

Even with the drastic action of the exchanges, the outcome of the silent battle with Bunker and his brothers remained undecided.

Chapter Forty-Five

Bunker Hunt's grumbling about the "shorts" on exchange boards seemed to imply that those asking him questions, demanding trading commitments, and imposing new rules were crooked insiders who were rightfully deceived. As part of the Hunt defense, Paul Curran called a witness to support the notion that despite all the talk, unbiased regulators had not supported the new regulations in January 1980—position limits and liquidation-only trading—and had not concluded that the silver markets were being rigged. We had an intense battle of direct and cross-examination with Dr. Andrew F. Brimmer, a public member of the COMEX Board of Governors and Chairman of its Special Silver Committee. Dr. Brimmer, a tall, broad-shouldered African American with a deep voice and a reticent manner, walked slowly to the stand.

Dr. Brimmer had a long list of impressive qualifications. He was Harvard economist, Deputy Secretary of Commerce, first African American appointed as a Governor of the Federal Reserve System, member of major corporate boards, and he had twenty honorary degrees. The Hunt examiner brought out that Brimmer and other members of the Special Silver Committee (who had no silver positions) had not voted for positions limits or liquidation-only trading—implying, as Bunker had suggested, that the shorts on the COMEX board with their conflicts of interest, were manipulating prices downward when the board imposed those restrictions. Continuing with this theme, Brimmer testified that in December 1979 the COMEX silver contract had liquidated "in an orderly manner." The Hunt examiner did not ask Brimmer to explain this technical term, which sounds like more than it is.

On cross-examination, I asked Brimmer about the Hunt theme that the shorts controlled the COMEX board. With his elbows on the witness chair and leaning slightly forward, Brimmer hesitated before answering. He was a very careful witness who seemed reluctant to take sides, which made him a dangerous witness—one who might give unhelpful testimony if pushed. I brought out that the COMEX board was made up of representatives of all segments of the industry, not just the shorts: floor brokers, metal traders, brokerage houses, and a general public group.

I moved on to the more pertinent subject, asking Brimmer to explain to the jury the technical meaning of an "orderly liquidation" of a silver futures contract. It meant, he said, the shorts had silver to deliver against their contracts— no shorts defaulted on their futures contracts. I continued:

"When you say that a contract liquidated in an orderly fashion, are you making any comment on the price of silver?"

"No," he responded in a low voice.

"And so when you say that the September and December 1979 silver futures contracts liquidated in an orderly fashion, you are not taking a position one way or the other as to whether those prices were manipulated or un-manipulated?"

"We were not taking a position."

After that answer I exhaled; I had not been sure what he would say. In response to my next question, Brimmer acknowledged that he had voted for position limits at the COMEX board meeting of January 7, 1980, even though his Silver Committee had not voted for the same regulation earlier that day, as the Hunt examiner had brought out. He was not at the meeting when the board had voted for liquidation-only trading.

Probing whether the COMEX board was biased against the Hunts, I felt he could give only one answer.

"Did you hear any evidence at the board table that the board members were acting in their self-interest when they decided to impose position limits?"

In the same low voice and restrained manner, Brimmer responded, "I have no such evidence." His answer was awkwardly stated, but I decided not to push him for a more emphatic one.

I tiptoed along, testing what Brimmer might say about the shorts. Early in my career, I had read about a famous cross-examination by Lizzy Borden's lawyer ("Lizzy Borden took an axe, gave her father forty whacks . . ." Surprisingly, it was a true murder trial). The lawyer had walked the maid slowly through the front door of the house, up the stairs, not sure whether she might place Lizzy at the scene, which was exactly the point he was trying to avoid. Step by step, he walked the maid into the bloody scene, ready to pivot to another subject if Lizzy appeared around the corner. She did not, and Lizzy Borden was acquitted, largely due to that daring cross-examination, according to commentators. I kept waiting for Brimmer to scream and point to the bloody axe.

About the shorts in pain from the price surge, I asked, "And your opposition to position limits did not arise from whether or not particular members had particular positions in silver; is that correct?"

"That is correct."

After I got that answer, it seemed safe to ask, "From the evidence that you heard at the board table or from any other source, is it your opinion that the board acted to impose position limits out of concern for the market and not out of concern for their self-interest?"

"In my opinion, the board acted out of concern for the market."

Still no bloody axe, but Brimmer also was not cooperating. Brimmer had been at an earlier meeting with CFTC

Vice Chairman Dunn in which Dunn had expressed the opinion that position limits were needed. Brimmer did not recall the meeting, even after I showed him a memo to refresh his memory. That seemed like a strange answer, but then I had been immersed in the story for the last five years and he had not. Nonetheless, Brimmer, for reasons I could not ascribe, was giving very reserved answers.

I changed course to points I had discussed with Brimmer before trial in his Washington, DC office. When the Hunts had listed Brimmer as a witness, my first instinct was to notice a pretrial deposition, but based on strategic insight from Herbert Deutsch—just go talk to him—I called and asked for an appointment. Brimmer agreed. From that conversation, I had several points that the defense may not have anticipated, but getting the answers I wanted also proved harder than I had anticipated.

Brimmer's report of December 12, 1979, said that the Silver Committee found no evidence that "Group A and Group B were acting together." Everyone in the courtroom by then knew from the earlier testimony that Group A was the Hunts and Group B was the Conti Group. But when I asked Brimmer, he did not recall who the two groups were, another strange answer for a regulator who had lived through the events. I pressed on.

The Silver Committee investigation included a meeting with Naji Nahas on December 18, 1979. From Norton Waltuch's testimony, we had learned that Nahas was very upset about the continued action by the COMEX against the longs.

Nahas had left for the COMEX from Waltuch's office and returned an hour later. Afterward, Waltuch's phone records showed calls to Fustok's home in Chantilly, France, Hunt Energy, and Crown Prince Abdullah. About that encounter, I asked Brimmer:

"Now, was one of your purposes in having a meeting with Mr. Nahas to determine whether he was acting with any of the other accounts that you were examining?"

"Yes."

"Did Mr. Nahas make any representations as to whether he was acting with or trading with any of the other accounts?"

"He did not indicate that he was."

"Do you recall him indicating that he was not?"

"No. But I remember what I said earlier."

That was another awkwardly stated answer that did not go far enough. This time I pressed by putting in front of him the Silver Committee's report about the interview and reading the quote:

"'In response to inquiries he [Nahas] stated that he has never purchased any silver futures contracts through the bank.' Do you see that?"

"I see that."

"And the bank in that case is Banque Populaire Suisse; is that correct?"

"Yes, that is the bank being discussed."

"At the time of this meeting, did you know that Naji Nahas had taken delivery of 300 silver futures contracts on the COMEX through Banque Populaire Suisse?"

"I do not recall whether I knew that."

Brimmer's memory was not my point; at least he had confirmed Nahas's statement, which had given me the opportunity to align Nahas's false statement with his trading activities. Nahas had denied that he was trading through Banque Populaire Suisse, and yet he had purchased 300 spot October 1979 contracts and taken delivery of 1,500,000 ounces of certificated bullion hidden in the bank's account at ContiCommodity.

Although that was significant testimony, I pressed on to a statement Nahas had reportedly made about the Hunts. But it was a struggle. At first Brimmer denied remembering Nahas saying anything about the Hunts. I had to show him his deposition testimony from another case.

"Does that refresh your recollection as to statements made by Mr. Nahas?" I asked, not sure it would.

"I remember this statement now that you have refreshed my memory," Brimmer said vaguely.

"What do you recall?" I asked, not sure what answer I would get. This time I may have been helped by our last exchange; Brimmer probably did not want to be shown again his prior testimony.

"I remember he said he had not had any communications," he whispered uncomfortably and stopped short.

That caught Judge Lasker's attention; he sat straight up: "Excuse me. You remember that he said what?"

"He said that he had not had any communications with the Hunt Group," Brimmer said, finally completing the thought.

"Thank you," the judge said, showing no emotion at what he undoubtedly understood was a significant falsehood. At that point in the trial, the jury also must have recognized Nahas's statement to be a gross falsehood. Bunker's later testimony describing Nahas as his good friend, plus their many meetings and telephone calls, put additional weight to that misstatement. If Nahas had nothing to hide, he could have readily admitted his meetings and conversations with Bunker Hunt. The fact that he hid those conversations showed a guilty mind, we argued. I sought to drive home the point to the jury through a still hesitant Dr. Brimmer.

"Were you," I asked him, "relying upon Mr. Nahas' statement as being truthful when he made it?" I thought it was an obvious point that would elicit an obvious answer.

But Brimmer surprised me, responding: "I accepted the statement as it was given."

What did that mean? So we continued to fence; I was caught off guard but had to quickly come up with another question. I asked:

"And in considering whether traders were acting in concert you accepted his statement as truthful?"

"I did."

"When he made the statement that he had no communications with the Hunts were you relying upon Mr. Nahas to be truthful?"

"Yes."

"And in analyzing the market, were you accepting Mr. Nahas' statement as truthful?"

"I did not make a distinction between his statements and other statements. I relied on the information presented by the staff to the committee." Brimmer again was sidestepping what I thought was an obvious point; I decided to press:

"And you relied upon them as truthful statements?"

"Yes."

I did not think it would be so hard to get a regulator to acknowledge he had been lied to. I might have asked him whether if he had known Nahas was lying, his committee would have voted for position limits and liquidation-only trading. But, by that time, I was not sure what he would answer. I felt I had made our point, although not as emphatically as I hoped. I sat down. Brimmer slowly stepped off the witness stand and walked out of the courtroom.

Chapter Forty-Six

Even after the liquidation-only trading rule, Bunker did not give up. He still thought he could defeat the exchange boards and the US Government. ContiCommodity's phone records showed another coordinated response to the new rule. On January 21, 1980, Norton Waltuch called Naji Nahas in Brazil and Bunker in Dallas for twenty overlapping minutes in an apparent conference call. Over the next two days, the trio held two more conference calls. Faced with our hard facts, Paul Curran had Bunker admit the obvious; he and Nahas had talked about the liquidation-only rule. But Bunker tried to diffuse the impact by adding another droll story: I "talked to 15 or 20 people," many he did not know, trying "to figure out if there was anything that could be done." And Bunker gathered unnamed minions to his side: the callers would say, "what the exchanges have done is a travesty of justice, changing the rules in the middle of the game, favor[ing] one side against the other. Why don't you sue them. And it was sort of a kind of deal, why don't you go fight someone and I'll hold your coat." The line was worth a laugh, but when Bunker delivered it with a dismissive sneer, nobody in the packed courtroom laughed; the smothering silence continued.

Finding alternative ways to stem the tide of silver bullion flowing into exchange warehouses became Bunker's preoccupation. After the conference calls, Bunker and Nahas began absorbing the flow of silver bullion through foreign markets, particularly London and Zurich. On January 22, 1980, the day after the liquidation-only rule was imposed, Bunker, Herbert, and IMIC began buying silver forward contracts on the London Metals Exchange (LME), which, similar to futures contracts, are commitments for the later delivery of silver bullion.

Any appearance of independent trading broke down; the activity became dizzying. Advicorp and Bunker placed trades for IMIC; Nahas made a trade for Bunker and the trade tickets said they were placed for Nahas's "friend"; and Bunker took silver contracts from Nahas's shell companies. As of February 1, 1980, Mahmoud Fustok's account at Swiss Bank Corporation showed 11 million ounces, about which he denied knowing anything. Within three weeks, Bunker, Nahas, Fustok, and IMIC had taken commitments of 34,708,000 ounces of silver bullion in London and Zurich, the silver bullion that would normally restock New York and Chicago warehouses if they were to be depleted.

When Curran asked Bunker whether he had made additional purchases of silver in 1980 outside of the United States, Bunker responded vaguely: "Yes. I think I did buy some silver after the rules changes or about that time or afterwards yes, sir."

Curran continued: "Did you understand that there was no impropriety or illegality in those [purchases]?"

"Absolutely ethical, legal and morally perfectly all right." Bunker responded with strong conviction in his voice.

"Why did you buy silver outside of the United States?"

"The American market was substantially closed and silver was offered to me and I bought it."

That was a general enough answer to sound convincing, but the details that Curran did not ask for at that point were damning.

Despite their drastic actions, the biggest problem for the exchanges remained right at home; the long legs of Bunker and Herbert's huge straddle positions from June 1979 could overwhelm the silver supply in exchange warehouses. In late January 1980, Robert Wilmouth had another conversation with Herbert Hunt during which he reminded Herbert of his commitment to roll forward his February 1980 contracts. To Wilmouth's dismay, although probably not surprise, Herbert demurred. He said the spreads between the New York and Chicago contracts were "out of line"; he would probably make a business decision to take delivery on his massive February 1980 contracts. Those massive deliveries would likely wipe out the remaining available supplies of bullion in Chicago, the regulators worried.

And that is what happened. Four months of talk with Herbert Hunt had been for naught; the Hunts had done exactly what the exchange had asked them not to. Despite their repeated promises to the CBOT, Bunker and Herbert Hunt took delivery on the residue of their positions after the exchange for physicals (EFPs) and swaps, a total of 12,875,000 ounces worth $432,312,500 but purchased for about a quarter of that price. Bunker and Herbert's deliveries represented about 85 percent of the deliverable open interest. The Conti Group took delivery of their few February 1980 contracts, another 220,000 ounces.

No major shorts defaulted. The major shorts on the COMEX board were already out of the market through transactions with the Hunts. The new flow of silver bullion into the exchange warehouses covered the remaining Hunt demand. But the gyrating prices were still inflicting untold losses on invisible traders.

The bullion deliveries propped up sagging silver prices, which jumped from $35.28 back up to $40.25, a momentary reprise for Bunker from margin calls and a renewed sign of hope for his plan. Robert Wilmouth made no more calls to Herbert Hunt. Any thought that the Hunts might cooperate was wiped out. Even though the deliveries exceeded the position limit rule, the exchanges took no action.

And consistent with Paul Curran's mocking theme of a "broad daylight conspiracy," Bunker was not being covert about his appetite for still more silver bullion. The *Wall Street Journal* reported that he made a public offer "to buy up to $5 million ounces at $40 an ounce, deliverable in Zurich, New York or London from anyone who has any silver that is deliverable." No one responded, according to the paper.

During Curran's direct examination, Bunker continued his theme of blaming the shorts on the exchange boards for the new rules that "caused the market to get weak for a period of time and, ultimately, destroyed the market." When Curran asked Bunker his theory of why the exchanges imposed liquidation-only trading, he had his ready answer: "Well, I think it's pretty clear now they did it at the urging and the insistence of the shorts because the shorts were having to put up variation margin . . . and they didn't like it."

Bunker jawboned several of the board members urging them to rescind the rule, "[b]ut it didn't do any good," he bemoaned, "Well, I told them, they were almost destroying their own market and it would probably take years to come back as a viable, trading market and they were violating their own rules. I think there's some federal rules that the market should be market neutral . . . it was pretty obvious they were favoring the shorts."

Bunker did not identify any specific members of the COMEX board who satisfied his definition of "shorts." I am not sure whom he could name. Henry Jarecki of Mocatta, Ray Nessim of Englehard EFP, and representatives from the Sharps Pixley and J. Aron were mollified by EFPs and swaps. That removed four of the seven metals firms from representatives on the COMEX board from the short side of the ledger. And two of the other three trade members either were not present or abstained. Plus, the Hunts or Conti Group held extraordinarily large futures positions at six of the seven brokerage firms represented on the COMEX board. Bunker could have called a quorum of the COMEX board to his conference room in Dallas and most of them might have shown up. His railing at the "shorts" had no substance.

The Hunt deliveries were an open challenge to the regulators, but the exchanges had done all they would; the markets would have to do the rest. Bunker was scrambling to offset the impact of the new exchange rules. But time was running out. His prospects did not look encouraging. The psychology of the squeeze had been broken. His scheme began unraveling over the next two months, slowly and agonizingly heading toward doom.

Chapter Forty-Seven

The Hunts and Conti Group deliveries and foreign purchases may have propped up silver prices but only for a time. They continued to soften. Through February 1980, prices continued to drop down to $30 in mid-month. And with falling prices, the direction of money flow shifted. During the upsurge in prices, the Hunts, IMIC, and the Conti Group could pyramid their silver positions by reinvesting their massive daily margin payments in more silver. Now, they were the ones paying nightly margin calls, which as February moving into March 1980 strained their once overflowing bank accounts. Financing the margin calls became Bunker's preoccupation as his bank accounts dripped, dripped, dripped toward empty.

Bunker Hunt and Naji Nahas started a frenzied transcontinental ferrying for forty-five days in February and March 1980 traveling Europe looking for financing and leaving a trail of receipts for us to follow. They flew together from Paris to Zurich, Hamburg, Geneva, and then bounced over to Riyadh, Saudi Arabia. Curran seemed to have little choice but to walk Bunker through their travels to give what explanations he could. As I watched, it seemed they were trying to tell the story by obscuring it with irrelevant details and without looking embarrassed, which would make it okay, I suppose.

Bunker acknowledged his finances were under pressure from margin calls. "Well, financing got to be more and more a problem, and particularly it became an insurmountable problem when the market started crashing or dropping and so I was in Europe trying to see if there wasn't some way to find some alternate financing." About Naji Nahas, Bunker testified: "*I got the impression* from him that he was having the same problem." The increased margin rates earlier imposed by the COMEX and CBOT were now having their intended impact of absorbing funds.

As silver prices fell and margin calls became relentless, Bunker and Herbert started borrowing from their brokers, particularly Bache and Merrill Lynch, which in turn borrowed from their banks. Paul Volcker's October 6th directive against lending for speculation in silver did not seem to matter; the banks later reasoned they were lending to brokerage firms or Placid Oil, the Hunt crown jewel, not funding the Hunts silver exploits, a shallow excuse when it became plain that they had set up the conditions for a panic and broad economic collapse. As the loan balances multiplied, the bankers and brokers comforted themselves with the illusion, stoked undoubtedly by dreams of extraordinary bonuses, that the Hunts were too wealthy to fail.

But Bunker still needed more money. About their forty-five days of travel together around Europe, Curran asked Bunker:

"Were you and Mr. Nahas trying to raise financing jointly?"

"No, not at all," Bunker responded quickly, "I just—he was a friend of mine and I would ask anybody that I thought was friendly if they had any idea where some financing could be done and I'd ask Nahas."

In response to Curran's questions, Bunker acknowledged that in early February 1980, he met with Nahas in Paris. While in Paris, Bunker had what he described as a "semi-board meeting" of IMIC with Mohammed Affara and Sheikh Mussalem. That led to a telling story about Nahas's reputation. When he told Nahas he was on his way to see Mussalem, Nahas reacted: "Excuse me. I'm anxious to meet him. Would you mind if I came along and met him and you would introduce me to him? I said sure be glad to," Bunker testified. "Nahas is the kind of fellow who likes to know a many people as he can. He came with me. I think we met in the lobby of the Maurice Hotel. I introduced him to Sheikh Ali [who] pretty quickly excused himself and left. Then we went up to the Sheikh's room and had the meeting."

At the IMIC board meeting, Mussalem gave Bunker a piece of his mind, as Bunker described it: "And, as a matter of fact, later when I was with the Sheikh and Affara, the Sheikh said, through Affara, that he specifically didn't want to have anything to do with doing business with Mr. Nahas." But Bunker brushed off the rebuke, continuing: "Frankly, he was a little bit prejudiced against Lebanese and the Sheikh's a Bedouin Sheikh and there seemed to a bit of friction there between a Bedouin and a Town Lebanese."

The theory, I suppose, is that if they do not like each other, they cannot be conspiring, but that is not how conspiracy law works. With a central character like Bunker, other conspirators do not even have to know or like each other. The "wheel and spoke" theory of conspiracy allows for a central organizing character—like Bunker—and spokes consisting of the other conspirators. But Curran's ploy could still have a sympathy effect on a jury.

When they flew on to Zurich, Bunker and Nahas purchased another 10 million ounces of silver bullion from Swiss Bank Corporation, the second of the joint transactions disclosed by the Swiss Bank Corporation documents. Bunker described a February 7, 1980 lunch that Swiss Bank's H. Kyburg hosted for Bunker, Nahas, and Jean-Jacque Bally from Advicorp. Bunker explained: "I been contacted by Mr. Kyburg of the Swiss Bank Corporation— he had some silver to sell . . . *I got the impression* from Nahas that Kyburg talked to him, also; he talked to him on the phone and invited him to come." Bunker's impression again was not from some ethereal source, he and Nahas flew to Zurich together.

Over a friendly lunch, Bunker and Nahas agreed to their second joint purchase of silver, following the late October 1979 pattern. They bought 10 million ounces of silver with Swiss Bank financing the deal. Bunker repeated several times that he did not know whether the bank was the principal or an agent in the deal, which seemed to be his only explanation for bank documents showing he purchased the silver with Nahas.

Once again, Curran did not confront the transaction directly; he asked Bunker why he was buying silver in Europe. Bunker pointed to the liquidation-only rules in the United States, saying: "the American markets were pretty much closing down," and then he added: "It just seemed like it was bullish time." Why it was a bullish time when the US markets were closed and prices were dropping was left without explanation.

Bunker bought 5 million ounces and Nahas bought an equivalent amount. The price was $36 or $38 per ounce. "It was quite expensive," Bunker admitted. But they were not buying "jointly," Bunker insisted, "I bought some silver from Swiss Bank, and as I recall Nahas said he was going to buy some and did agree to buy some at that time." Of Bunker's allotment, the supposedly independent trading IMIC and Herbert Hunt each took one-third.

According to Bunker, he was "bullish as ever" in February 1980, testifying: "Well, I was overconfident and, in hindsight, I was wrong. But obviously at the time I felt that the usage in the world and the supply, the ratio had finally come into effect and seeing the price go from $1.60 in Libya to $40 a barrel, so I could see silver stabilizing at those prices or higher." Obviously it was better to be wrong than guilty.

On February 13, 1980, the COMEX board lifted the liquidation-only trading rule despite the huge overhang of the Hunt positions in the March 1980 contract, but it maintained position limits. The resolution acknowledges the "continuing undue concentration in the silver futures market and in the cash silver market resulting in a continuing emergency situation in the silver market." Charles Mattey abstained. Henry Jarecki departed the meeting after the discussion of market conditions but before the vote. Two weeks before, Jarecki had opposed a resolution of the Board Trade Group and Precious Metals Committees recommending to the COMEX board to continue liquidation-only trading.

The reopening of the US exchanges, however, did not solve Bunker's problems; he continued to scramble to prop up prices.

Chapter Forty-Eight

After a month of traveling, Bunker Hunt and Naji Nahas were back at the Bristol Hotel in Paris on February 23 to 27, 1980, just as the March 1980 silver futures contract was about to expire. The now desperate effort to absorb silver bullion continued when Bunker and Herbert Hunt, Nahas, and Mahmoud Fustok took delivery of a total of 14,890,000 ounces of bullion. Many of the Conti Group deliveries were taken through bogus accounts to evade the COMEX position limit rule. Silver prices jumped up from $32.80 to $36.31 per ounce. That must have been cause for some optimism.

However, any remaining façade of independent trading had broken down. The account records revealed secret transactions that left little doubt about the joint trading among Bunker, Nahas, Herbert, and IMIC. The Swiss Bank records reveal two more secret joint transactions. On February 25, 1980, Bunker purchased 474,000 ounces of silver bullion from Nahas, and on February 28, 1980, another 3,500,000 ounces. The proceeds of those purchases appeared to finance

Nahas's bullion deliveries on his March 1980 contracts. But on March 10 and 11, 1980, Bunker bought about half of Nahas's March bullion deliveries in two transactions: 325,000 ounces and 1,690,000 ounces. It appeared the Nahas had become a surrogate for Bunker. The price of the four transactions was about $190 million; Bunker paid $108 million and Nahas financed the remaining $82 million while holding onto the silver bullion as collateral. Friendship apparently goes only so far. The supposedly freethinking Herbert Hunt and IMIC each again took one-third of the deals.

Curran could not avoid asking about the purchases because the $82 million financed portion of the deal became a saga of its own as the year progressed. In response to Paul Curran's question, Bunker told a vague story: "[Nahas] called me, I was in the United States, don't know where he was calling from but it was either Brazil or in France, and said that he needed to sell and wondered if I was interested in buying it. I asked what the price was and he said well, the market close yesterday . . . I did buy some from him."

This vague, breezy story sounded very different when I asked Bunker:

"You were traveling around in Europe looking for financing at that time, right?"

"Yea, I was looking for financing, very proud of it," Bunker snapped at the touchy subject, "I think anybody who wasn't looking out for financing in my situation, there would be something wrong with them."

He was worried about financing, looking for a reserve, but supposedly still too optimistic about the future. Bunker's two purchases from Nahas on February 25 and 28, 1980, came while they were together at the Bristol Hotel, not as Bunker had suggested when he was home in Dallas, which I forced Bunker to concede.

And the prices were not right; they were not market prices. Bunker appeared to have guaranteed Nahas against the price drop that occurred between January and February 1980. I walked him through Jim Parker's records showing he had paid Nahas a premium, not the market price for the day of the trade. Bunker did not have an explanation. "Well you will have to ask Parker," Bunker snapped again, "Whatever the records say, I'm not going to try to interpret somebody else's records . . ."

Bunker had testified to two purchases, but we had found four; he had omitted the two mid-March purchases of Nahas's March deliveries, also at the higher price than Nahas had paid. Bunker stubbornly maintained the transactions were conducted "based on the market close that day," even as I went over each transaction in Parker's records, which showed a higher price. In other words, he could not rebut the appearance of a guarantee, which I hoped the jury understood even in the face of Bunker's defiant demeanor.

Bunker and Herbert's tax returns for 1980 show a combined loss of $47 million from something vaguely called the "Nahas option." Jim Parker had no explanation for that entry, testifying: "I have no knowledge of any Nahas option . . . Some accountant may have presumed it was that, but it's not with respect to options at all." That seemed unlikely. Although Bunker repeatedly denied it in response to my questions, the documents that I confronted him with strongly suggested he had guaranteed his friend Nahas's silver buying and provided Nahas the resources to stay in the scheme once the prices turned downward.

For the jury, I suggested the reason for Bunker's purchases from Nahas was to support silver prices as they deflated, but Bunker denied it. Bunker had supported his children's silver positions for just that reason, because, he said, "if [traders] hear a Hunt selling it's going to be very damaging to the market. So, if you'll hold up, it might help me."

"And if Mr. Nahas sold it would have had the same effect as if your children sold, isn't that true?" I asked.

"No. Mr. Nahas is a guy from Brazil. My children are a bunch of people that people know," Bunker harrumphed.

After more than an hour of these details, Bunker's shoulders slumped but he remained stoic with a strong voice. I had not cracked his demeanor that suggested he thought he had done nothing wrong. How much the jury was absorbing of the contradictions I had no way of knowing. I turned to a point that finally evoked an emotional reaction.

When he appeared later in the year, Bunker had misled Congress about the depth of his relationship with Nahas. After pointing out that at first he refused to appear in response to Congressional subpoenas—the committee had to threaten him with contempt—I asked:

"You attempted to insist that three Congressional committees have a joint session for your convenience, is that what occurred?"

Curran shot up to object, but Judge Lasker quickly overruled him before he could get out of his chair. Bunker turned toward the judge, pleading. "He really tries to make me look like a criminal, your Honor. I'm a nice guy," Bunker implored, sounding truly hurt, "I've never heard such a question in my life . . ."

The judge looked down at him expressionless, his brow furrowed, but he said nothing. I paused momentarily, wondering what he was thinking, but then kept going:

"In May 1980 did you testify before Congress that you had only one transaction with Mr. Nahas?" I barked in order to get the bewildered Bunker to turn back toward me.

"I may have," he shrugged swallowing his words. "Sometimes I just can't remember all the different transactions."

Bunker had to concede the testimony came only two months after the transactions had occurred. After I quoted his testimony before the Subcommittee on Agricultural Research and General Legislation that: "I bought a couple of million ounces of bullion from him one time," I asked:

"Well, that testimony wasn't correct, was it?"

"It was not completely accurate," he conceded. "It was inaccurate, not intentionally. I certainly wouldn't try to deceive anyone," he huffed with boyish innocence.

Chapter Forty-Nine

After spiking to $36.31, silver prices reversed themselves and began spiraling downward again, dropping all the way to $16.60 by March 18, but rebounding to $23.05 by March 24. Margin money was flowing out and then in like the tides. Bunker's search for additional financing continued. Bunker and Nahas flew to Saudi Arabia looking for a lender. Among their meetings was a dinner with Prince Faisal, one of the young nephews of the King. Bunker set the scene around a large lavish table with the prince at the head. When I asked him whether he was sitting on the prince's right, "Yes," he responded with a quizzical look. It was a throwaway question; where else would the guest of honor be sitting? I heard later Bunker thought that Nahas must have turned on him; how else would I know where he sat?

The duo was not successful finding financing from Prince Faisal; Bunker may have been an honored guest but not a reliable risk apparently. Bunker testified: "I went to Saudi Arabia hoping that they wouldn't be affected by the same inhibitions about silver lending as the U.S. and European banks." They visited three banks, but "the bankers just felt the market had gotten weak to the point where there wasn't anything that could be done." Bunker rejected, flew home to Dallas.

As March 1980 progressed, the Conti Group scurrying further exposed their joint trading and led to later conflicts. On March 13, 1980 after selling silver bullion to Bunker, Nahas sought to make use of the funds. He ordered Norton Waltuch to buy an additional 500 long silver contracts on the COMEX and give them up to various accounts at other brokers. But Nahas's credit was wearing thin; E.F. Hutton refused to accept the 182 contracts. When I asked Waltuch about those contracts, he said Nahas "acted very surprised." He told Waltuch to give them up to Merrill Lynch, some Beirut account, but he later called back and said Mahmoud Fustok would take them. Waltuch called Jean-Jacque Bally to confirm the instruction.

Fustok later sued ContiCommodity denying he authorized that instruction, which led to the courtroom confrontation between Peter Fleming and, another illustrious litigator, Arthur Liman before Judge Lasker that I had sat in on before our trial. When I asked about the 182 contracts, Fustok's testimony gave insight to the growing tension falling silver prices were having:

"Did you ever get angry at Mr. Nahas for having Advicorp put these [182] contracts in your account?"

"You mean openly or deep inside?"

"Openly?"

"Openly, no, I was very cautious." He had other business interests with Nahas in Brazil.

"But deep inside you were disappointed in him?"

"I was burning."

"Because this is not the way you would treat Mr. Nahas?"

"No, or any other person, not only Mr. Nahas."

Bunker got further intertwined with the wily Nahas on March 17, 1980, when he got on yet another plane and flew to Zurich where he signed a document he later regretted. Paul Curran tried to have Bunker explain away his pledge of 4,296,000 of Hunt silver to guarantee Nahas's Litardex account at Swiss Bank Corporation, asking:

"Do you recall signing the original of that document in that form on March 17, 1980 at Swiss Bank Corporation?"

Bunker stammered with emotion, "I, I, I signed a document that day. I don't remember Litardex Traders, Inc. being on the paper. I had been up all night and, like I said, I was tired, but I didn't know who Litardex Traders were, and if it had been mentioned to me I'd have asked them, but— that's why I don't recall it being on the document."

Four or five days later, Jim Parker questioned him about what he had done; Bunker claimed he was tricked, he thought he was pledging $30 million of silver collateral for his own account. "I thought they were in extremely bad faith, if not fraud," Bunker complained but the bank would not relent.

The deteriorated situation continued on March 20, 1980 when Norton Waltuch called Jean-Jacque Bally for money to cover margins in a series of Advicorp accounts; he was told to talk to Nahas. "That was the first indication that Nahas had anything to do with these accounts," Waltuch testified. When I pressed Waltuch about Nahas's guarantee of the Advicorp accounts, we had a testy exchange:

"Now, once you found out that Mr. Nahas was guaranteeing these accounts, did you tell the COMEX that Nahas apparently was violating the position limit rule by trading through the accounts?"

"That was not my job, Mr. Cymrot. Our compliance people are responsible for any communications with the exchanges."

"You weren't concerned that Mr. Nahas had used these accounts and you had entered the orders in violation of the position limit rule?"

"You're darned right I was concerned. They owed a lot of money and I was on the line for this, but that did not necessarily mean I had to notify the COMEX. It was up to Conti to do it . . . COMEX was operating fine."

That was about all I could get from Waltuch about his concern for emergency rules. In late March 1980, Bunker, Herbert, and Jim Parker were back in New York staying at the Berkshire Hotel to talk to their brokers at Merrill Lynch, Bache and perhaps E.F. Hutton. Their credit was also wearing thin. Bunker and Nahas met. A senior ContiCommodity official later came by to have breakfast with Bunker in a small, cramped breakfast room. The Conti official tried to convince Bunker to buy Nahas's positions before they sold them into the market. Bunker's response was curt: "I said no, I was having enough margin problems of my own. I didn't want to buy any more silver than I had."

The end was less than a week away. The financial institutions now were scrabbling to cover their massive advances to both the Hunts and Conti Group. If Bunker was watching an hourglass empty, he was beginning to panic. And panic breeds mistakes.

Chapter Fifty

The frantic two months of February and March 1980 ended with a press release that looked very much like a written conspiracy agreement. With silver prices down from $51 to $23.05 and dropping, relentless margin calls prompted Bunker Hunt into his final, ruinous blunder. On March 24, 1980, Bunker Hunt and Naji Nahas met at the President Hotel in Geneva. Mahmoud Fustok was also there visiting Advicorp; they went to his room. It was another huddle about financing. According to Fustok, Bunker needed money: "I think he mentioned that he was in debt of so many hundreds of millions or whatever and that he had to cover that and he needed a loan from some banks . . ."

"How did you feel about that?" I asked.

Fustok continued his theme of being detached: "Can I kick them out? Can I tell them get out of my place?"

"Was it your impression that Nahas needed money, too?"

"According to him, no. He told me he is in good shape and he does not need anything."

Nahas must have been drawing quite handily on Bunker's wallet at the time. I urged Fustok to continue, asking:

"Did he tell you why he was traveling with Bunker Hunt?"

"He said Bunker Hunt consults him all the time, he helps Bunker Hunt and he was feeling pity for Bunker Hunt." That was quite a breathtaking image.

Bunker was visiting a Geneva bank based on an introduction from Jean-Jacque Bally. Fustok was facing his own problems in Geneva; he learned he had debts at Swiss Bank Corporation and Banque Populaire Suisse. When he learned he also had debts at ContiCommodity, he was "raving mad."

Apparently, the group flew to Paris. The next day, they met at Fustok's home in Chantilly, France. "They came into the house," Fustok testified, "and they told me they are going to put all the silver they had in the *pool* and with that pool they want to sell bonds backed by this pool." Nahas proposed they "pool" the silver, to put the silver "in one basket" in order to make the price go back up. According to Fustok, Nahas said that the three of them owned half the world's silver. Fustok "was scared of the problems that happened. I said, let me think about it and get back to you on it," putting them off, according to his version, "I never got back to them on it. That was it."

"What was the purpose of pooling this silver . . . ?" I asked to keep him talking.

"I think they said it will *regain its price*," Fustok acknowledged.

III.

An Announcement

1) Nelson Bunker Hunt announces the conclusion of ~~negotiations~~ discussions to form a company with the following persons.

H.R.H. PRINCE FAISAL oF SAUDI ARABIA
MAHMOUD FUSTOK oF SAUDI ARABIA
NAJI NAHAS of BRAZIL
SABAH AL ARISS of KUWAIT
SHEIK MOHAMED AL AMOUDI oF SAUDI ARABIA

2) Together these ~~individuals~~ ~~and~~ ~~their~~ ~~associates~~ own in excess of 200 million ounces of physical silver.

3) This silver ~~bullion~~ was purchased for investment purposes.

4) This silver is not available to the usual commercial market.

5) It is the plan of the aforenamed to use this silver for the backing of an international silver backed bond.

6) It is anticipated these bonds will be distributed through normal financial institutions. They will be in denominations small enough that persons of low income can purchase.

Nelson Bunker Hunt

That interchange was a direct admission of an illegal conspiracy. But what came next was viewed as a public admission. After this meeting, Bunker wrote out a press release in his own handwriting and edited it along with Nahas.

On March 26, 1980, at 8 a.m. in Paris, Bunker Hunt issued the press release through a Nahas associate, announcing a public offering of silver-backed bonds "by a group of silver owners" comprised of Bunker, Nahas, Fustok, Sheikh Al-Amoudi from IMIC, and HRH Prince Faysal bin Abdulla al Saoud of Saudi Arabia. "Together these persons and their associates own in excess of 200 million ounces of physical silver purchased for investment," the release continued.

Over the next several days, Nahas's press agent was peppered with inquiries, including reports that commodity houses were selling Hunt silver without their permission. He also was quoted responding to various angry accusations by saying: "Hunt and the Group were not manipulating the market, but the authorities have been."

The regulators at the CFTC, COMEX, and CBOT must have been red-faced and livid seeing Bunker, Nahas, and Fustok together in the same press release after the Hunts and Nahas had assured them they were not trading together. But surprisingly, we never asked any of the regulators for their reactions at trial. No one responded to the press release with an offer of financing. The silver markets responded badly, viewing it as a sign of desperation. Silver prices in New York opened on March 26 at $21.25 and began dropping. By the next day, Silver Thursday, prices landed at an intraday low of $10.80.

The Hunts were finished; they could not pay their margin calls. Herbert and Lamar were in New York assigned to the grim task of visiting brokerage houses that had served them well for many years. They had to announce they could not pay their margins and begin the process of unwinding the catastrophe.

Those named on the press release scrambled to distance themselves from the bond proposal. Fustok denied he authorized Bunker to use his name. Mohammed Affara said he spoke to Bunker only once about the proposal, when Bunker called Sheikh Al-Amoudi's telephone number. He also expressed Sheikh Mussalem's viewpoint, "He said it was a madness proposal . . . He said it can't work. They can't expect to have something like the OPEC cartel for silver." That was an interesting response; we could imagine that if the Sheikhs had shown up at trial, they would have been saying the Hunts misled them about IMIC's purpose.

Paul Curran had to deal with the appearance given by the press release that Bunker, Nahas, and Fustok were acting together. He did it by trying to bury the story with details. Bunker explained how silver-backed bonds work. Bunker was hoping to "bring out somebody that would be interested in getting involved in this type of financing and that was my hope." While in Paris, he talked to several people Nahas suggested who were also having margin problems.

Bunker said Prince Faisal was a friend of Nahas who authorized use of his name, and Nahas also authorized Fustok's name. Mohammed Affara authorized the use of Sheikh Al-Amoudi's name. According to Bunker, his brother Herbert opted out. "Herbert didn't think it was a very good idea. He didn't think that anything could be done and he said you better count me out, that I don't think it's a very good idea."

I started my attack on Bunker by reading from his testimony before the CFCT about Herbert:

> "Q. Was some of the silver or silver in his name going to be used to back the bonds?"
> "A. He was anxious to participate in that, yeah."

I moved on to other details in the press release. He and Nahas would each put up 100 million ounces of silver, Bunker testified. That left Fustok out, so I turned to Fustok's role. Referring back to Bunker's answer to Curran, I asked:

> "You got the impression that Mr. Fustok wanted to participate from talking to Mr. Fustok?"
> "No, I couldn't say that. I got the impression he was interested. But I may have misinterpreted the man because I can't quote him."

That answer worried me; he backed off from his testimony that Fustok had agreed to the plan. Judge Lasker saw the same point and interrupted with a question about Bunker repeated use of "impression," asking:

"Can you tell us what you mean, Mr. Hunt, when you say you got the impression? From what do you think you got the impression, what or whom?"

"Well, I believe I talked to him on the telephone about that time, your Honor. At least I'm pretty sure I said hello to him and said a few words to him and passed the phone. That was after Nahas had passed the phone to me and then I passed it back to Nahas."

The judge continued with a question that Fustok's lawyer might have been thinking at that moment:

"But you're not sure now what he said; is that right?"

"I'm really not, no, sir."

"You didn't have a face-to-face conversation with him?"

"No, I don't have any recollection of that."

"Thank you," the judge concluded and turned back toward me.

I did not want to leave that version unchallenged. I turned back to our all-important timeline, asking about his dinner with Fustok the night before the press release:

"And at that time you discussed the silver-backed bonds?"

"I don't know that they were discussed with Fustok there to tell you the truth."

That was not helpful; I had to adjust. I pulled out Fustok's testimony about the dinner, asking: "Mr. Fustok has testified that you talked about putting all your silver in one basket. Do you recall that conversation?"

Curran popped out of his chair, objecting. But the judge ignored him at first. Curran persisted, asking to have the question reread. "I heard it," the judge snapped, "I didn't see anything objectionable. It was leading." Curran tried one more time but could not move the judge; he sat down. Bunker responded rambling:

"I don't recall that ever being discussed, that there would be a combining and compiling of silver or putting it in one basket as you say. I think it was—what was discussed, with people that I spoke with, they would make silver available to a bond issue and various people might issue the bonds separately."

That was another new and troubling story; I went back to the press release: "Well, now, there's nothing about issuing bonds separately in that press release, is there, Mr. Hunt?"

"There's nothing about one as I read the press release, there is nothing about one bond being issued. It could be either way."

The judge interrupted to ask me when the dinner was. March 25, 1980, the night before the press release was released, I responded. The judge turned to Bunker who agreed it was "thereabouts."

I again went back to the press release to try to get back to inconvertible facts, first asking about the "agreement in principle."

"And that was discussed at dinner at Mr. Fustok's house where you and Mr. Fustok and Mr. Nahas had dinner shortly before this press release was issued?"

"It was discussed sometime thereabouts. I don't recall that Fustok came and went and I don't recall whether he was there the whole time it was discussed."

That answer seemed to bring the story back to a joint plan. I turned to the 200 million ounces of silver. He and Nahas would contribute 100 million ounces each, Bunker testified. But he did not recall that Fustok had said he had 30 to 40 million ounces of silver to contribute.

"If Mr. Fustok gave that testimony, you wouldn't say that's wrong?"

"No. I wasn't there the entire evening and I came and went and the other people were moving back and forth and so, you know, he could have told him anything outside of my hearing."

I continued to go through the remaining details of the press release. Bunker admitted they had not approached a financial institution, the mechanics had not been worked out, and there was no formal papers drawn up.

"Indeed, none of the details of this arrangement had been worked out at all at the time the press release was issued; is that correct?" I asked in a more emphatic voice.

"That's right. It was a press release, as I've testified, to see what the interest was." Bunker responded sounding frustrated.

I then gave the jury our explanation for the press release:

"Isn't it true, Mr. Hunt, that with none of the details of this program worked out and none of the participants formally committed to you, the reason for issuing this press release at that time was to let the world know that you had the resources to support the price of silver."

"No." Bunker barked.

I had made my point; it was a stunt that backfired. Silver prices had crashed, the Hunts could not pay their margins to brokers, and the scheme was finished. But a surprise confronted Federal Reserve Chairman Paul Volcker the day the press release was issued.

Part Nine

Hovering Near Disaster

Chapter Fifty-One

On March 26, 1980, Federal Reserve Chairman Paul Volcker was called out of a Board of Governors meeting to take a panicked call from a senior executive of Bache, the nation's second largest brokerage firm. The frantic Bache executive had just walked out of a meeting with Herbert and Lamar Hunt, he told Volcker; the Hunts could no longer meet their margin calls. As the member of the exchange that had placed Hunt trades, Bache was on the hook to pay the Hunt margins to other exchange members. If the Federal Reserve did not intervene, he continued, Bache would be bankrupt and the markets would suffer huge losses. Volcker hung up worried that a major bank might fail starting a chain reaction that could crash the economy. Volcker had been largely in the dark about the brewing storm.

Volcker quickly worked the phones to officials of the CFTC, Securities and Exchange Commission (SEC), and Comptroller of the Currency. They identified First National Bank of Chicago as the most vulnerable with $175 million in loans to the Hunts or their brokers. If silver prices dropped below $7 per ounce, the bank's collateral would not cover the loans. The bank might fail, starting a chain reaction of failures. After consulting with other financial regulators, however, Volcker decided not to intervene, particularly not to support Bache's request to close the silver markets. The CFTC wrote Bache declining to declare an emergency.

The next day, Thursday, March 27, 1980, when silver prices plummeted to $10.80, some thought it was the beginning of a panic that would bring on the next Great Depression. The *Wall Street Journal* headline the next morning read: "*Dealers Say Mart Went 'Nuts' on Hunt Woe.*" The effects of the Hunt collapse were reverberating throughout the money markets as investors looked for safe havens. *The New York Times* breathlessly reported under the headline, "*Silver's Plunge Jolts Hunts' Empire and Brings Turmoil to Wall Street*": "The upheaval threatened at least one major brokerage house, prompting Government intervention to prevent stampede selling in its shares and driving the price of silver still lower." But, in fact, the government had not intervened. The Dow Jones Industrial Average was down significantly in "hectic trading." The Hunts problems were now threatening the general economy.

According to the *Times*, officials were shaken. Coming out of a meeting with Paul Volcker, "Treasury Secretary G. William Miller, preoccupied by the crash in silver prices and its far-reaching repercussions, was late for National Press Club luncheon speech on March 27 and made a number of errors in the speech." Deputy Secretary Robert Carswell cancelled plans to attend the luncheon in order to deal with the fallout from the Hunts' default on $100 million Bache Group margin call, the *Times* reported.

On Friday silver prices steadied closing at $13.99, allowing brokers to sell Hunt collateral to cover some of their outstanding margins deficits. The reason for that bounce was to surprise Congressional investigators just months later. Bache announced it had liquidated the Hunt silver futures and bullion, and "the liquidation did not result in any loss to Bache." That turned out to be untrue. The Federal Reserve thought the worst was over.

Paul Volcker later learned that his October 6th directive instructing banks to refrain from lending for speculative investments had been ignored when applied to the Hunts. As silver prices pulled back in February and March 1980, major banks had lent more than $800 million to the Hunt brokers to support their silver escapade, the equivalent of 10 percent of all bank lending in the United States the previous two months. Bache had lent the Hunts $233 million, Merrill Lynch a whopping $492 million, and E.F. Hutton added $104 million. Some banks accused the brokers of misleading them, claiming they had no idea they were indirectly lending to the Hunts for their silver speculation.

On Friday evening, Volcker learned he had another problem. The $1 billion exchange for physical (EFP) that had saved Engelhard from the price spike in January was about to unravel. The Hunts were due on Monday, March 30, 1980, to take delivery of silver bullion from Engelhard at the high mid-January prices. When the silver markets crashed, Engelhard executives rushed to Dallas to negotiate with the Hunts. Engelhard was demanding $665 million in cash, which the Hunts did not have.

Now, a major metals dealer was teetering too. As Volcker later described the situation to a Congressional committee: "Engelhard, felt they might be faced with a decision on Monday to sue the Hunts for payment, forcing probable bankruptcy and possibly triggering massive liquidation of silver positions to the peril of all creditor institutions (and indirectly placing in jeopardy the customers and creditors of those institutions in a financial chain reaction). The alternative, as the company saw it, was to negotiate, with the help of some banks, a credit to the Hunts or intermediaries that could provide time for repayment and avoid forced liquidation of silver in an already nervous, depressed market."

This time, Volcker did not want to stand aside. That likely would have meant Engelhard's failure, followed by the failure of its banks, and a chain reaction leading to general economic chaos. The question for Volcker was whether a loan to the Hunts to pay off Engelhard would breach Volcker's October 6th directive regarding lending for speculative purposes. Volcker had just reissued the directive on March 14, 1980, accompanied, for the first time, with bank examinations to act as an enforcement mechanism.

Volcker decided to grace the negotiations. By coincidence, the Association of Reserve City Bankers was meeting that weekend in Boca Raton, Florida, which brought Volcker together with senior executives from the vulnerable banks. Bunker, Herbert, and Lamar Hunt flew in from Dallas with Engelhard representatives. During an all-night negotiating session on Sunday night, Volcker received hourly updates.

After midnight on Sunday, the bankers walked away; they did not want to take on the risk associated with a billion dollar loan to the Hunts. An Engelhard lawsuit and a Hunt bankruptcy appeared imminent on Monday morning. However, working feverishly through the remainder of the night, Engelhard and the Hunts negotiated a workout under which Engelhard kept its silver bullion and the Hunts gave it valuable oil leases in the Beaufort Sea in Canada in return for a release from Engelhard's claims to $665 million. Monday, March 31, 1980, passed without a crisis.

The Hunts still had other debts to pay to their brokers and banks. For instance, the Bache announcement that it had not suffered any loss was $50 million short of the truth. On Monday, March 31, 1980, Bache had to issue another press release to correct its error. A Bache audit committee report later explained the self-inflicted damage to its reputation: "The uncertainties carried by the successive press releases served to further undermine confidence in [Bache] at a time when its viability was threatened . . ." Bache never recovered. In 1981, Bache was acquired by Prudential Financial, renamed Prudential-Bache Securities. In 1991, the Bache name was dropped. The firm that traced its roots

to 1879 was no longer due to its miscalculation in supporting Bunker Hunt's scheme.

The bank negotiations resumed over the next several
weeks, eventually resulting in a $1.1 billion loan from a
consortium of twenty-three banks to a partnership created
with the Hunt's oil company, Placid Oil Company. Volcker
informally blessed the deal. The Hunts and their brokers
were, thus, bailed out. Silver prices bounced back to the $10
to $15 range over the next several months. The reason for
that bump also was not known until Henry Jarecki testified before Congress two months later.

Volcker was widely criticized for his decision. Federal
Reserve Governor Henry Wallich, a former member of
President Eisenhower's Council of Economic Advisors and
an economic columnist for *Newsweek*, was quoted as saying: "Suppose a large firm had gone bust. It wouldn't have
been the end of the world. It would have been a great tragedy, but it would have been a disaster on a smaller scale.
The argument against doing anything was: let the bankers
and the brokers take their lumps." Retired Reserve Governor Philip Coldwell expressed a similar view: "I was very
unhappy with the chairman that he let Bunker Hunt off the
hook. Hunt clearly was trying to corner silver, and I thought
he should pay the price. In my very simplistic way of looking at it, I didn't see anything wrong with the banks paying the price too."

The Federal Reserve put out a statement denying the
Federal Reserve or Volcker had "initiated" efforts to obtain

bank loans, and the Federal Reserve had not "approved" the loans. Volcker, who was at an IMF meeting in Hamburg, Germany, was not available for comment. But he had to come home some time, and when he did, he had to endure months of grilling at Congressional hearings. One subcommittee chairman, Benjamin Rosenthal, suggested that Volcker was "naïve" to believe loan terms could keep the Hunts from using the money to speculate in silver. Volcker responded that their investments would be monitored "to the extent humanly possible," but he added, "I am not running a police department."

In a dry recitation at trial, Bunker explained that he and his two brothers got the loan by pledging all their personal assets and their interests in the family oil company, Placid Oil. The brokerage houses were repaid with the loan, as were all other creditors. At that point, most of their silver futures contracts and most of their silver had been sold. Over time IMIC's silver positions were sold to pay its debts, Bunker testified, "IMIC essentially just discontinued doing business after that."

In 1980, the crisis passed quickly. If Bache or Merrill Lynch had failed in 1980, the financial wreckage might not have been contained. Their failure likely would have brought down several major banks, which in turn would have spread economic pain throughout the economy. That scenario was played out almost three decades later when Lehman Brother, the fourth largest investment bank, was allowed to fail, brought down by uncontrolled derivative trading. Ironically, a decade before the 2008 Great Recession, the lead lawyer for Banque Populaire Suisse, Brooksley Born, warned of the dangers of unregulated derivatives trading in her new position as chairman of the CFTC. An impressive array of public officials admonished her. According to her CFTC colleagues, the blood drained from her face from a tongue-lashing by White House Chief of Staff Larry Summers—more from fury than intimidation, I suspect. But, she and Volcker were proven right when the turmoil from the Lehman failure drove stock prices down by 57 percent; unemployment skyrocketed from 5% to 10%; housing values declined by 30%; and mortgage foreclosures exploded. US gross domestic product (GDP) was not anticipated to recover for a decade.

I ran into Paul Volcker yet another decade later. Tall and stately looking, he did not look like he had aged much when he sat down opposite me on an Acela Express from New York to Washington. After I got up the nerve to introduce myself, he quizzed me about what ever happened to Bunker and Herbert. I asked him how he felt about the Congressional criticism he took for bailing out the Hunts; he paused for a minute thinking, shook his head, and then responded: "I don't remember losing any sleep over it." I suppose you sleep well when you are right.

Chapter Fifty-Two

The police departments for the futures markets were supposed to be at the CFTC and the exchanges, but the Congressional hearings disclosed that at least one member of
the COMEX police force had done quite well in the midst of
the silver crisis. After Black Thursday, silver prices bounced
back to the $15 to $20 range for the remainder of 1980. Henry
Jarecki explained the reason to the Senate Subcommittee
on Agriculture, Nutrition and General Legislation in May
1980. "Mocatta, together with a number of commercial and
investment bankers," he said, "organized a syndicate of
buyers to purchase the entire overhang of silver at reasonable
prices. Clients throughout the world had expressed an interest after that Silver Thursday in purchasing this silver . . ."

That sounded like the same type of illegal cartel that the
Hunts had just executed, which was not lost on Subcommittee Chairman Donald W. Stewart who interrupted
asking:

"I assume this was out of the goodness of your heart, or
to save your market?"

Jarecki, not hesitating, responded: "Not at all, Senator. I was motivated by man's noblest motive, greed. As I am sure you are aware from your studies of history, Chunilal Sayara, chairman of the India Specie Bank, tried to corner the silver market from the years 1910 to 1913. He kept buying up silver confident that the Chinese and Indian Governments would eventually buy it from him because they would need silver for monetary purposes. When, in 1913, they failed to do so, the Indian Specie Bank failed, Chunilal committed suicide, and Mocatta organized a syndicate that took over the 26 million ounces that he had acquired. Mocatta and its associates sold that silver to the market over the next 3 to 6 months at a good profit. And so 57 years later, we would have been happy to do it again."

To which Senator Stewart had a quick retort: "Carrying on that tradition?"

"Carrying on the tradition of being there to help," Jarecki responded without embarrassment and quickly added a speech, which mischaracterize the results of the Hunts escapade, saying, "the only group which suffered any substantial economic harm were those who believed that the price of silver would continue to climb and backed that belief with speculative capital . . . It is not a national calamity when people who are hoping to profit by accepting a risk lose money."

He continued with a lecture on the value of markets free from government interference. He left out of his self-serving lecture, Minpeco, a hedger, thousands of companies that relied upon silver, and thousands of traders relied upon an unmanipulated market . . .

After Senator Stewart took a recess for a vote, he returned to express his skepticism, which prompted the following exchange:

"Dr. Jarecki, I am going to put this on the record. Did you receive an invitation from Agriculture Committee staff to appear here today?"

"That is correct," Jarecki responded.

"When is the first time you had any contact with me, personally, at this hearing or in connection with this hearing?"

"During the last half hour," Jarecki responded.

"OK, thank you. Go ahead," Senator Stewart continued, "*I just wanted to disassociate myself with some of your remarks.*"

That prompted laughter, according to the Congressional Record. But not everyone was laughing.

And even Jarecki was not so full of himself several months later when he asked for a meeting with CFTC Commissioner Read Dunn. Jarecki told Dunn that Mocatta "had made lots of money selling this on the market." He wanted "to discuss conflict of interest problems," according to Dunn's memo. "He expressed concern that [COMEX] and Mocatta might get criticized unduly for their activities in the silver market during last winter." Jarecki seemed to be lobbying Dunn to keep the CFTC's investigation of the silver debacle confidential. "His concern was for how it might be used in private legal actions."

Beyond his admission of a silver cartel to prop up prices, Jarecki does not appear to have disclosed to Commissioner Dunn or anyone else in an official capacity at that time, the 800 March 1980 long contracts that Mocatta bought with IMIC's guarantee. Mocatta held onto those 800 long contracts through the price peak of $51 on January 21, 1980 when they represented a potential $120 million profit and began selling on March 14, 1980, netting a profit in the range of $20 million with little risk due to IMIC's guarantee. Jarecki certainly should have known the likely price impact of liquidation-only trading that shut the longs out of the futures markets in January 1980. As *Fortune* pointed out: "A market . . . comprising only sellers obviously could only collapse." With a collapsing price, Jarecki must have known his 800 long contracts would lose value, but his contract with IMIC required him to hold onto the contracts until March 1980. Even his sale in mid-March 1980 put downward pressure on silver prices, which led to IMIC to sue Mocatta in Bermuda.

Nonetheless, Jarecki's boast that he made a killing on silver seems well founded with Mocatta's profits from the Bache positions and the hidden 800 long contracts guaranteed by IMIC. Jarecki later bought not one, but two, Caribbean islands, and he was elected to the Futures Industry Association Hall of Fame.

I wonder what the inscription said?

Chapter Fifty-Three

During the spring and summer 1980, Bunker Hunt, Naji Nahas, and Mahmoud Fustok had to unwind the shambles of their scheme. These negotiations provided considerable insights into their relationships. That is when we could get it into evidence.

Sitting in one of the seemingly endless sessions of Bunker's pretrial deposition, my colleague, Paul Clayman, started reading upside down an unfamiliar document entitled "Agreement" sitting on the table in front of one of the Hunt lawyers. When we questioned them about it, they claimed it was irrelevant, but when we persisted, they hurdled various ugly invectives at our ethics. When Judge Lasker ordered the document produced, it was another stunner. It was an agreement dated April 1980 among Bunker and Herbert Hunt, Mahmoud Fustok, and Naji Nahas to share their silver losses, unimpeachable evidence of a conspiracy we thought.

After the silver markets crashed, ContiCommodity and Banque Populaire Suisse began chasing Advicorp, Nahas, and Fustok to cover their losses. At a meeting in early April 1980 at Banque Populaire Suisse, Nahas and Fustok agreed to pool funds to save Advicorp. According to one of the bankers, Fustok dictated a proposed loss-sharing agreement to compensate Banque Populaire Suisse for its silver losses.

Fustok also told a ContiCommodity official that he would help Nahas in settling his accounts. On April 2, 1980 at Mahmoud Fustok's home in Chantilly, France, Nahas, Norton Waltuch, and another ContiCommodity executive gathered to discuss Nahas's outstanding balances. The Conti official testified:

"Was there a proposal put forward by Mr. Fustok concerning the settlement of those accounts?"

"Yes. There was a proposal of perhaps a guarantee that would be provided."

"By whom?" Judge Lasker jumped in.

"Well, Mr. Fustok was suggesting that, and he was at that time also suggesting that perhaps Mr. Hunt would."

"During this meeting, was it proposed that Mr. Nahas and Mr. Fustok and Mr. Hunt would all execute this particularly guarantee?"

"I believe that's correct," the Conti official responded, "that was the suggestion made."

According to the Conti official, Fustok called Bunker and "suggested some form of document to be drafted."

However, when we tried to get the Agreement in evidence, we ran into a roadblock. Bob Perry, our elder statesman, usually dispensed wisdom from the background, but we wanted an experienced advocate arguing for the admission of such an important document. After Bob's perfectly structured presentation, Judge Lasker studied the document briefly and barked: "Denied. *That's crappy evidence!*" Bob looked shocked, as was I. The usual mild-mannered Judge Lasker did not often show such bite. Bob recovered and tried to argue with him but the judge just repeated: "That's crappy evidence." We could not fathom the ruling; the judge did not cite a rule for crappy evidence.

Bob took solace when the team named a new principle of law after his effort: the "Crappy Evidence Rule." Raoul Gonzalez blew up the quote from the transcript to hang on Bob's office door, an honor saved for only the best trial quotes. The jury never saw the division of losses agreement.

Fustok and ContiCommodity, however, could not settle their differences about the 182 contracts that Nahas had told them to put in Fustok's account. Fustok adamantly would not accept responsibility for them. We got to play to the jury two telephone conversations record by a Conti official with Fustok on May 19, 1980. Fustok came across as much more sophisticated and knowledgeable than he tried to appear in his testimony. And he further tied Bunker to Nahas, telling the Conti official: "You know very well that these are Mr. Nahas' and Mr. Hunt's . . . This is what Mr. Nahas says." Fustok stayed adamant about those contracts, and after ContiCommodity liquidated his account to cover loss on those contracts, Fustok sued and the dispute was not settled until several days into the Fustok's trial against ContiCommodity in 1987.

Bunker also had scores to settle. His dispute with Swiss Bank Corporation about the $90 million in Hunt silver he had pledge for Litardex, Nahas's company, remained unresolved, and Bunker owed Nahas $4.5 million from his February and March 1980 silver purchases. Bunker, Herbert, and IMIC had transferred a total of $108 million to Nahas, but Nahas had financed the remaining $82 million and held Bunker's silver bullion as collateral. When the markets crashed, Bunker's good friend, Nahas, had liquidated the bullion for a $4.5 million loss. Those two transactions were negotiated together.

On April 18, 1980, Bunker sent Swiss Bank Corporation a letter attempting to withdraw his March 17 instruction to guarantee Litardex's debt, which, of course, the bank would not accept. According to Bunker, "the Swiss lawyers said, 'Well, the bank is just like the government of Switzerland, you can't sue it.'" Six or eight months later, Bunker, Nahas, and the bank worked out a settlement. The bank would release the Hunt silver subject to its settlement with Nahas. After an extended negotiation, the Hunts paid Swiss Bank $14.5 million to release their $90 million in silver bullion. Nahas released his $4.5 million debt and gave the Hunts a remote property in Brazil that proved worthless to them because Brazilian law did not permit the sale of land to foreigners.

At the end of 1980, Bunker also resolved matters with his children to release the debt they owed him for covering their margin calls in March 1980. He took all their assets.

"Yes. I talked to them about it. I talked to Mrs. Hunt, my wife, and, unfortunately, that was the only thing that could be done that I knew of because the debt was just clearly beyond their capacity to pay it."

This was more of the poor-Hunt routine that the judge had ruled was irrelevant, but I did not object. I did not find it sympathetic and I did not think the jury would.

Surprisingly, Bunker was still not through with Naji Nahas who seemed to have an unusual hold over him. Bunker continued to sell thoroughbred horses to Nahas. Several years later, Nahas came through Dallas to ask Bunker for a loan. "He's a very persuasive talker. I guess maybe I got a little soft touch attitude toward him," Bunker added quizzically. Nahas said he needed $2 million for thirty days and he would exchange checks with him for one on a French bank. Even after the silver crash, Bunker apparently still had $2 million to lend Nahas. Nahas kept talking but not paying for two years until Bunker sued him in France. That prompted Nahas to pay.

But Bunker still would not cut him off entirely. "He still calls me occasionally, three, four, five times a year in the last couple of years . . . I never want to turn against someone I consider a friend," Bunker lamented.

Part Ten

Closing, Verdict and Afterwards

Chapter Fifty-Four

The trial crawled to an exhausted conclusion six months after it began. After the major players testified, the defense called a series of forgettable witnesses before they rested their case. We finished with a rebuttal expert who presented a report that concluded the Hunts owned 70 percent of the US silver supplies at the height of their accumulation, which amount to a *per se* monopoly. I ran into the expert years later playing tennis; he remembered how attentive the jury had remained even at the close of the trial.

Once the testimony finally ended, the big guns for the defense—Paul Curran, Peter Fleming, and Paul Perito— gave their final arguments. Curran started with the theme for the defense: "Nonsense is precisely what the record shows Minpeco's distorted version of conspiracy is . . . your common sense, your everyday experience will tell you Minpeco's claim of conspiracy just does not add up." He and his colleagues spent hours dissecting our case before the alert jurors.

Closing argument before the jury

Paul Perito continued the assault by defending IMIC as an ordinary business company, but also including a well-deserved compliment to the judge, "I would be remiss if I didn't mention to you that as heavy as your burden has been to sit here, you have also had a unique opportunity. You have sat and participated before a federal judge who has conducted this trial with decorum, with politeness, with respect for the participants and with a sense of humor that has kept some perspective on what we are about."

Peter Fleming concluded with one more attack on Ismael Fonseca's trading decisions, and saying, "The fact that these defendants, by any ordinary terms, are men of wealth does not make it right to give Minpeco money Monpeco does not deserve . . . That would be wrong . . . I believe you have a chance to right a wrong . . ."

I split Minpeco's final argument with Tom Gorman. I opened our final argument with an emotional plea: "Ladies and gentlemen, I would like to start my summation on a somewhat personal note. I wouldn't do that except I feel that it has relevance to your deliberations. This case has been an enormous burden. It's been a burden for me. I know that Mr. Gorman has felt it and our team has too. It has been a burden because it's not an ordinary case. This is a case that involves major economic events that occurred in the United States. The defendants are a small group of men—Bunker Hunt, Herbert Hunt, Lamar Hunt, one of their companies, IMIC, Mahmoud Fustok, and other men who have chosen not to come here—who created a near catastrophe of the American economy and a catastrophe for Minpeco. Only you, the jury, can tell these men that they were wrong and only you, the jury, can compensate Minpeco for its losses."

Tom and I spent the remainder of the day bashing the defense. I concluded by quoting Ismael Fonseca, "I thought we were dealing in an honest and trustworthy environment, which not only assigned responsibilities, but had its own too." And I continued, "Minpeco has fulfilled its obligations. It traded in what it believed was an honest market. It took responsibility and paid [its] margins. It closed it positions in a responsible manner. The defendants didn't do that. They rigged the market. They intentionally hurt innocent people."

The Judge Lasker gave the weekend off. After about an hour of legal instructions from the judge on Monday morning, the jury retired to their room at the back of the courtroom to decide whether the defendants had intentionally increased silver prices in December 1979 and damaged Minpeco. Two hours later they sent out a note with a question about damages. That implied they had already decided the defendants were liable. We were elated, imaging a quick victory.

But Tuesday melded into Wednesday and then Thursday. Euphoria flowed into concern. On Friday, the jury reported they were deadlocked on damages. Concern turned to distress. Would we have to do this again? The judge gave the jury what is commonly known as an "Allen charge," which reminded them that we all had spent an enormous time, expense, and energy to try the case.

The next morning, August 20, 1988, they returned the verdict, $65.7 million in damages, which when trebled under the racketeering and antitrust laws meant a $197.1 million recovery for Minpeco which less the $63 million in pretrial settlements from the financial institutions, resulted in a judgment of $134 million. Only Lamar Hunt was spared a finding of racketeering, although he was found liable on the other charges.

On our team, there was a lot of laughing, clapping backs, and handshakes, but in reality, I was too numb and relieved for the impact to set in. We learned later that the jury had indeed decided liability in two hours, but the nurse and the retired policeman had argued for the remaining six days over damages. She held out for the full amount and he wanted to give Minpeco $20 million, an amount that the Hunts had leaked to the press as their mid-trial settlement offer. Although they had leaked the amount—or at least I thought they had—the Hunt lawyers blamed me for the leak, which led to an extraordinary exchange in his robing room; Judge Lasker turned to me and entered a gag order of me personally, over my protests.

The verdict was a glorious victory. Thirty years later I can see the many ways the verdict changed my life, but at the time, I had no conception. We did not have any experience dealing with the now swarming reporters. We walked down the courthouse steps to the waiting cameras and gave a few ill-prepared quotes. *The New York Times*, with a headline "*Hunts Are Ruled Part of a Scheme to Control Silver*," reported: "The Hunts looked grim as they left the court after the verdict was read shortly before noon. All three, who had testified in the trial and who sat impassively through six days of intense, suspenseful jury deliberations, declined to answer questions from reporters." The *Wall Street Journal* headline announced "*Jurors Order Hunt Brothers to Pay Minpeco*." In Peru, the headline read "*Round ganado por el*

Hunt brothers walking out of court

Peru." The Hunts generally did not comment; Paul Curran announced they would appeal, and added: "The Hunts lost money in the 1980 silver market too, resulting in a $1.1 billion bailout loan. If they were in a conspiracy . . . it was the most poorly executed, disorganized conspiracy."

As I was packing the next morning to return home, I got a call from our public relations firm; the *Today* show wanted me to appear on Monday morning. I could not fathom what I would say to Bryant Gumbel and a morning TV audience, but it obviously was a unique career opportunity. However, I hesitated only a moment before turned it down. I was feeling exhausted and accepted a guilty about what my family had endured during the long absence of trial. I was not going to stay another day in New York. I heard that Herb Deutsch took the *Today* show appearance. Although I did not see him, I imagine he told the story in a more entertaining way than I might have.

That probably was not my smartest career move, but I was already moving on to my next big case. In the middle of the Hunt trial, a market maker in index options had called me. He had been one of the big losers during the October 1987 stock market crash when Bear Stearns had taken over his positions without a margin call. He was in the midst of a $50 million dispute and wanted a lawyer gutsy enough to sue the exchanges. I had to prepare for an important hearing just weeks after the verdict.

I quickly learned that my status in a courtroom had changed with the Hunt verdict. The hearing was before a different judge in the same courthouse. When I confidently walked in, the courtroom deputy greeted me with a big hello; she had substituted several times in Judge Lasker's courtroom. The judge, however, was frosty, examining my every word. I was no longer the young underdog who got the benefit of the doubt when confronting more experienced opponents. That status was forever gone.

Minpeco organized a post-trial celebration, but Ismael Fonseca did not attend. Years later, Luis Galliani found his daughter for me. She told us his fate. Once a new democratic government replaced the military dictatorship, the courts rejected the criminal charges against him and Juan Munar. Fonseca tried to start an export–import business, but it failed; then he tried to work on the Lima stock exchange as a broker. He always felt his past haunted him. In later years, he spent time helping old-age pensioners get better treatment, much like the work he had done for Minpeco's workers. He had a heart attack and died at the age of sixty-eight years on August 20, 2002, fourteen years to the day after the verdict.

Within weeks of the verdict, Bunker and Herbert Hunt filed for bankruptcy because the Internal Revenue Service (IRS) was threatening to impose jeopardy assessments due to an unrelated tax dispute. The IRS feared we would take the bulk of the Hunt assets not in one of their many trusts. Lamar Hunt who owned the Kansas City Chiefs football team and world team tennis avoided bankruptcy by settling with us. Judge Lasker suggested at a post-verdict hearing that he might dismiss the case against Lamar because he had a minor role in the conspiracy and perhaps we had not proved enough about him. That prompted a settlement that ended the case against Lamar.

Since I had already moved to my next case, Tom Gorman took over as lead counsel for the Hunt bankruptcy. I heard one early story that made me laugh. The Hunt lawyers had to get approval from a Dallas judge for their representation of Bunker and Herbert in the bankruptcy. When they explained their hefty hourly rates, the skeptical judge cracked, "Can't we get some lawyers from Brooklyn?" Aaron Rubinstein, Paul Curran's young partner, had the unfortunate job of bearing that indignity.

The bankruptcy, however, seemed to depress all of Dallas, according to one news report: "The outcome of the

Hunts' story could have a significant psychological impact on how this city sees itself and how it is seen by others," said Dan Weston, an associate dean at Southern Methodist University's business school. "If people see J.R. (Ewing) lose his fortune, they're going to think Texas must be going down the tubes," said Weston, referring to the fictional Ewings of the "Dallas" TV series.

Bunker and Herbert won that tax trial, and later settled other charges with the IRS. Bunker and Herbert also settled with the CFTC, which had charged them with manipulating silver prices. They paid fines of $10 million and accepted a lifetime bar on future trading. The settlements helped them emerge from bankruptcy. Bunker retired from public view and died in 2014 from heart failure; he had been battling Alzheimer's disease for many years. Herbert continued in business and reportedly returned to the ranks of billionaires by 2013.

The other key trial participants made news in later years in various ways. In 1989, Naji Nahas, in another financial fiasco, bounced $29 million in checks to Brazilian brokerage houses, forcing Brazilian authorities to close the stock and options markets for a day. The scandal reportedly caused $500 million in losses and the liquidation of five brokerage houses.

Two decades after our trial, Mahmoud Fustok was hit by a car and killed while jogging across the street from the Pompano Park racetrack in Florida, ironically a few hundred yards from where my parents once owned a condominium. I had attended that racetrack during my regular visits to see my parents without knowing I must have been watching Fustok's horses race. Fustok had realized one of his lifelong dreams just months before his death when his horse, Silver Train, won the prestigious Breeders Cup Sprint.

Norton Waltuch also spent time with his thoroughbred horses. His horse "Miss Legality" won the Black-Eyed Susan Stakes in 1992 at Pimlico Racetrack outside of Baltimore.

In 2002, the State Department wrote Swiss prosecutors accusing Sheikh Ali bin Mussalem of indirectly funding Al Qaeda. Shortly after the letter became public, Mussalem was found dead in his home in Lausanne, an unsolved mystery worthy of a John Le Carré novel. His partner, Mohammed Aboud Al-Amoudi, never lost his stride after the trial. In 2013, *Forbes* estimated he was worth $8 billion and did an interview about his focus on philanthropy.

Paul Curran remained the head of litigation at his Park Avenue law firm. *The New York Times* later in his obituary said: "He was most at home in a trial courtroom, winning many civil and criminal cases and the admiration of colleagues." Aaron Rubinstein eventually took over as the head litigator of the law firm. I heard one story about Rubinstein that touched home. Twenty years after our trial, he ran into my niece who had been hired as a young associate out of Harvard Law School apparently without his knowledge; he reacted: "Cymrot! Are you related to . . .

How did you get in here!" which I hope was a good-natured jest.

Three years after our trial, Peter Fleming caught the Washington limelight, when as special counsel to the US Senate he investigated Anita Hill's allegations of sexual harassment against Supreme Court nominee Clarence Thomas. In 1998, Fleming won yet another high-profile acquittal for Don King, the boxing promoter. "The guy saved my life," King said of Fleming and continued, "I think that Clarence Darrow will be standing there welcoming Peter to lawyer's heaven."

Paul Perito continued as one of Washington, DC prominent trial lawyers until 1999 when he left private law practice to become the General Counsel and eventually the Chairman of Star Scientific, Inc., a public company listed on the NASDAQ that developed smokeless cigarettes. Perito also became Chairman of the Board of the Washington Workshops Foundation, a nonprofit that received the Freedom Foundation Award for its excellence in bringing thousands of qualified junior high and high school students to Washington to understand the functioning of the federal government. Years later, we joined the same country club and enjoyed many friendly conversations.

In 1989, 180 major banks sued the Peruvian government for nonpayment of commercial loans. Peru was bankrupt and could not pay, and a young, brash president was not willing to negotiate with the banks. Following our victory for Minpeco, Peru knew a trial lawyer. I organized a team to defend $10 billion in fifty-five lawsuits worldwide with the fifteen lead cases in same New York courthouse that I had just left.

But that is another story for another day.

Acknowledgments

Compared to impressive credentials of the ten major law firms of the defense, Cole Corette & Abrutyn was unknown to the stage of major litigation. We had assembled a trial team largely at the beginnings of their careers. Often sitting down the trial table, Scott Andersen would lean back surveying the scene, fiddling with his pen and notepad. Scott and I had spent our first months plowing through thousands of subpoenaed documents. When he found a small gem, Scott would come charging down the hall, waving his long arms with unbound enthusiasm, shouting: "Look what I found! Look what I found!" I always flinched when this tall, broad-shouldered, blond freight train came bursting into my office. He molded hundreds of thousands of documents into a chronology of events that became the framework for almost all the work we did in preparing the case and helped with almost every task that could be done during trial, including preparing "Way Beyond Greed," a summary of the evidence that he named after a book by Stephen Faye. I used Scott's work to write this book.

Tom Gorman, our recruit from the Securities and Exchange Commission (SEC), would sit next to me, leaning forward with his fist clenched, listening intently when he was not the examiner. Tom, a tall, lanky, muscular jogger was a quiet and intense guy who mostly kept to himself. Tom led the team prosecuting our case against Merrill Lynch until it settled; he also took major depositions, like Herbert Hunt's, and examined key witnesses at trial. He was so cantankerous that the defense lawyers would plead with me to rein him in. Apparently, I was viewed as the nice guy. I never understood why they thought I would back him off, but I always talked in soothing tones when they brought it up.

The third original team member, Raoul Gonzalez, had organized this treasure trove of hundreds of thousands of pages of documents from the Hunts, their brokers, others around Wall Street, Swiss banks, hotels, travel agencies, telephone companies, and many others. Raoul would sit looking painfully nervous at the end of our table. A slim Cuban refuge, he had been a flight attendant who had survived two plane crashes before becoming a paralegal. In the second crash, the pilot was circling to drop fuel in preparation for an emergency landing but instead dropped all the fuel. That experience convinced Raoul crashing around courtrooms was safer than crashing in airplanes.

Today we use computers to scan and word-search voluminous documents for relevant information. In those days, we read everything and made multiple copies to organize them by date, subject matter, and various other categories. We had a storeroom packed with paper. But Raoul could find anything. A typical conversation he had with Tom Gorman went: "Raoul, I remember a telex; there were several copies, but I want the one with a handwritten note in the lower right corner of the second page. That note is essential. I am in the middle of a deposition. I need it now!" Raoul invariably came back promptly with an innocent: "Is this it?" which he knew very well was it. He had not only organized the documents, but also read and understood their importance.

Raoul had another asset for an overwrought litigation team: he told funny stories on himself. My favorite story was Raoul's first assignment as a flight attendant, a story he told while adding a particularly thick accent. He was just out of flight training school when a dispatcher called him in Seattle and said: "Gonzalez, ferry on down to San Francisco, I have a flight for you." When he got off the phone, he thought to himself, "Ferry, ferry; this is an airline, why is he telling me to ferry to San Francisco? Oh well, that's what the man said." He scurried on down to the docks, found a boat heading to San Francisco (who knew boats ferried between Seattle and San Francisco), and eagerly showed up at the dispatcher's office.

"Gonzalez, Gonzalez? I don't have a plane for Gonzalez . . . Wait a minute! Wait a minute! You're the Gonzalez who was supposed to be here two days ago! Where have you been?"

"You said ferry down to San Francisco," Raoul said meekly, "I came directly from the docks."

One wonders why his flying career did not end in its infancy. From then on whenever he met a new crew, they would say: "Gonzalez, you're the guy who took the boat!" And everyone would laugh, including Raoul. Although he was immune to plane crashes, angry dispatchers, and late night drives through snowstorms to file pleadings, Raoul died in one of the first waves of the AIDS epidemic shortly after trial. But before that tragedy, he was the heart of a team that grew to twenty professionals, I recounted in his eulogy. At the time, we barely understood the cause of our loss.

Reynaldo Pastor, our Peruvian intern, only spoke broken English when he first joined us. We established a rule: he could speak only English in the mornings but could revert to Spanish in the afternoons. He would speak with Raoul and another young lawyer, Pedro Pierluisi, or with Luis Galliani, Minpeco's General Counsel when he was in town. Pedro took his first deposition on the eve of trial when defendants added another expert to their witness list. After Pedro's two hours of examination, the defense thought better of the idea and withdrew the expert. Lucho was our invaluable window into Minpeco and Peru, and a steady source of well-thought-out advice. He also provided me with a steady supply of Manzania, a Peruvian chamomile tea, to keep me calm throughout the trial.

Bob Perry, our graying eminence, would take his usual modest place at the end of our trial table. Shortly before trial, we added his many years of experience to the team to assuage our anxiety about our first appearance on the big stage. No one on our team had experience with a trial of this magnitude. Bob provided thoughtful advice throughout the trial and kept us calm during some of the more intense moments. Several years after trial, Bob Perry retired, sold his home, moved onto a sailboat, and lived on it for years touring the Caribbean. Periodically, I would hear stories about him from Ted Sonde, like he was blown into the ocean during a storm, saved by a safety line and his wife's quick thinking.

Herbert I. Deutsch, the counsel to one of the class action lawsuits that paralleled our case, shared the pretrial discovery tasks with us and taught me a lot about litigating. When my first instinct was to pull out a subpoena to get information, Herb had a much more direct approach. He would pick up the telephone or get on a plane to meet a potential witness and simply ask questions. Herb's technique has proved to be much more efficient and effective over the years. Nobody ever accused Herb of being dull in performing any task. Watching him cross-examination a witness was always an entertaining—if not hair-raising experience—I could never imitate but I could try to emulate.

Many of our team continued to show their great skills and dedication as they went on to great success: Tom Gorman, Roger Colazzi, and Bill McGrath later led litigation departments at prominent law firms, and Scott Andersen became managing partner of the Geneva office of a major international law firm. Pedro Pierluisi became Attorney General of Puerto Rico, later its elected representative in the US Congress, and a successful senior statesman for Puerto Rico. Reynaldo Pastor became the World Bank's chief lawyer for Latin America. Paul Clayman became Chief Counsel to the Senate Foreign Relations Committee and head of the DC office of the UN Development Program; he left our firm before trial, a decision we continue debate these many years later over lunch. Kathy Milton defended the United States in international arbitration cases at the State Department. Gigi Murphy, a paralegal before trial, was our first witness; she became a diplomat, left the State Department to home school her kids, and then returned to law school and a legal career at a Delaware law firm.

Bill McGrath married Brenda Nelson, the secretary to our senior partner who pitched in during trial. Brenda had a lasting effect on me. During one tense evening of preparation, she turned to me and said: "Do you realize that you never say thank you. We all know that you mean thank you, but you never say it." I was shocked, of course. And I have never forgotten to say thank you ever since. But more than that, I realized that in the tense world of trial law, taking the time to stop and exchange a few words of greetings or a personal story lightens the mood, binds the team, and makes everyone's life more pleasant, including mine. She made me a nicer guy.

Other member of our trial team who worked tireless days, nights, and weekends for many months included Jim McNamara, Michelle Bartoli, Mark Weinress, Carol Ann Brideau, Jeanette Roberts, Lorie Goode, Susan Herlick, and many others. I appreciate the confidence that Ted Sonde and the founding partners of Cole, Corette & Abrutyn showed in me. Hendrik Houthakker, Leslie Jordan, Maurice J. Whalen, and Bruce Malashevich were our excellent expert witnesses. Steve Groo and his colleagues at FTI Consulting were masters of trial graphics and spent many late nights in the cumbersome process in those days of editing the deposition transcripts that we showed to the jury. Art Patterson and Ann Greeley, now with DecisionQuest, helped us with very insightful jury research and during the all-important days of picking a jury.

Judge Lasker continued his distinguished career on the bench of the Manhattan federal court and then transferred to the Boston federal court to be closer to his children and grandchildren. He died at ninety-two. US District Judge Nina Gershon (when she was a US Magistrate) had the unenviable task of herding us through the pretrial discovery process. I remember one hearing when Tom Kavaler, counsel for E.F. Hutton, was unloading on me while she was trying to control his bombastic style. She succeeded. But I remember thinking that if I had accepted the job offer from his law firm, we would have been in the same freshman class, and he would have buried me before I could grow up some. I also thank Maureen Cloonan for her fine work on sourcing the research.

This book came about after I joined the board of the Writer's Center (writer.org) and attended our workshops. My good friend, Mier Wolf, who I like to say gives me my public service assignments, sponsored my membership. Barbara Eastman, one of our instructors, got me started with her insightful writing advice. And Kate Blackwell gave me a figurative slap across the face to get me to pay attention to Barbara. After all, I was a successful lawyer at that point who had written many winning legal briefs, wasn't that enough? Well, no. My workshop colleagues enlightened me on that score also and were very helpful with thoughtful advice. Our chairman, Sally Mott Freeman, who became successful author during her tenure, introduced me to James Morgan (publishersmarketplace. com-/member/jamesmorgan), who helped me mold an ungainly manuscript into this book.

I must thank my daughter Erin for her editing advice and lessons in social media, and my daughter Isabella for the idea for the cover.

Gorman, Galliani, Cymrot, Mario Mesia, Shaun Corette

Raoul Gonzalez

Reynaldo Pastor, Scott Andersen

Bob Perry, Mario Mesia

Reynaldo, Mesia, Pedro Pierluisi

Erin, Mark, Isaac

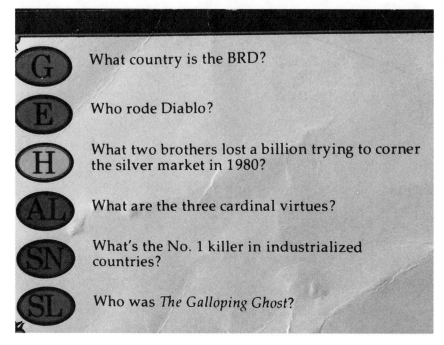

What country is the BRD?

Who rode Diablo?

What two brothers lost a billion trying to corner the silver market in 1980?

What are the three cardinal virtues?

What's the No. 1 killer in industrialized countries?

Who was *The Galloping Ghost*?

Trivial Pursuit

Endnotes

This book was written principally from the trial transcripts and exhibits of *Minpeco S.A. v. Hunt*, Civil No. 81 Civ. 7619 (MEL) (S.D.N.Y.) and from opinions of US District Judge Morris E. Lasker, the most important of which are reported at 724 F. Supp. 259 (Nov. 8, 1989), 127 F.R.D. 460 (Oct. 6, 1989), 718 F. Supp. 168 (Aug. 15, 1989), 693 F. Supp. 58 (Aug. 25, 1988), 686 F. Supp. 420 (May 3, 1988), 686 F. Supp. 427 (May 12, 1988), 677 F. Supp. 151 (Jan. 6, 1988), 118 F.R.D. 331 (Jan. 6, 1988), 676 F. Supp. 486 (Dec. 22, 1987), 673 F. Supp. 684 (Nov. 17, 1987), 116 F.R.D. 517 (Jul. 9, 1987), 653 F. Supp. 957 (Feb. 20, 1987) aff'd 832 F.2d 739 (2d Cir. 1987), 558 F. Supp. 1348 (Mar. 21, 1983), 552 F. Supp. 332 (Nov. 24 1982), 552 F. Supp. 327 (Nov. 24, 1982), 549 F. Supp. 857 (Oct. 26, 1982). The author also reviewed additional sources, including:

Prologue

- Opening Statement of Chairman Proxmire, "Margin Requirements for Transactions in Financial Instruments." Hearings before the Senate Committee on Banking, Housing and Urban Affairs, 96th Cong., 2d Sess., May 29 and 30, 1980 ("Senate Banking Hearings").

- McFadden, Robert D. "Paul Curran, Who Fought Corruption in New York, Dies at 75." *New York Times*, September 6, 2008, p. A30.

Chapter One

- *Commodity Futures Trading Commission v. Hunt*, 591 F.2d 111 (7th Cir. 1979), *cert. denied*, 442 U.S. 921 (1979).
- Labaton, Stephen, "Trial of Hunt Brothers in Silver Case Begins." *New York Times*, February 25, 1988.
- "Hunts Drove up Silver Prices, Jury Told." *Los Angeles Times*, February 25, 1988.

Chapter Two

- Porterfield, Bill, "H.L. Hunt's Long Goodbye." *Texas Monthly*, March 1975.
- Applebome, Peter, "The Hunts: A Dynasty Built on Poker and Oil." *New York Times,* August 29, 1986.
- Jenkins, John A. "The Hunt Brothers: Battling a Billion-Dollar Debt." *New York Times*, September 27, 1987.
- Coll, Steve. "Hunts Still Fighting Losses from Silver Crisis; Family Faces Lawsuits Seeking Millions in Damages and Fines, Owes Banks More Than a Billion Dollars." *Washington Post*, March 20, 1988, p. H1.
- Hayes, Thomas C. "Hunt Deal on Penrod Is Reached." *New York Times*, July 1, 1988.

- Hayes, Thomas C. "Hunts Propose a $663 Million Bankruptcy Settlement for Placid Oil." *New York Times*, July 24, 1988.
- Simnacher, Joe. "Nelson Bunker Hunt, Second Son of Legendary Wildcatter H.L. Hunt, Dies." *Dallas Morning News*, October 21, 2014.

Chapter Three

- Gerth, Jeff. "Hunts Again Charged in 1979-80 Silver Deals." *New York Times*, March 1, 1985.
- Eichenwald, Kurt. "2 Hunts Fined and Banned from Trades." *New York Times*, December 21, 1989.
- Hagedorn, Ann. "Nelson Hunt Denies Trying to Corner the Silver Market." *Wall Street Journal*, June 1, 1988.
- Hagedorn, Ann. "Quest Spans Globe to Prove Silver Scheme—Was Hunt's Jet-Setting Social or Part of Plot?" *Wall Street Journal*, June 13, 1988.

Chapter Four

- Asser, Martin. "The Muammar Gaddafi Story." *BBC News*, October 21, 2011.
- "Muammar Al-Gaddafi, Dictator 1942-2011." *Biography.com*.

Chapter Five

- "Mohammad Reeza Shah Pahlavi." *Iran Chamber Society.*

Chapter Seven

- Martin, Douglas. "Khalid bin Mahfouz, Saudi Banker, Dies at 60." *New York Times,* August 27, 2009, p. A24.
- Paul L. Perito, President and Chief Operating Office at Rock Creek, Corporate Biography.

Chapter Eight

- *Gordon v. Hunt,* 116 F.R.D. 313 (S.D.N.Y. 1987).

Chapter Ten

- "AW Galadari Dubai's First Bankrupt 1983." *Dubai as It Used to Be.*
- "Falling from Grace: Dubai Tycoon Abdul Wahab Galadari Loses Global Business Empire." *India Today,* January 15, 1984.
- "Galadari Free on Bond." *Chicago Tribune,* May 22, 1986.
- "Ruhollah Khomeini Iranian Religious Leader." *Biogra phy.com.*

- Anderson, Raymond H. "Ayatollah Ruhollah Khomeini, 89, the Unwavering Iranian Spiritual Leader." *New York Times*, June 4, 1989.

Chapter Thirteen

- "Lamar Hunt—Kansas City Chiefs." *Football Hall of Fame.*
- "Resignations over Scandal in Brazil." *Reuters*, June 19, 1989.
- "Brazilian Court Seizes Assets." *Reuters*, July 4, 1989.
- Brayton, Colin, "The Man Who Broke the Brazilian Bourse." *cbrayton.wordpress.com*, July 4, 2007.
- "Article about Naji Nahas." *Los Angeles Times.*

Chapter Fourteen

- "Mohammed Al Amoudi." *Forbes.*
- Serafin, Tatiana. "Sheikh Mohammed Al Amoudi on Philanthropy." *Forbes*, June 5, 2013.
- Vaught, Jason Jonathan. "Al Taqwa Bank." *A Thesis Presented to the Faculty of San Diego State University*, May 11, 2011.

Chapter Sixteen

- "Selling Horses at Keeneland—Graduating Success." *Keeneland.*

- Arnold, Jobe, "Kentucky Sales Attract Turf's Rulers." *New York Times,* July 23, 1979.

Chapter Seventeen

- Crist, Steve. "A Saudi Invests in Bluegrass." *New York Times,* April 2, 1982.
- *Fustok v. ContiCommodity Service, Inc.,* 577 F. Supp. 582 (1984) 103 F.R.D. 601 (1984), 610 F. Supp. 986 (1985), 618 F. Supp. 1069 (1985), 618 F. Supp. 1074 (1985), 618 F. Supp. 1082 (1985), 106 F.R.D. 590 (1985), 122 F.R.D. 151 (S.D.N.Y.) aff'd 873 F.3d 38 (2d Cir. 1989).
- *Fustok v. Banque Populaire Suisse,* 546 F. Supp. 506 (S.D.N.Y. 1982).
- Haberman, Clyde. "Arthur L. Liman, a Masterly Lawyer, Dies at 64." *New York Times,* July 18, 1997.
- Hevesi, Dennis. "Peter E. Fleming Jr., 79, Dies; Defense Lawyer Who Relished the Limelight." *New York Times,* January 15, 2009.

Chapter Twenty

- "Heard on Street: Silver's Price Rise." *Wall Street Journal,* September 21, 1979.
- "Silver Broker Reportedly Told by COMEX to Sell Some Holdings." *Wall Street Journal,* September 21, 1979.

Chapter Twenty-One

- "1979: Remembering 'The Siege of Mecca'." *NPR*, August 20, 2009.

Chapter Twenty-Two

- Nelson, John. "At 29, He Runs a Commodities Market." *New York Times*, April 4, 1982.

Chapter Twenty-Three

- "Corner Feared in Silver Futures." *Wall Street Journal*, October 26, 1979.
- Maidenberg, H.J. "Commodities Regulator Criticizes British Policy; Regulator Criticizes Britain." *New York Times*, November 4, 1979, p. D1.
- "Squeeze in December Silver Thought Overrated; Price Falls." *Wall Street Journal*, November 30, 1979.

Chapter Twenty-five

- Strengold, James. "Talking Business with Jarecki of Mocatta Metals; Gold's Future: Cautious View." *New York Times*, January 1, 1985.
- "Mocatta" *Jewish Virtual Library*.

Chapter Twenty-Six

- Francke, Linda Bird. "A Day at the Races, French Style." *New York Times*, May 21, 1989.
- Kay, Mary. "Prix De Diane 2012—Hats and Horses! (Part 1)." *Out and About With Mary Kay*, June 18, 2012.
- McKenzie, Sheena. "Ascot vs L'Arc: The Glitz and Glamor of France's Great Monument." *CNN Sports*, October 5, 2012.

Chapter Thirty-Five

- "Gold and Silver Prices Rise and Worry of Heavy Mideast Buying." *Wall Street Journal*, December 3, 1979.
- Maidenberg, H.J. "Silver Soars to Records; Swiss Bank Sued by U.S." *New York Times*, December 4, 1979.
- Knight, Jerry. "CFTC Acts to Get Swiss Bank to Name Clients for Futures; CFTC Challenges Swiss Banks' Account Secrecy." *Washington Post*, December 4, 1979, p. E1.
- Maidenberg, H.J. "Commodities." *New York Times*, December 4, 1979, p. D16.
- "Information Bank Abstracts." *New York Times*, December 5, 1979, p. 12.
- "Swiss Bank Hasn't Heard from CFTC about Sanctions." *Wall Street Journal*, December 6, 1979.

Chapter Forty-One

- "Silver Ended '79 at $35 an Oz., Five Times Year-Earlier Price." *Wall Street Journal*, January 2, 1980.

- "Silver-Price Surge Taking Toll on Consumers, Manufacturers." *Wall Street Journal*, January 4, 1980.
- "Information Bank Abstracts." *New York Times*, January 7, 1980, p. 3.
- "COMEX Puts Limits on Amount of Silver Contracts Traders Hold." *Wall Street Journal*, January 8, 1980.
- Bennett, Robert A. "Position Limits Adopted in Comex Silver Futures; Position Limits Adopted in Comex Silver Futures Few Actually Take Delivery 5,000 Ounces in a Contract." *New York Times*, January 8, 1980, p. D1.
- "Hunt Says He Thinks Trading Curbs Won't Sway Silver Margin." *Wall Street Journal*, January 10, 1980.
- Tully, Shawn. "Who Guards Whom at the Commodity Exchange?" *Fortune*, May 8, 2011.
- Goldfield, Hannah "Tavern on the Green." *New Yorker*, June 9, 2014.

Chapter Forty-Four

- "COMEX Bans New Positions in Silver, Boosts Margin Run." *Wall Street Journal*, January 22, 1980.
- Maidenberg, H.J. "Comex Curbs Trade in Silver Futures; How Futures Protect Merchants Trade in Silver Is Curbed Near Chaos in Markets Actions to Curb Trade." *New York Times*, January 22, 1980, p. D1.
- Cohen, Laurie. "Ban on Some Silver Futures." *Chicago Tribune*, January 23, 1980.

- "Heard on Street: Kodak 'Silver Risk'." *Wall Street Journal*, January 23, 1980.
- "Silver Price Falls $10 to $34 an Ounce in Record 1-Day Drop." *Wall Street Journal*, January 23, 1980.
- William, Robbins. "Chicago Board Limits Silver Futures Trading; Sharp Response in Market Averting Squeeze on Shorts." *New York Times*, January 23, 1980, p. D12.

Chapter Forty-Five

- DeBonis, Mike. "Andrew F. Brimmer, 1926-2012." *Washington Post*, October 11, 2012.
- Strom, Stephanie. "Andrew Brimmer, First Black Member on Fed Board, Dies at 86." *New York Times*, October 12, 2012, p. B15.

Chapter Forty-Eight

- "Price Fluctuations Seen in Silver." *Wall Street Journal*, March 3, 1980.

Chapter Fifty-One

- "T-Bill Rates Drop; Dealers Say Mart Went 'Nuts' on Hunt Woe." *Wall Street Journal*, March 28, 1980.
- Lohr, Steve. "Silver's Plunge Jolts Hunts' Empire and Brings Turmoil to Wall Street." *New York Times*, March 28, 1980, p. 1, 10.

- "CFTC Regulatory Review." Hearings before the House Subcommittee on Conservation and Credit of the Committee on Agriculture, 96th Cong., 2d Sess., February 12, May 21, 22, and 29, 1980.
- "Silver Prices and the Adequacy of Federal Actions in the Marketplace, 1979-1980." Hearings before the House Subcommittee on Commerce, Consumer and Monetary Affairs of the Committee on Government Operations, April 30, May 2, 22, 1980.
- "Price Volatility in the Silver Futures Markets." Hearings before the Senate Subcommittee on Agricultural Research and General Legislation of the Committee on Agriculture, Nutrition and Forestry, 96th Cong., 2d Sess., May 1 and 2, 1980.
- "Margin Requirements for Transactions in Financial Instruments." Hearings before the Senate Committee on Banking Housing and Urban Affairs, 96th Cong., 2d Sess., May 29 and 30, 1980.
- "Report to the Congress in Response to Section 21 of the Commodity Exchange Act, Pub. L. No. 96-276, 96th Cong., 2d Sess. Section 7, 94 Stat. 542 (June 1, 1980)," Commodity Futures Trading Commission, May 29, 1981.
- "The Silver Market of 1979/1980, Actions of the Chicago Board of Trade and the Commodity Exchange, Inc." Investigative Report, Division of Trading and Markets, Commodity Futures Trading Commission.
- "The Silver Crisis of 1980": A Report of the Staff of the U.S. Securities and Exchange Commission, October 1982.

- Greider, William. "Secrets of the Temple: How the Federal Reserve Runs the Country." *Simon & Schuster*, 1987, p.192.
- Tavakoli, Janet. "Rehypothecation Is an Old Story: MF Global's Story Is a Different Story of Filched Funds." *Huffpost*, December 16, 2011.
- "Lehman Revisited: The Blackout that Never Was." *New York Times*, September 30, 2014, p. A1.
- Wiggins, Rosalind Z., Piontek, Thomas, and Metrick, Andrew. "The Lehman Brothers Bankruptcy A: Overview." Yale Program on Financial Stability, October 1, 2014.
- "Case Study: The Collapse of Lehman Brothers." *Investopedia*, March 3, 2016.

Chapter Fifty-Two

- Testimony of Dr. Henry G. Jarecki, Chairman, Mocatta Metals Corp. of New York, N.Y. and Statement of Paul A. Volcker, Chairman, Board of Governors of the Federal Reserve System before Senate Agriculture Committee Hearings.
- Collins, P. Daniel. "Henry Jarecki: Jarecki's Law." *Futures Magazine*, May 1, 2011.
- Liberman, Si. "Ex-New Haven psychiatrist Dr. Henry Jarecki made a killing in the market." *New Haven Register*, September 20, 2014.

Chapter Fifty-Four/Afterward

- Coll, Steve. "$20 Million Offered Firm by Hunts." *Washington Post*, May 17, 1988, p. C3.
- Hagedorn, Ann. "Jurors in Battle between Hunt Brothers and Peru's Minpeco Begin Deliberating." *Wall Street Journal*, August 16, 1988.
- Hagedorn, Ann. "Minpeco Jury Is Near Verdict in Silver Suit." *Wall Street Journal*, August 18, 1988.
- "Jurors Order Hunt Brothers to Pay Minpeco." *Wall Street Journal*, August 21, 1988.
- Lueck, Thomas J. "Hunts Are Ruled Part of a Scheme to Control Silver." *New York Times*, August 21, 1988.
- Kennedy, J. Michael. "Hunts Guilty of Scheme to Corner Silver: Texans Order to Pay $130 Million to Firm in Fraud Convictions." *Los Angeles Times*, August 21, 1988.
- Hagedorn, Ann and Apcar, Leonard M. "Peru Firm Is Awarded over $130 Million in Case Involving Hunts' Silver Scheme." *Wall Street Journal*, August 22, 1988.
- Hundley, Tom. "Hunt Saga Rivals Story of 'Dallas'." *Chicago Tribune*, August 28, 1988.
- Adler, Stephen J. and Hagedorn, Ann. "Peruvian Concern Seeks to Force Hunts to Post a Bond in Silver-Market Case." *Wall Street Journal*, August 30, 1988.
- Apcar, Leonard M. and Hagedorn, Ann. "Two Hunts File for Personal Bankruptcy in an Effort to Thwart Legal Challenges." *Wall Street Journal*, September 22, 1988.

- Hagedorn, Ann. "Lamar Hunt Will Pay $17 Million to Resolve Silver Conspiracy Case." *Wall Street Journal*, October 20, 1988.
- Hagedorn, Ann. "Lamar Hunt Settles Minpeco Judgment with $17 Million." *Wall Street Journal*, October 21, 1988.
- Berry, John M and Knight, Jerry. "A Fall from Wealth; Nelson Bunker Hunt Talks of Reasons and Regrets." *Washington Post*, July 16, 1989, p. H1.
- Eichenwald, Kurt. "2 Hunts Fined and Banned from Trades." *New York Times*, December 21, 1989.
- Williams, Jeffrey. "The Hunt Family Silver Venture." *Manipulation on Trial: Economic Analysis and the Hunt Silver Case*, 1995, p. 244.
- Gwynne, S.C. "Bunker Hunt." *Texas Monthly*, September 2001.
- Rudolph, Barbara. "Down to Their Last Billion?" *Time*, June 24, 2001.
- Lindsey, David E., Orphanides, Athanasios, and Rasche, Robert H. "The Reform of October 1979: How It Happened and Why." Finance and Economics Discussions Series Divisions of Research & Statistics and Monetary Affairs Federal Reserve Board, Washington, D.C., February 2005.
- Cain, Glenye, "Mahmoud Fustok, 70, Killed in Accident." *Racing Daily Form*, February 9, 2006.
- "Brother-in-Law of Saudi King Hit, Killed in Pompano Beach." *Local10.com*, February 9, 2006.

- Hammonds, Evan. "Mahmoud Fustok Killed in Florida Accident." *BloodHorse.com,* February 9, 1980.
- Burrough, Bryan. "The Man Who Was Texas." *Vanity Fair,* October 2008.
- McFadden, Robert D. "Morris Lasker Dies at 92; Made City Clean Its Jails." *New York Times,* December 29, 2009.
- "Obituary: Morris E. Lasker." *The Martha's Vineyard Times,* December 31, 2009.
- Cui, Carolyn. "From Healing to Making a Killing." *Wall Street Journal,* April 24, 2010.
- Coffey, Brendan. "Hunt Becomes Billionaire on Bakken Oil after Bankruptcy." *Bloomberg,* March 28, 2013.
- McFadden, Robert D. "Nelson Bunker Hunt, 88, Oil Tycoon with a Texas-Size Presence, Dies." *New York Times,* October 21, 2014.
- McFadden, Robert D. "Nelson Bunker Hunt, 88, Oil Tycoon with a Texas-Size Presence, Dies." *New York Times,* October 22, 2014, p. A24.
- Peppard, Alan. "Oil in the Family." *Vanity Fair,* May 7, 2008.
- Moore, Heidi N. "Hunt Petroleum and the Death of the Family-Run Company." *Wall Street Journal,* June 10, 2008.
- Wiggins, Rosalind Z., Piontek, Thomas, and Metrick, Andrew. "The Lehman Brothers Bankruptcy A: Overview." Yale Program on Financial Stability Case Study 2014-3A-V1 (Yale School of Management, Oct. 1, 2014).

- "Texas Oil Tycoon, Thoroughbred Owner-Breeder Nelson Bunker Hunt Dies." Paulick Report, October 22, 2014.
- "Telling Fortunes: No. 19: William Herbert Hunt." *Texas Monthly.*

Additional Sources

- "Business: Bunker's Busted Silver Bubble." *Time,* May 12, 1980.
- "Joint Agency Report on the Silver Markets." Hearing before the House Subcommittee on Conservation, Credit and Rural Development of the Committee on Agriculture, 97th Cong., 1st Sess., October 1, 1981.
- Barbanel, Jack A. An Introduction to the Rules and Regulations Governing National Banks and Their Use of Financial Futures, 38 Wash. & LeeReportr Rev. 813 (1981).
- Cole, Robert J. "Bache Firm Fined $400,000 for Role in '80 Silver Crisis." *New York Times*, October 12, 1982, p. D4.
- Tomeck, William G. "Margins on Futures Contracts: Their Economic Roles and Regulation." *American Enterprise Institute for Public Research*, 1985.
- Mathewson, William. "World Wire." *Wall Street Journal*, November 1, 1989.
- Markham, Jerry. "Law Enforcement and the History of Financial Market Manipulation." Routledge, Taylor & Francis Group, 2014.

- Parts of the story were previously written in two articles: "Squeezing Silver" *Litigation*, Journal of the ABA Litigation Section (Summer 1991)(co-authored with Thomas O. Gorman); "A Case Study in Foreign Discovery: Minpeco S.A. v. Nelson Bunker Hunt" ABA National Institute on International Litigation (1989); reprinted *The Journal of the Society of English and American Lawyers*, Vol. 1, No. 2 (1989); *International Quarterly* (Jan. 1990); *Themis*, in Spanish (Jan. 1990)(co-authored with Thomas O. Gorman).